THE HISTORY OF AL-ṬABARĪ

AN ANNOTATED TRANSLATION

VOLUME XIV

The Conquest of Iran

A.D. 641–643/A.H. 21–23

The History of al-Ṭabarī

Editorial Board

Ihsan Abbas, University of Jordan, Amman

C. E. Bosworth, The University of Manchester

Franz Rosenthal, Yale University

Everett K. Rowson, The University of Pennsylvania

Ehsan Yar-Shater, Columbia University (*General Editor*)

Estelle Whelan, *Editorial Coordinator*

Center for Iranian Studies
Columbia University

SUNY

SERIES IN NEAR EASTERN STUDIES

Said Amir Arjomand, Editor

The preparation of this volume was made possible in part by a grant from the National Endowment for the Humanities, an independent federal agency.

Bibliotheca Persica
Edited by Ehsan Yar-Shater

The History of al-Ṭabarī

(Ta'rīkh al-rusul wa'l-mulūk)

VOLUME XIV

The Conquest of Iran

translated and annotated
by

G. Rex Smith

The University of Manchester

State University of New York Press

Published by
State University of New York Press, Albany

Printed in the United States of America

For information, address State University of New York
Press, State University Plaza, Albany, N.Y., 12246

Library of Congress Cataloging-in-Publication Data

Ṭabarī, 838?–923.

[Ta'rīkh al-rusul wa-al-mulūk. English. Selections]

The conquest of Iran / translated and annotated by
G. Rex Smith.

p. cm.—(The history of al-Ṭabarī = Ta'rikh al-rusul
wa'l-mulūk; v. 14) (Bibliotheca Persica) (SUNY series in Near
Eastern studies)

Translation of extracts from: Ta'rīkh al-rusul wa-al-mulūk.

Includes bibliographical references (p.) and index.

ISBN 0–7914–1293–8 (alk. paper).—ISBN 0–7914–1294–6
(pbk. : alk. paper)

1. Iran—History—640–1256. 2. Islamic Empire—History—
622–661. 3. 'Umar ibn al-Khaṭṭāb, Caliph, d.644.
4. Caliphs—Biography. I. Title. II. Series. III. Series:
Ṭabarī, 838?–923. Ta'rīkh al-rusul wa-al-mulūk. English; 14.
IV. Series: Bibliotheca Persica (Albany, N.Y.)

DS38.2.T313 1985 vol. 14
[DS287.3]
909'1 s—dc20
[955'.02] 92–25776
CIP

10 9 8 7 6 5 4 3 2 1

Preface

The History of Prophets and Kings (*Ta'rīkh al-rusul wa'l-mulūk*) by Abū Ja'far Muḥammad b. Jarīr al-Ṭabarī (839–923), here rendered as *The History of al-Ṭabarī*, is by common consent the most important universal history produced in the world of Islam. It has been translated here in its entirety for the first time for the benefit of non-Arabists, with historical and philological notes for those interested in the particulars of the text.

Al-Ṭabarī's monumental work explores the history of the ancient nations, with special emphasis on biblical peoples and prophets, the legendary and factual history of ancient Iran, and, in great detail, the rise of Islam, the life of the Prophet Muḥammad, and the history of the Islamic world down to the year 915. The first volume of this translation contains a biography of al-Ṭabarī and a discussion of the method, scope, and value of his work. It also provides information on some of the technical considerations that have guided the work of the translators.

The *History* has been divided here into thirty-nine volumes, each of which covers about 200 pages of the original Arabic text in the Leiden edition. An attempt has been made to draw the dividing lines between the individual volumes in such a way that each is to some degree independent and can be read as such. The page numbers of the Leiden edition appear in the margins of the translated volumes.

Al-Tabarī very often quotes his sources verbatim and traces the chain of transmission (*isnād*) to an original source. The chains of transmitters are, for the sake of brevity, rendered by only a dash (—) between the individual links in the chain. Thus, "According to Ibn Ḥumayd—Salamah—Ibn Isḥāq" means that al-Ṭabarī received the report from Ibn Ḥumayd, who said that he was told by Salamah, who said that he was told by Ibn Isḥāq, and so on. The numerous subtle and important differences in the original Arabic wording have been disregarded.

The table of contents at the beginning of each volume gives a brief survey of the topics dealt with in that particular volume. It also includes the headings and subheadings as they appear in al-Ṭabarī's text, as well as those occasionally introduced by the translator.

Well-known place names, such as, for instance, Mecca, Baghdad, Jerusalem, Damascus, and the Yemen, are given in their English spellings. Less common place names, which are the vast majority, are transliterated. Biblical figures appear in the accepted English spelling. Iranian names are usually transcribed according to their Arabic forms, and the presumed Iranian forms are often discussed in the footnotes.

Technical terms have been translated wherever possible, but some, such as dirham and imām, have been retained in Arabic forms. Others that cannot be translated with sufficient precision have been retained and italicized, as well as footnoted.

The annotation aims chiefly at clarifying difficult passages, identifying individuals and place names, and discussing textual difficulties. Much leeway has been left to the translators to include in the footnotes whatever they consider necessary and helpful.

The bibliographies list all the sources mentioned in the annotation.

The index in each volume contains all the names of persons and places referred to in the text, as well as those mentioned in the notes as far as they refer to the medieval period. It does not include the names of modern scholars. A general index, it is hoped, will appear after all the volumes have been published.

For further details concerning the series and acknowledgments, see Preface to Volume 1.

Ehsan Yar-Shater

Contents

Preface / v

Abbreviations / xi

Translator's Foreword / xiii

Map 1. The Area of the Conquests of Iran, 21–23/641–44 / xxi

The Events of the Year 21 (cont'd) (641–642) / 1

What Happened in This Year, 21—'Umar's Previously Mentioned Orders to the Two Armies / 2
Iṣfahān / 6
The Account of [the Attack on Iṣfahān] / 10

The Events of the Year 22 (642–643) / 17

The Conquest of al-Rayy / 24
The Conquest of Qūmis / 27
The Conquest of Jurjān / 28
The Conquest of Ṭabaristān / 30
The Conquest of Azerbaijan / 31
The Conquest of al-Bāb / 34
Information on ['Umar's Division of the Conquered Lands] / 43

The Reason for [the Dismissal of ʿAmmār] / 47
Yazdajird's Journey to Khurāsān and the Reason for It / 51

The Events of the Year 23 (643–644) / 64

The Conquest of Tawwaj / 64
The Conquest of Iṣṭakhr / 66
The Conquest of Fasā and Darābjird / 70
The Conquest of Kirmān / 73
The Conquest of Sijistān / 75
The Conquest of Makrān / 77
Bayrūdh in al-Ahwāz / 78
Salamah b. Qays al-Ashjaʿī and the Kurds / 83
ʿUmar's Assassination / 89
The Sources of [the Conflicting Report of ʿUmar's Death] / 93
ʿUmar's Genealogy / 95
The Sources of [the Report that Muḥammad First Called ʿUmar al-Fārūq] / 96
The Sources of [the Report that the People of the Book Did That] / 96
A Description of ʿUmar / 96
His Birth and Age / 97
Some of the Sources of [the Report that He Was Fifty-Five Years Old] / 98
The Sources of [the Report that He Was Fifty-Three Years Old] / 99
The Sources of [the Report that He Was Sixty-Three Years Old] / 99
The Sources of [the Report that He Was Sixty-One Years Old] / 99
The Sources of [the Report that He Was Sixty Years Old] / 99
The Names of His Children and Wives / 100
When He Became a Muslim / 102
The Sources of This Report / 102
Some of His Memorable Deeds / 103
Relevant Information on [ʿUmar's Night Visits] / 109
ʿUmar's Being Called Commander of the Faithful / 113
Information on This Matter / 114
His Institution of the [Islamic] Dating System / 114

['Umar's] Carrying a Whip and His Instituting the State Registers / 115
Some Excerpts from His Addresses / 123
Another Address / 124
Another Address / 125
Another Address / 126
Those Who Have Lamented and Elegized 'Umar—Some of the Elegies Written about Him / 129
Some of 'Umar's Meritorious Deeds Not Previously Recorded / 131
The Account of the Electoral Council / 143
'Umar's Governors in the Garrison Towns / 164

Bibliography / 167

Index / 173

Abbreviations

Cairo: al-Ṭabarī, *Ta'rīkh*, Cairo edition.
CHIr: *Cambridge History of Iran.*
CHIs: *Cambridge History of Islam.*
EIr: *Encyclopaedia Iranica.*
EI[1]: *Encyclopaedia of Islam*, 1st ed.
EI[2]: *Encyclopaedia of Islam*, 2nd ed.
GAS: F. Sezgin, *Geschichte des arabischen Schrifttums.*
Glossarium: Glossary in al-Ṭabarī, *Ta'rīkh: Indices, Introductio, Glossarium, Addenda et Emendanda.*
SEI: *Shorter Encyclopaedia of Islam.*
Selection: M. de Goeje, ed., *Selection from the Annals of Tabari.*
Ṭabarī: al-Ṭabarī, *Ta'rīkh*, Leiden ed.
Translation: al-Ṭabarī, *The History of al-Ṭabarī.*

Translator's Foreword

This volume of Ṭabarī's text (I, pp. 2634–2798 of the Leiden edition and IV, pp. 137–241 of the Cairo edition) covers the period 21–23/641–43 and can be divided into two distinct and almost equal parts: the first concerning the conquests under ʿUmar b. al-Khaṭṭāb in Iran and the east, which gives this volume its title, and the second concerning ʿUmar himself, his assassination, and an assessment of the caliph and the man.

The text translated in this volume owes much to Ṭabarī's informant Sayf b. ʿUmar, a controversial figure who has occasioned some comment. Although much trusted by Ṭabarī for the early period of Islamic history, Sayf is not used as an informant by others. He has, for example, been accused of presenting inconsistent accounts and of overemphasizing the role of his own tribe, Tamīm. References to assessments of the mysterious Sayf are given below, p. 1 n. 3.

Historical Background

ʿUmar had assumed the caliphate in 13/634, the immediate successor of the first caliph, Abū Bakr (11–13/632–34). Abū Bakr's first major problem had been how to hold together the young Islamic community that had been built by the Prophet and that immediately after his death threatened to disintegrate. Some tribes of the Peninsula felt no further loyalty to the community and its leader, and they had anyway, increasingly with their geographical distance from Medina, only tenuous links with Muḥammad and the religion of Islam. This cannot be the place for a detailed discussion of Abū Bakr's determined efforts to bring these tribes back into the fold, efforts that have gone down in history as the so-called Riddah wars or the wars of Apostasy. What can be said with confidence is that these Riddah wars, as the Muslim warriors fighting them moved farther and farther away from the center of Islam and out of the control of the head of the Islamic community (a point to which I shall return below in the context of ʿUmar himself), gradually merged into wars of conquest. Whatever one's view of the military activities of the Muslims during the brief caliphate of Abū Bakr, it is true to say that by the time of ʿUmar's assumption of the caliphate in 13/634 we are talking only in terms of conquest.

The Conquests

Two fronts initially opened up, the Syrian and the Iraqi. The former attracted less attention from Ṭabarī, who compiled all history in terms of an eastern center with every other area or province on the periphery. Without becoming too involved in the massive problem of the discrepancies in the dates of the conquests (a second point to which I feel compelled to return briefly below), we can probably say that the majority of Greater Syria had fallen to the Muslims by 15/636 and that the Byzantines under Heraclius were in full retreat from the area. On the second front, according to Ṭabarī's accounts, Iraqi towns such as Babylon; al-Madāʾin, the old Sasanian capital; and Tikrīt had been taken by the Muslims in the year 16/637–638. Of tremendous importance was the resounding victory secured by the Muslim forces under Saʿd b. Abī Waqqāṣ at al-Qādisiyyah, when a huge Sasanian army under Rustam dissolved in panic. Such a victory left the Sasanian empire to the east vulnerable to attack and penetration by the forces of Islam. As we shall see from Ṭabarī's accounts of the eastern conquests in this volume, they were not slow to take advantage of their success and of the weakness of a once mighty empire. In the following year (17/638–639), again according to Ṭabarī, al-Kūfah was founded as a Muslim garrison town in southern Iraq, and the conquering armies began to raid into the province of Fārs.

Turning aside almost incidentally from his other accounts under the year 20/640–641 to chronicle the events of the conquest of Egypt and Alexandria, Ṭabarī then recounts the details of one further major Muslim victory in the east, the last before the text of which this volume is the translation opens. This victory happened in 21/641 at a place called Nihāwand, east of Baghdad and south of Hamadhān (see map). Sa'd once again led the Muslim forces. The defeated Persians were on this occasion led by their last Sasanian emperor, Yazdajird III, who, however, survived the defeat. His further attempts to undermine the Islamic eastern conquests can be read below. With two such major victories behind them, al-Qādisiyyah and Nihāwand, the Muslims stood poised to penetrate into the territories of the Sasanian empire and beyond. At this point this volume opens.

The following text covers the last two years of 'Umar's life, 21–23/641–643. Under those years Ṭabarī's accounts of the territorial gains of the Muslim armies, who move out of the two garrison towns of al-Kūfah and al-Baṣrah, include such important centers and areas as Isfahān (21/641–642), Hamadhān, al-Rayy, Qūmis, Jurjān, Ṭabaristān, Azerbaijan, Khurāsān (all in 22/642–643), parts of Fārs province, Kirmān, Sijistān, and Makrān as far as the Indus (all listed under 23/643–644, also the year of 'Umar's assassination).

Neither Ṭabarī himself nor his informants were at all interested in military strategy, and it should be stated at the outset that the reader only rarely finds reference to tactics, and then usually of a very primitive kind. The almost stereotyped pattern that emerges is as follows. The Muslim supreme commander reaches his goal; frequently the names of his generals in the van, in the rear, and with the two wings of the army are all given as a prelude to the battle. A siege may ensue; there may even be personal combat to decide the issue, and this frequently provides an interesting anecdote. If battle is actually joined, the divinely guided Muslim army defeats the polytheist enemy. Muslims are occasionally killed, but they are invariably heroes who lay down their life in God's cause and who frequently have a premonition of their fate and prepare for the supreme sacrifice. The enemy may, however, see the strength and moral superiority of the Muslim forces and that is sufficient to bring about a quest for peace without fighting.

The Peace Documents

The several peace documents given verbatim by Ṭabarī in this text are of some interest and would indeed repay deeper study. On the important question of authenticity, perhaps all that can be said in such a brief introduction is that it might be wise to assume that the texts, although presented verbatim, represent the fourth/tenth-century view of what such texts might have said rather than the first/seventh-century original. In particular, the relationship between the circumstances of the peace and the contents of the document itself might perhaps be further investigated. Invariably, in return for their safe-conduct and the freedom to practice their faith and live in accordance with their own laws, the conquered peoples are required to assist the Muslims in various ways. They are required to give sound advice, to provide hospitality, to keep the roads free of highwaymen, to guide the Muslims, and so on. Most important, they must in all cases pay tribute to the Muslims, this payment being imposed on all those above the age of puberty, although at a rate that they can afford to pay. The tantalizing hints in this volume of the associated questions of military service and exemption from the tribute should also be looked at more closely. The document spells out the dire consequences, should the conquered peoples harm the Muslims in any way or break the terms of the document.

Control of the Conquests

With the peace document signed and witnessed, Ṭabarī tells the reader of the Muslim commander's despatch of trusty messengers to inform the caliph in Medina of the victory and to deliver the fifths of the booty for the community treasury in accordance with early established Islamic practice. 'Umar frequently uses the messenger's return to send further directions and military orders to his commanders in the field. Indeed, letters and documents pass freely between caliph and general. The reader should perhaps, however, be aware that 'Umar may not have controlled the Muslim military effort in quite the way in which Ṭabarī's accounts would have us believe. Such reports appear to ignore entirely the sheer geographical impossibility of delivering documents hundreds of miles in frequently appallingly difficult terrain, perhaps through only half-subdued regions, in short periods of time. The occasional message from Medina is of course possible, but one can perhaps assume that the military and administrative decisions in connection with the conquests that had to be taken were taken by commanders on the spot in the front line.

Dates of the Conquests

One of the greatest problems facing students of early Islamic history is that of the precise dates and chronology of the conquests. It is a problem that can be seen at its most acute in Fred Donner's *The Early Islamic Conquests*, in this case with particular reference to the Syrian front. The serious discrepancies in the dating of campaigns and battles of conquest have even been used to discredit in general the early Muslim sources that touch on the conquest. One can do little more here than to indicate that such a serious problem does exist and that perhaps the reader should beware. It should be stressed, however, that, serious though these discrepancies in the accounts of the conquests, and in particular in the dates provided, undoubtedly are, they certainly cannot be used to discredit the text as a whole.

ʿUmar—the Caliph and the Man

The second part of the text here translated begins with the graphic account of ʿUmar's assassination by a Christian slave, Abū Lu'lu'ah, in 23/643. Several dates are given for his death. We are further presented with his genealogy, physical descriptions, different accounts of his birth date and age, the names of his children and wives, and the period of time that he was a Muslim. A lengthy section follows recounting in anecdotal form the deeds of ʿUmar, followed by examples of several of his Friday addresses. Some poetic eulogies are quoted. The volume ends with ʿUmar's appointment of the electoral council, five senior figures in the Islamic community, to decide on his successor and the fascinating account of the workings of the council, with all the cut and thrust of debate and the politicking behind the scenes.

Physically ʿUmar was immensely tall, head and shoulders above the crowd. Although he was dark, we are told that his skin was pale and perhaps blotchy. He had a bald patch on the top of his head. He was never elegantly dressed, quite the opposite in fact, and is invariably portrayed in a simple waist wrapper. By natural disposition, he was rough and ready, eating at home inferior food with some greed and toting a stick or whip, which he was never afraid to use on the person. A blow dealt, however, might be regretted later and the victim of his brusque behavior eventually compensated in some way. He was never afraid of stripping down and throwing himself into some hard, sometimes dirty, work, whether it be feeding hordes of the poor in the midday sun or treating camels with tar. He is portrayed as absolutely scrupulous in all his dealings with money. Wealth set aside by the community for the public good was inviolate; he was often personally short of money. Gifts, however insignificant, taken from campaign booty with the approval of the troops on the front and delivered to him in Medina brought only an angry response, sometimes a box round the ears, as the messenger was sent away to return the gift to its rightful place with the rest of the spoils. He could be extremely kind and compassionate and the anecdote of the woman and her starving children, which is given below, is famed as an example of ʿUmar's pity toward those suffering great hardship.

The Texts Used and Parallel Texts

The texts used in this translation are those of Leiden and Cairo (see Bibliography). This section of the text in the First Series of the Leiden edition was edited by E. Prym. Muḥammad Abū al-Faḍl Ibrāhīm's Cairo text in fact adds little or nothing to Prym's editorial effort, though on occasions it is preferred for the purposes of translation. The Egyptian scholar's punctuation often helps the process of interpretation, though again sometimes it is misleading. Serious problems clearly remain in both editions, although all one's sympathies are fully on the side of Prym, and his editorial endeavors deserve nothing but praise.

Such problematic passages are quoted here in transliteration in footnotes, at times at some length.

The only truly parallel text—and then it does not cover all the ground of the *Ta'rīkh* by any means—is Ibn al-Athīr's *Kāmil*, which is, however, a slavish, verbatim copy of Ṭabarī. It is therefore of very limited use, but I have nevertheless kept the reader informed of the parallel text in the footnotes. Ya'qūbī's *Tārīkh* is extremely thin at this early period, although I have where necessary referred to it in the footnotes. Bal'amī's so-called abridgment of Ṭabarī's text in Persian I have found useful; from time to time it is extremely so, not only clarifying, but even adding to, the Arabic text. Balādhurī's *Futūḥ* has proved invaluable. It is an excellent check on facts and figures, although it frequently presents an entirely different view of a particular conquest. The *'Iqd* of Ibn 'Abd Rabbih, who was a contemporary of Ṭabarī, quotes the latter's account of the electoral council almost verbatim. References to it have been given in the footnotes, particularly where they help with the interpretation of the text.

The Translation

Two problems in connection with the translation of the text have been dealt with in a manner that requires clarification. The first is the constant use in the original of pronouns—sometimes referring to nouns distant from them, sometimes referring to no noun at all! In this I have followed what seems to be the sensible method of the translator of Volume XV of this series (see his Translation and Editorial Conventions p. xxi). I use parentheses ( ) to surround the noun to which the pronoun refers where merely to use a pronoun in English would be to create ambiguity, possibility even incomprehension. I have also used brackets [ ] to surround any additions supplied for the purpose of a clearer and smoother understanding of the text.

The second problem arises because of the total nonexistence in Arabic of reported or indirect speech. All conversations in the original are in direct speech and always introduced by nothing more precise than *he said/she said/they said*. Where it seems to me important to retain the original direct speech, I have done so.

Where, however, the constant direct speech appears ridiculous, I have not hesitated to convert it to indirect speech. In either case I have also not hesitated to use a little imagination and to introduce verbs like *reply, retort, exclaim,* instead of the ubiquitous *said.*

Footnotes and Bibliography

I have made every endeavor to identify all personal, place, and tribal names found in the text. As for the first, there is a great problem in particular with the narrators whose names appear by the dozens. In this case I have consulted the standard biographical dictionaries. Where persons remain unidentified, I have indicated this clearly in my footnotes. Thanks to the excellent geographical coverage of the eastern part of the Islamic empire by Yāqūt and other geographers and to such studies as Le Strange's *Lands of the Eastern Caliphate,* among others, place names have not been difficult. Reference works on tribes, too, are on the whole adequate. I have also used the footnotes to add explanations where it seems to me that the text requires them, particularly for the non-Arabist and to quote the original Arabic in transliteration in the cases of problematic and corrupt passages. The bibliography lists those works quoted in the footnotes, with in addition one or two other works that I have found particularly valuable during my work on this translation.

Acknowledgments

There remains the pleasant task of acknowledging the kind assistance of Professors C. E. Bosworth and J. Derek Latham. Both gave extremely generously of their time and effort to read through the manuscript of this volume; both made numerous suggestions for the improvement of the text and the notes. I am enormously grateful to them both. Successive postgraduate seminars in Durham and Manchester have benefited me greatly, and I must finally mention Mushallaḥ al-Muraykhī with particular thanks.

G. Rex Smith

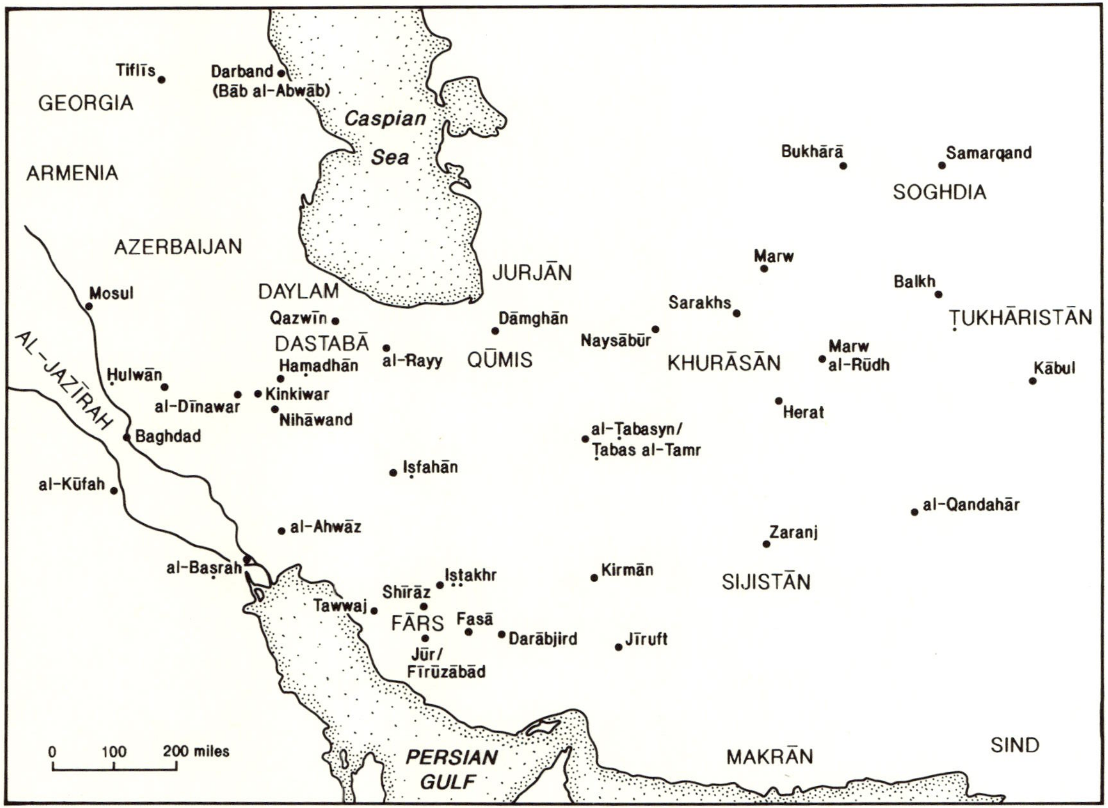

Map I. The Area of the Conquests of Iran, 21–23/641–44

The Events of the Year

21 (cont'd)

(December 10, 641–November 30, 642)

In this year 'Umar [b. al-Khaṭṭāb] gave the armies of Iraq the command to seek out those of Persia,[1] wherever they might be. He commanded some of those Muslim troops who were in al-Baṣrah and its surrounding areas to march on the region of Fārs, Kirmān, and Iṣfahān and some of those who were in the district and regions[2] of al-Kūfah [to march] on Iṣfahān, Azerbaijan, and al-Rayy. Some said that 'Umar did this in the year 18 [January 12, 639–January 2, 640]. This is [also] the version of Sayf b. 'Umar.[3] [2634]

1. Fārs here in the text refers broadly to the land of Persia, not specifically the province of that name, indeed including the provinces of Fārs, Kirmān, Iṣfahān, Azerbaijan, and al-Rayy, listed below. The text of this volume thus begins with this general command on the part of the caliph, 'Umar b. al-Khaṭṭāb, to his forces in Iraq to move eastward and begin the conquest of Iran.

2. For the Persian word *māh*, see Le Strange, *Lands*, 190; Barthold, *Geography*, 208.

3. Sayf b. 'Umar (d. ca. 180/796) appears as the major source for Ṭabarī's account of the conquest of Iran; see Translation, XIII, xiii–xviii; XV, xvi–xvii. See also Hinds, "Sources," 3–16, with an assessment on p. 12; Hinds also discusses Sayf in the context of the conquest of the province of Fārs in "Con-

What Happened in This Year, 21—'Umar's Previously Mentioned Orders to the Two Armies

According to al-Sarī—Shu'ayb—Sayf—Muḥammad, Ṭalḥah, al-Muhallab, 'Amr, and Sa'īd:[4] When 'Umar realized that Yazdajird[5] was making war on him every year and when it was suggested to him that he would continue to do this until he was driven out of his kingdom, ('Umar) gave the army permission to penetrate into Persia to wrest from Yazdajird his imperial possessions. He therefore dispatched the commanders of the Basran and Kufan armies after the victory of Nihāwand.[6] Between the appointment of Sa'd b. Abī Waqqāṣ[7] [as commander of al-Kūfah] and that of 'Ammār b. Yāsir,[8] there were two [other]

quest," 39, 47–49; Duri, "Iraq School," 49–50; Duri, *Rise*, especially 46–47. See also Hill, *Termination*, 26–27.

4. Al-Sarī is al-Sarī b. Yaḥyā. It should be noted that he invariably conveys his information in writing. See Ibn Ḥajar, *Tahdhīb*, III, 460–61; Translation, I, 6–7. Shu'ayb is Shu'ayb b. Ibrāhīm al-Tamīmī. Muḥammad is Muḥammad b. 'Abdallāh b. Sawād, first appearing in the account of the year 12/633–634, Ṭabarī, I, 2026; cf. Duri, *Rise*, 140. Ṭalḥah is Ṭalḥah b. al-A'lam al-Ḥanafī, first appearing in the account of the year 11/632–633, Ṭabarī, I, 1796; cf. Duri, *Rise*, 140. Al-Muhallab is al-Muhallab b. 'Uqbah al-Asadī, first appearing in the text in the account of the year 12/633–634, Ṭabarī, I, 2023. 'Amr is 'Amr b. Muḥammad (d. 199/814–815), who first appears in Ṭabarī, I, 380; cf. Ibn Ḥajar, *Tahdhīb*, VIII, 98–99. Sa'īd is Sa'īd b. al-Marzubān, Abū Sa'd al-Baqqāl, who first appears in Ṭabarī, I, 19. Cf. Ibn Ḥajar, *Tahdhīb*, IV, 79–80. All are important sources of Sayf b. 'Umar. Cf. Hill, *Termination*, 20 no. 23.

5. That is, the last Persian emperor, Yazdgard III, son of Shahriyār, who was killed in 31/651. A brief survey of his career is given in Zarrīnkūb, "Conquest," 18–26. See also Spuler, *Iran*, 18–20; Translation XIII, passim. For the Sasanian family tree, see Nöldeke, *Geschichte*, table, 436a. For these and following events, cf. Bal'ami, *Chronique*, III, 480ff.

6. A town some 40 miles south of Hamadhān (Le Strange, *Lands*, 196), the site of the famous battle earlier in 21/641–642, in which the Muslims won a resounding victory to pave the way for the later conquests of Iran. Cf. Ṭabarī, I, 2596–2631; Translation, XIII, 179–214; Zarrīnkūb, "Conquest," 16.

7. Sa'd was the Qurashī commander of the Muslim forces at al-Qādisiyyah in 16/637. A relative and Companion of the Prophet, Sa'd had been appointed to lead the forces by 'Umar. See Spuler, *Iran*, 8; Shaban, *History*, 30: Zarrīnkūb, "Conquest," 10; Translation, XIII, passim. Cf. Bal'ami, *Chronique*, III, 386.

8. Son of the client of Abū Ḥudhayfah of Makhzūm, Companion, and later follower of 'Alī. He died at Ṣiffīn in 37/657. Cf. Shaban, *History*, 69; Ibn Sa'd, *Ṭabaqāt*, I, 234, 241, etc.; *EI*², s.v. "'Ammār b. Yāsir" (Reckendorf).

commanders, ʿAbdallāh b. ʿAbdallāh b. ʿItbān,[9] in whose time the battle of Nihāwand took place, and Ziyād b. Ḥanẓalah, confederate of B. ʿAbd b. Quṣayy,[10] in whose time the order to penetrate was given. ʿAbdallāh b. ʿAbdallāh was removed and sent elsewhere. Ziyād b. Ḥanẓalah, an emigrant, was appointed. But he served for [only] a short time, persistently asking to be relieved. So he was relieved of his post, and ʿAmmār b. Yāsir appointed after him. (ʿUmar) reinforced the army of al-Baṣrah with ʿAbdallāh b. ʿAbdallāh and that of al-Kūfah with Abū Mūsā [al-Ashʿarī],[11] appointing ʿUmar b. Surāqah[12] in his place. Standards came from ʿUmar to certain individuals in al-Kūfah during the time of Ziyād b. Ḥanẓalah.[13] One of (these standards) came to Nuʿaym b. Muqarrin.[14] The people of Hamadhān[15] had reneged [on their] peace [agreement], so (ʿUmar) ordered (Nuʿaym) to march on Hamadhān, saying, "If God gives you victory, [go] on beyond, onward to Khurāsān!" (ʿUmar) also dispatched ʿUtbah b. Farqad[16] and Bukayr b. ʿAbdallāh,[17] confirming them in charge of Azerbaijan. He divided (the country) [2635]

9. Companion and military commander. See Translation, XIII, 80, 88–89, and passim; also Zarrīnkūb, "Conquest," 21, erroneously ʿAtabān; Donner, *Conquests*, 436; Ibn Ḥajar, *Iṣābah*, VI, 145.

10. For Ziyād, a prominent commander and administrator, see Ibn Ḥajar, *Iṣābah*, IV, 28; Ibn al-Athīr, *Usd*, II, 213; Donner, *Conquests*, 365 (at Yarmūk). B. ʿAbd b. Quṣayy is a tribal division (*fakhdh*) of Kilāb b. Murrah. See Zubayrī, *Quraysh*, 256; Ibn Ḥazm, *Jamharah*, 14; Kaḥḥālah, *Muʿjam*, II, 726; Caskel, *Ğamharat*, I, Table 4.

11. Important Companion and commander, who died ca. 42/662. See Morony, *Iraq*, 433; *EI*², s.v. "Abū Mūsā" (Veccia Vaglieri).

12. That is, over al-Baṣrah. See Ibn Ḥajar, *Iṣābah*, VIII, 26, and Ibn al-Athīr, *Usd*, IV, 79, both giving little information on this military commander.

13. The dispatch of standards from the caliph to Muslim commanders in the field marked the beginning of a general mobilization eastward of their armies.

14. Nuʿaym was, with al-Nuʿmān and Suwayd, one of the famous Ibn Muqarrin brothers and heroes of the eastern campaigns. See Ibn Ḥajar, *Iṣābah*, X, 178. See also note 26, below.

15. A famous town in the Jibāl, northeast of Baghdad and southwest of al-Rayy, about equidistant from both. See Yāqūt, *Muʿjam*, V, 410–17; Le Strange, *Lands*, 194–95.

16. Al-Sulamī, Companion, military commander, and *kharāj* official. He was the conqueror of Mosul in 18/639. Cf. Translation, XIII, 60.

17. Al-Laythī, first mentioned in the text in the account of the year 14/635–636, when he was appointed military commander. See Ṭabarī, I, 2232. Cf. also Translation, XIII, 4–5.

between them, ordering one of them to take [troops] there from Ḥulwān[18] to [form] the right section [of the army] and the other to take [troops] from Mosul to [form] the left. Thus one was on the right of his colleague and the other on his colleague's left. ('Umar) sent a standard to 'Abdallāh b. 'Abdallāh, ordering him to march on Iṣfahān. Now he was courageous, a hero of the
[2636] noble Companions and a prominent Helper, confederate of Banū al-Ḥublā of Banū Asad.[19] ('Umar) reinforced him with Abū Mūsā from al-Baṣrah and appointed 'Umar b. Surāqah commander of al-Baṣrah.

The account concerning 'Abdallāh b. 'Abdallāh is that, when 'Umar heard of the victory at Nihāwand, he determined to give permission [to his armies] to penetrate [further eastward]. He therefore wrote to ('Abdallāh), giving him instructions to march out of al-Kūfah and halt in al-Madā' in;[20] he should call on [the Muslim commanders to volunteer], not select them, and write to him [to inform him that all] this [had been carried out]. 'Umar was intending to despatch him to Iṣfahān. Among those who answered his call [to volunteer] were 'Abdallāh b. Warqā' al-Riyāḥī and 'Abdallāh b. al-Ḥārith b. Warqā' al-Asadī.[21] Those who do not know think one of them was 'Abdallāh b. Budayl b. Warqā' al-Khuzā'ī because of mention of [the name] Warqā'. They were under the [mistaken] impression that (Warqā') was ('Abdallāh al-Riyāḥī's) grandfather. But when he was killed at Ṣiffīn 'Abdallāh b. Budayl b. Warqā' was twenty-four years old and in 'Umar's time he was a young lad.[22]

---

18. A well-known town of the Jibāl province. See Yāqūt, *Mu'jam*, II, 290–94; Le Strange, *Lands*, 191.

19. Al-Ḥublā was the nickname of pot-bellied Sālim b. Ghanm b. 'Awf b. al-Khazraj, the word meaning "pregnant." Banū al-Ḥublā is a tribal division (*baṭn*) of al-Khazraj. There would appear to be nothing, however, linking al-Khazraj with a Banū Asad. See Wāqidī, *Maghāzī*, 166; Ibn Ḥazm, *Jamharah*, 248, 354–55; Kaḥḥālah, *Mu'jam*, I, 239; Caskel, *Ǧamharat*, I, Table 189.

20. The Sasanian capital, seven leagues below Baghdad on both banks of the Tigris, the twin towns of Ctesiphon and Seleucia. See Yāqūt, *Mu'jam*, V, 74–75; Le Strange, *Lands*, 33.

21. The editor of the Cairo edition enters these two under the name 'Abdallāh b. Warqā' al-Riyāḥī al-Asadī in his index (X, 316). This is their first mention in the text, and no further information on them would appear to be available.

22. Ṭabarī here corrects others (e.g., Balādhurī, *Futūḥ*, 312) who make the error of suggesting Ibn Budayl was playing a major military role at this time.

When ʿUmar heard of ʿAbdallāh's departure, he sent Ziyād b. Ḥanẓalah [to al-Kūfah]. When he heard of the departure and [continuing] penetration of the troops, he appointed ʿAmmār commander, reciting God's words, "And We want to show favor to those who were considered weak on earth, to make them leaders and to make them heirs."[23] Ziyād had been sent in the middle of Saʿd's period as commander to the office of judge of al-Kūfah after Salmān and ʿAbd al-Raḥmān, the sons of Rabīʿah,[24] had been relieved [of the post], to act as judge until ʿAbdallāh b. Masʿūd[25] arrived from Ḥimṣ. Al-Nuʿmān and Suwayd, the sons of Muqarrin,[26] had been put in charge on behalf of ʿUmar of [the lands] watered by the Euphrates and Tigris, but they asked to be relieved, saying, "Relieve us of a position that is changing and becoming attractive to us like a prostitute!"[27] So he relieved them of their posts, appointing in their places Ḥudhayfah b. Asīd al-Ghifārī[28] and Jābir b. ʿAmr al-Muzanī.[29] Then they [too] asked to be relieved, so he relieved them, appointing in their places Ḥudhayfah b. al-Yamān and [2637]

However, Ṭabarī himself erroneously mentions Ibn Budayl in connection with the conquest of Kirmān (Ṭabari, I, 2704); see also note 328, below. In 23, when Kirmān was taken by the Muslims, Ibn Budayl would have been only ten years old! Ibn Budayl played a prominent part at the battle of Ṣiffīn in 37/657–658 on the side of ʿAlī; see Ṭabarī, I, 3292ff.

23. Qur'ān 28:5. See p. 47, the dismissal of ʿAmmār.

24. For Salmān, see Ibn Saʿd, *Ṭabaqāt*, VI, 34; Ibn Ḥajar, *Iṣābah*, IV, 220–21. For ʿAbd al-Raḥmān, see Ibn Ḥajar, *Iṣābah*, VI, 278–79. See also Donner, *Conquests*, 395–96.

25. Ibn Masʿūd was a Qur'ān reader who died in 32/652–653; see Ibn Ḥajar, *Tahdhīb*, VI, 27ff.; see also Translation, I, 206 n. 280.

26. For the administrative and military activities of the two brothers, see Translation, XIII, passim. Al-Nuʿmān has an entry in Ibn Ḥajar, *Tahdhīb*, X, 456–57, and is mentioned by Abū Yūsuf; see Ben Shemesh, *Taxation*, III, 96. For Suwayd, see Ibn Ḥajar, *Tahdhīb*, IV, 279–80. This passage would seem to indicate that they were charged with land survey duties in the areas described; see Ṭabarī, I, 2456, and Translation, XIII, 36, where the land-survey aspect of the appointment is clearer. Cf. also Morony, *Iraq*, 69, 150, 157.

27. This would appear to mean that their official position proved too much of a temptation for them! For the Arabic *mūmisah*, see Bosworth, *Underworld*, I, 20.

28. Ḥudhayfah died 42/662–663; see Ibn Ḥajar, *Tahdhīb*, II, 219.

29. Jābir is mentioned in Ibn Saʿd, *Ṭabaqāt*, VII, 236, though with no further details.

ʿUthmān b. Ḥunayf,[30] Ḥudhayfah over [the lands] watered by the Tigris and beyond and ʿUthmān over all [the lands] watered by the Euphrates belonging to the Sawād [of al-Kūfah and of al-Baṣrah] together.[31] (ʿUmar) wrote to the troops of al-Kūfah, [informing them] that he had sent ʿAmmār b. Yāsir to them as commander and appointed ʿAbdallāh b. Masʿūd as teacher and administrative assistant.[32] [He also informed them that] he had appointed Ḥudhayfah b. al-Yamān in charge of [the lands] watered by the Tigris and beyond, whereas he had appointed ʿUthmān b. Ḥunayf in charge of [the lands] watered by the Euphrates.

Iṣfahān[33]

ʿAmmār arrived as commander in al-Kūfah and ʿUmar's letter
[2638] reached ʿAbdallāh [b. ʿAbdallāh with the order] to march on Iṣfahān, leaving Ziyād in charge of al-Kūfah. ʿAbdallāh b. Warqāʾ al-Riyāḥī was to be over his vanguard and ʿAbdallāh b. Warqāʾ al-Asadī and ʿIṣmah b. ʿAbdallāh—that is ʿIṣmah b. ʿAbdallāh b. ʿUbaydah b. Sayf b. ʿAbd b. al-Ḥārith[34]—over his two wings. ʿAbdallāh marched at the head of the army and came to Ḥudhayfah [b. al-Yamān], who returned to his post. ʿAbdallāh left Nihāwand at the head of his followers and those of the army of al-Nuʿmān who had departed with him to face [another] army that had assembled against him, [comprising] some of the in-

30. Both renowned for their work in land survey and *kharāj* assessment; see Zarrīnkūb, "Conquest," 20; Morony, *Iraq*, 101, 108, 121; Ben Shemesh, *Taxation*, 80, 87, 93, 97, 100, 103.

31. For the general meaning of al-Sawād, see Le Strange, *Lands*, 24. I have here translated the dual of the Leiden and Cairo texts. The variant reading, al-Sawād, in the singular, however, should be noted, and Abū Yūsuf, when referring to the appointments of Ḥudhayfah and ʿUthmān, also uses the singular, presumably the Sawād of al-Kūfah. See Ben Shemesh, *Taxation*, 80, 87; Morony, *Iraq*, 121. Perhaps the following mention that ʿUmar wrote only to the Kufans about his appointments also points to the Sawād of al-Kūfah alone being meant here.

32. In this early period, this seems the most appropriate rendering of *wazīr*; see Morony, *Iraq*, 536.

33. For the conquest of Iṣfahān, see Balādhurī, *Futūḥ*, 312–14; Ibn al-Athīr, *Kāmil*, III, 9; Balʿami, *Chronique*, III, 480ff. Cf. Donner, *Conquests*, Appendix N.

34. Ibn Ṭarīf, an early military commander under Khālid b. al-Walīd in Syria, later in the east. See Ibn Ḥajar, *Iṣābah*, VII, 8.

habitants of Iṣfahān, led by the district governor.[35] In charge of his vanguard was Shahrbarāz Jādhawayh,[36] an important leader (*shaykh*) at the head of a large force. The Muslims and the vanguard of the polytheists met in one of the districts[37] of Iṣfahān, and they fought a hard battle. The leader called for single combat, so ʿAbdallāh b. Warqāʾ came out against him and killed him. The army of Iṣfahān fled. The Muslims named this district Rustāq al-Shaykh, and this is its name to this day. ʿAbdallāh b. ʿAbdallāh called out, "Who's next?!" so the district governor sued for peace, which (ʿAbdallāh) granted them. This was the first district of Iṣfahān to be taken.

Then ʿAbdallāh marched out from Rustāq al-Shaykh in the direction of Jayy and finally arrived there.[38] The ruler in Iṣfahān [2639] was at that time al-Fādhūsafān.[39] (ʿAbdallāh) settled the army around Jayy. He besieged them, but after a period collecting together a huge army, they came out against him. When they met, al-Fādhūsafān said to ʿAbdallāh: "Do not kill my men, and I shall not kill yours. Rather come out against me in single combat. If I kill you, your men will withdraw. If you kill me, my men will make peace with you, but only if no arrow falls on them."[40] So ʿAbdallāh came out against him in single combat, saying, "Will you make the [first] attack on me, or shall I on you?" He replied that he would attack. So ʿAbdallāh stood still before him, and al-Fādhūsafān made an attack on him, thrusting at him and hitting the pommel of his saddle and breaking it. He also cut through the breast girth and the girth and the saddle

35. *Ustandār* in the text; see *CHIr*, 218; Morony, *Iraq*, 536, suggests Sasanian official in charge of royal property or a crown prince. The first interpretation, however, seems most appropriate to the context. *Chronique*, III, 483, says that the town was governed by a Persian called Pâdouspân. Cf. *EI*², s.v. "Bādūspānids" (Nikitine).

36. Cf. Justi *Namenbuch*, 278, where there is brief mention of this Persian general.

37. For the Persian word *rustāq*, see Steingass, *Dictionary*, 575; Morony, *Iraq*, 534.

38. Jayy is the name of one of the two towns making up Iṣfahān; see Yāqūt, *Muʿjam*, II, 202–3; Le Strange, *Lands*, 203–4, 206.

39. Cf. Nöldeke, *Geschichte*, 151 n. 2. Cf. also note 35, above.

40. Arabic: *wa-in qatalta-nī sālama-ka aṣḥābī wa-in kāna aṣḥabī lā yaqaʿu la-hum nushshābah.*

cloth, and the saddle came away, with ʿAbdallāh still on the horse. But he came off, though he was still standing, then regained a firm seat on the horse, riding bareback. (ʿAbdallāh) told him to stand still, but (al-Fādhūsafān) agreed with him not to fight [further]. He said: "I do not want to fight you [further], for I see you are a perfect man. Rather I shall come back with you to
[2640] your camp and make peace with you. I shall hand over the town to you, allowing anyone who wishes to stay, but [he must] pay tribute, keeping his property, and on condition that you grant anyone whose land you have taken by force equal status with them and they return [to their property]. Anyone who refuses to enter into the same [agreement] as we will go where he wishes, and his land will be yours." (ʿAbdallāh) replied that he accepted his terms.

Abū Mūsā al-Ashʿarī arrived [to join] ʿAbdallāh from the area of al-Ahwāz[41] when al-Fādhūsafān had already made peace with the latter. All the troops left Jayy and entered into the contract except for thirty Iṣfahānīs who opposed [the majority of] their people. They assembled and made off for Kirmān, along with their dependents, [to join] a group already there. ʿAbdallāh and Abū Mūsā entered Jayy, the town of Iṣfahān, and (the former) wrote to ʿUmar to this effect. Those who remained rejoiced, whereas those who left regretted [their decision]. ʿUmar's reply to ʿAbdallāh commanded him to march and join up with Suhayl b. ʿAdī[42] to fight with him those in Kirmān. He was also to leave behind in Jayy those who would defend the town. He was to appoint as his deputy over Iṣfahān al-Sāʾib b. al-Aqraʿ.[43]

According to al-Sarī—Shuʿayb—Sayf—a group of al-Ḥasan's informants, who included al-Mubārak b. Faḍālah—al-Ḥasan[44]—

41. On the Dujayl, capital of Khūzistān. See Yāqūt, *Muʿjam*, I, 284–86; Le Strange, *Lands*, 232–34.

42. Al-Azdī. See the brief entry in Ibn Ḥajar, *Iṣābah*, IV, 286.

43. A client of Thaqīf who fought at Nihāwand and was governor of al-Madāʾin. See Ibn Ḥajar, *Iṣābah*, III, 16ff.; Ibn al-Athīr, *Usd*, II, 249; Translation, XIII, 182 n. 624.

44. Al-Ḥasan is the famous al-Ḥasan al-Baṣrī (b. 22/641 [Ṭabarī, I, 2646], d. ca. 110/728). See Ibn Ḥajar, *Tahdhīb*, II, 263–70; *EI*², s.v. (Ritter); Sezgin, *GAS*, I, 591–94. For al-Mubārak (d. ca. 164/780), see Ibn Ḥajar, *Tahdhīb*, X, 28–31; Translation, I, 268 n. 641.

Asīd b. al-Mutashammis, the nephew of al-Aḥnaf:[45] I was with Abū Mūsā at the conquest of Iṣfahān, but he was there only in a supporting role.

According to al-Sarī—Shu'ayb—Sayf—Muḥammad, Ṭalḥah, al-Muhallab, 'Amr, and Sa'īd: the Iṣfahān peace document: [2641]

> In the name of God, the Compassionate, the Merciful; a document from 'Abdallāh to al-Fādhūsafān and to the people of Iṣfahān and the surrounding areas. You will [remain] in a state of security as long as you pay the tribute. This is imposed upon you annually at a rate within your capacity [to pay]. You will pay it for everyone who has attained puberty to whoever is governor of your region. The Muslim must be guided, be afforded safe passage; he must be given hospitality for a whole day and a night and given a mount, if he is on foot, up to a distance of one stage. You are not to put [anyone] in authority over a Muslim. The Muslims must have your good counsel and be paid what you are obliged [to pay]. You will have safe-conduct as long as you carry out [all these stipulations]. If you go against [this] in any way or if anyone of you goes against it and you do not hand him over, you will have no safe-conduct. Anyone abusing a Muslim will be dealt with severely. If anyone physically abuses him, we shall kill him.

He wrote [this document] and it was witnessed by 'Abdallāh b. Qays [al-Ash'athī], 'Abdallāh b. Warqā', and 'Iṣmah b. 'Abdallāh.

When 'Umar's letter reached 'Abdallāh, in which he was ordered to join up with Suhayl b. 'Adī in Kirmān, he left at the head of a detachment of cavalry. He appointed al-Sā'ib as his deputy and joined up with Suhayl before he arrived in Kirmān.

According to Ma'qil b. Yasār,[46] it was al-Nu'mān b. Muqarrin who was in command of the Muslim army when it attacked Iṣfahān.

---

45. I find no information on Asīd. Al-Aḥnaf is al-Aḥnaf b. Qays al-Tamīmī, the leader of Tamīm in al-Baṣrah. See *EI*², s.v. "Al-Aḥnaf b. Ḳays" (Pellat).

46. Al-Muzanī (d. 60–70/679–689); see Ibn Ḥajar, *Tahdhīb*, X, 235.

The Account of [the Attack on Iṣfahān]

According to Ya'qūb b. Ibrāhīm[47] and 'Amr b. 'Alī[48]—'Abd al-
[2642] Raḥmān b. Mahdī[49]—Ḥammād b. Salamah[50]—Abū 'Imrān al-Jawnī[51]—'Alqamah b. 'Abdallāh al-Muzanī[52]—Ma'qil b. Yasār [al-Muzanī]: 'Umar b. al-Khaṭṭāb consulted al-Hurmuzān,[53] asking him what he thought; should be begin with Fārs, Azerbaijan, or Iṣfahān? He replied: "Fārs and Azerbaijan are the wings; Iṣfahān is the head. If you cut off one of the wings, the other one [can still] work. But, if you cut off the head, the wings collapse. Begin with the head!" 'Umar went into the mosque while al-Nu'man b. Muqarrin was praying and sat down beside him. When he had finished his prayers, ('Umar) told him that he had a job for him to do. (Al-Nu'mān) replied that, if it was collecting taxes, he was unwilling, but, if it was a military task, [he was willing]. ('Umar) told him that he would be engaged in a military matter. He despatched him to Iṣfahān and wrote to the people of al-Kūfah to give him reinforcements. He arrived in (Iṣfahān), but there was the river between him and [the enemy]. So (al-Nu'mān) sent al-Mughīrah b. Shu'bah[54] to them, and he reached them. Their ruler, called Dhū al-Ḥājibayn,[55] was told that the envoy of the Arabs was at the door. So he took counsel

47. Al-Jūzajānī (d. ca. 256/870); see Ibn Ḥajar, *Tahdhīb*, I, 181–83; Rosenthal, *Historiography*, 278; Translation, I, 26, note 96.

48. 'Amr b. 'Alī b. Baḥr al-Fallās (d. 249/864); cf. Ibn Ḥajar, *Tahdhīb*, VIII, 80–82; Rosenthal, *Historiography*, 392; Translation, I, 26 and n. 96.

49. Died 198/814. See Ibn Ḥajar, *Tahdhīb*, VI, 279–81; Translation, I, 201 n. 252.

50. Ḥammād died in 167/783. See Ibn Ḥajar, *Tahdhīb*, III, 11–16; Rosenthal, *Historiography*, 518.

51. An unidentified narrator.

52. 'Alqamah died in 100/718. See Ibn Ḥajar, *Tahdhīb*, VII, 275.

53. Ruler of Khūzistān, who, after leading much opposition against the Muslim forces, surrendered to 'Umar earlier in 21/641. Only later did he become a Muslim. See Zarrīnkūb. "Conquest," 14–15. See also Mas'ūdī, *Murūj*, IV, 230ff., recounting the same anecdotes on the authority of 'Alqamah and Ma'qil. Cf. also Bal'ami, *Chronique*, III, 481.

54. A veteran Muslim administrator and commander and a Thaqafī (d. 50/670). See Shaban, *History*, 58, 84, 187; Zarrīnkūb, "Conquest," 19, 21; Translation, XIII, passim.

55. "He of the two eyebrows." See Bal'ami, *Chronique*, III, 468; Nöldeke, *Geschichte*, 226 n. 1. On such names, see Goldziher, "Ueber Dualtitel"; see also Translation, XIII, 180 n. 618.

with his advisers, saying: "What do you think? Shall I sit down to [receive] him in royal splendor?" They replied that he should. So he sat on his throne and put the crown on his head, while the royal princes sat in two ranks, wearing earrings, gold bracelets, and silk-brocade garments. Then [the ruler] allowed (al-Mughīrah) to enter, carrying his lance and shield. He began to [2643]
poke at their carpets with his lance to unnerve them.[56] Two men took him by the arms, and he stood before their ruler, who spoke to him, saying: "You Arabs, vehement hunger has afflicted you, so you have left [your homelands]. If you wish, we shall give you provisions, and you can return home." Al-Mughīrah spoke, praising and extolling God; then he said: "We Arabs used to eat corpses and carrion; people used to trample us under foot, not we them. God has sent forth from us a prophet, the best of us in rank, the most truthful in what he says." (And he mentioned the Prophet in the fashion he deserves.) "He made us promises that we discovered were [fulfilled] as he had said. He promised us that we would conquer you and take possession of everything here. I see you are wearing [fine] garb and apparel. I do not think that [the Muslim army] coming after me will go away until they seize them." (Al-Mughīrah) continued: "Then I wondered what if I were to collect up my garments, leap up in one bound, and sit with this huge infidel on his throne! Perhaps [then] he would be unnerved." He continued: "I waited for a time when he was not expecting it and jumped. There I was with him on his throne!" (The account) continues: They seized him, beating him repeatedly with their hands and trampling him under foot. (Al-Mughīrah) continued: I said, "Is this how you treat envoys? We do not act thus. We do not do this with your envoys." The ruler replied, "If you wish, you can cross over to us or we over to you [to fight]."[57] (Al-Mughīrah) said that they would cross over to [the army of Iṣfahān]. He continued: "So

56. *Li-yataṭayyarū*, literally, "so that they might augur evil."

57. An indication that the audience was over and battle would ensue. A similar story involving al-Mughīrah has already appeared in the text in the context of the events leading up to the battle of Nihāwand (Ṭabarī, I, 2601–3). If it is a genuine account in either case, we learn much here and in the anecdote recounted below (about his appointment) of al-Mughīrah, who had clearly failed miserably in his diplomatic mission! He was later appointed governor of al-Kūfah (see p. 4) and remained in office until ʿUmar's murder.

[2644] we crossed over against them. They formed themselves into a chains of men, ten in one chain, or five, or three. We drew ourselves out in rank to meet them, and they shot arrows at us, finally rushing in among us." Al-Mughīrah said to al-Nu'mān, "God have mercy upon you, they have rushed in among our men; attack!" But he replied: "You are indeed a man of fine qualities. But I was with the Messenger of God when he went into battle. If he did not fight early on in the day, he would postpone the battle until the sun went down, the winds blew, and victory descended!" Then (al-Nu'mān) said, "I shall wave my standard three times: At the first wave everyone will relieve himself and perform his ablutions; at the second everyone will inspect his weapon and his sandal thong and fasten it tight; at the third attack, with no one turning aside to another. If al-Nu'mān is killed, let no one turn aside to him. I am going to make a single prayer to God. I conjure every one of you to say amen after it: 'O God! Give martyrdom this day to al-Nu'mān in the aid of the Muslims! Grant him victory over (the army of Iṣfahān).'" He waved his standard once, then a second, then a third time. Then he put on his coat of mail and attacked. He was the first man to be struck down.

Ma'qil said:[58] I came over to him and, remembering his conjuring [us all to say amen after his prayer], put a marker over him, then went away. Now [usually] when we kill a man his followers are distracted away from us [to investigate him]. Dhū al-Ḥājibayn fell from his mule, his belly split open, so God put (the Iṣfahānī army) to flight. Then I came [back] to al-Nu'mān, bringing with me a skin containing water. I washed the dust from his face, and he said, "Who are you?" I replied I was Ma'qil b. Yasār. He asked how the army had done. I replied that God had given them victory. He said: "Praise be to God! Write to
[2645] 'Umar about this." And his soul departed. The [Muslim] army, including Ibn 'Umar,[59] Ibn al-Zubayr,[60] 'Amr b. Ma'dī Karib[61]

58. See Ibn al-Athīr, *Kāmil*, III, 9, on the same authority.

59. This must be 'Abdallāh b. 'Umar b. al-Khaṭṭāb, who had been sent from Medina to join al-Nu'man's army prior to the battle of Nihāwand; see Ṭabarī, I, 2597, 2601, 2618.

60. 'Abdallāh b. al-Zubayr, the famous anticaliph (d. 73/692); see *EI*², s.v. (Gibb).

61. Al-Zubayrī (d. 16/637 or 21/641); cf. *EI*², s.v. (Pellat).

and Ḥudhayfah, rallied to al-Ash'ath b. Qays.[62] They sent for (al-Nu'mān's) concubine[63] and asked her what testament he had left with her. She replied, "Here is a casket containing a document." They took it, and in it was [the following]: If al-Nu'mān is killed, so-and-so [will take over]; if so-and-so is killed, so-and-so [will take over].

Al-Wāqidī[64] said that Khālid b. al-Walīd died during this year—that is 21—in Ḥimṣ. He exhorted [his followers to] continue their support for 'Umar b. al-Khaṭṭāb.[65]

(Al-Wāqidī) also reported: In (this year) 'Abdallāh and 'Abd al-Raḥmān, the sons of 'Amr, and Abū Sirwa'ah made a military expedition and arrived in Egypt. 'Abd al-Raḥmān and Abū Sirwa'ah drank wine, and something happened to them![66]

(Al-Wāqidī) also reported: In (this year) 'Amr b. al-'Āṣ marched on Anṭābulus, which is Barqah. He conquered it and made peace with its inhabitants on [payment] of 13,000 dinars and [on condition] that they sell off what they wanted of their sons as part of their tribute.[67]

---

62. Famous shaykh of Kindah who settled in al-Kūfah and died in 40/661. See Morony, *Iraq*, p. 93; Donner, *Conquests*, 433–34; Mad'aj, *Yemen*, 12, 13, 45–51, and passim; *EI*^{2}, s.v. (Reckendorf).

63. Arabic: *umm walad*; strictly speaking a concubine who has given birth to a child by her master; see Translation, XIII, 58.

64. Muḥammad b. 'Umar (d. 207/823), famous author of *K. al-Maghāzī* and a narrator used extensively by Ṭabarī. See Duri, *Rise*, 37ff.; Sezgin, *GAS*, I, 294–97.

65. Khālid b. al-Walīd was a famous early Islamic general; see *EI*^{2}, s.v. (Crone). This would appear to be the meaning here of *awṣā ilā*. See in particular Kazimirski, *Dictionnaire*, II, 1551.

66. These are perhaps the sons of 'Amr b. al-'Āṣ. Abū Sirwa'ah is perhaps Abū Sirwa'ah 'Uqbah b. al-Ḥārith b. 'Āmir b. Nawfal b. 'Abd Manāf; see Ibn Ḥajar, *Tahdhīb*, VII, 238–39, XII, 105; Translation, XII, 105; Iṣfahānī, *Aghānī*, IV, 42. There appears to be no record of what exactly happened to the offending pair.

67. Also Balādhurī, *Futūḥ*, 224; and Ya'qūbī, *Tārīkh*, II, 156; and Ibn 'Abd al-Ḥakam, *Futūḥ*, 170, with the rather strange suggestion that sons were sold, presumably for the purpose of providing military service to the Muslims, as part of a tribute arrangement. Barqah is ancient Barce in present day Libya; Balādhurī, *Futūḥ*, 224–25; Yāqūt, *Mu'jam*, I, 388; Abun-Nasr, *Maghrib*, 315, map. It is spelled Barqā in Wāqidī, *Futūḥ*, 102. Whereas Balādhurī, ibid. calls Barqah the town of Anṭābulus, Yāqūt, ibid., says the town of Barqah is Anṭābulus.

(Al-Wāqidī) also reported: In (this year) ʿUmar b. al-Khaṭṭāb appointed ʿAmmār b. Yāsir governor of al-Kūfah, Ibn Masʿūd treasurer, and ʿUthmān b. Ḥunayf in charge of land survey.[68] But the inhabitants of al-Kūfah complained about ʿAmmār, and he asked ʿUmar b. al-Khaṭṭāb to be relieved. (The latter) approached Jubayr b. Muṭʿim[69] in confidence and appointed him governor of al-Kūfah, telling him not to mention it to anyone. But al-Mughīrah b. Shuʿbah heard that ʿUmar had held a private meeting with Jubayr b. Muṭʿim, returned to his wife, and told her to go to the wife of Jubayr b. Muṭʿim and offer her some food [prepared especially] for a journey. She came to her and
[2646] offered her [the food], but she remained silent [at first], then said, "Yes, give me it." When al-Mughīrah had verified all this, he came to ʿUmar and said, "God bless you in the one whom you have appointed governor." "What governor have I appointed?" asked ʿUmar. So he mentioned that he had appointed Jubayr b. Muṭʿim. ʿUmar said, "I do not know what to do!" He [in fact] appointed al-Mughīrah b. Shuʿbah governor of al-Kūfah, an office in which he remained until ʿUmar died.[70]

(Al-Wāqidī) also said: In [this year] ʿAmr b. al-ʿĀṣ sent ʿUqbah b. Nāfiʿ al-Fihrī,[71] and he acquired Zawīlah by treaty, the whole area between Barqah and Zawīlah being already pacified in Muslim control.[72]

---

68. See *EI*[2], s.v. "Misāḥa" (Bosworth and Pellat).

69. A leader of Quraysh and a genealogist, although appearing in the text mainly as an early narrator; see Ibn Ḥajar, *Tahdhīb*, II, 63–64. Cf. a slightly different, and more informative, version of the story that follows in Balʿami, *Chronique*, III, 485–86. See also Ibn Saʿd, *Ṭabaqāt*, VIII, 59.

70. This anecdote, which represents ʿUmar as somewhat weak and indecisive and al-Mughīrah as ambitious and cunning, is also recounted in Ibn al-Athīr, *Kāmil*, III, 10.

71. Famous Muslim military leader on the North African front, entering the Maghrib in 46/666, and founder of al-Qayrawān. Killed in 64/682 near al-Qayrawān. See Abun-Nasr, *Maghrib*, 68–69; *CHIs*, I, 79.

72. Balādhurī, *Futūḥ*, 224, confirms that ʿUqbah took control of the Maghrib and reached Zawīlah. See also Yaʿqūbī, *Tārīkh*, II, 156, who reports the dispatch of ʿUqbah to Nubia. Yāqūt, *Muʿjam*, III, 159–60, says that Zawīlah was between Bilād al-Sūdān and Ifrīqiyah and also confirms that ʿUqbah took it after the conquest of Barqah. Cf. Hill, *Termination*, 56, erroneously Zāwilah.

According to Ibn Ḥumayd[73]—Salamah[74]—Ibn Isḥāq:[75] There took place in Syria in the year 21 [December 10, 641–November 30, 642] the campaign of the commander, Mu'āwiyah b. Abī Sufyān,[76] while 'Umayr b. Sa'd al-Anṣārī[77] was in charge of Damascus, al-Bathaniyyah,[78] Ḥawrān, Ḥimṣ, Qinnasrīn,[79] and al-Jazīrah and Mu'āwiyah in charge of al-Balqā',[80] the Jordan, Palestine, the coastal regions (al-Sawāḥil), Antioch, Ma'arrat Maṣrīn,[81] and Cilicia. At this point Abū Hāshim b. 'Utbah b. Rabī'ah b. 'Abd Shams[82] made a peace treaty covering Cilicia, Antioch, and Ma'arrat Maṣrīn.

It was said that in (this year) both al-Ḥasan al-Baṣrī and 'Āmir al-Sha'bī were born.[83]

Al-Wāqidī said: 'Umar b. al-Khaṭṭāb led the pilgrimage this year, leaving Zayd b. Thābit[84] as his deputy over Medina. His governors of Mecca, al-Ṭā'if, the Yemen, al-Yamāmah, Bahrain, [2647] Syria, Egypt, and al-Baṣrah were the same as those in the year 20

73. Muḥammad b. Ḥumayd al-Rāzī (d. 248/862), one of Ṭabarī's teachers in al-Rayy and one of his leading authorities. See Sezgin, *GAS*, I, 29ff., 79, 242, 253.

74. Salamah b. al-Faḍl al-Azraq (d. after 190/805). He transmitted Ibn Isḥāq's *Maghāzī* and *Mubtada'*. See Ibn Ḥajar, *Tahdhīb*, IV, 153ff.

75. Muḥammad b. Isḥāq (d. 150/767), author of the famous *Sīrah*. See Ibn Ḥajar, *Tahdhīb*, IX, 38–46; *EI*², s.v. (Jones).

76. The famous Umayyad governor in Syria and later (41–60/661–680) first Umayyad caliph.

77. Prominent figure in the Syrian conquests. See Ibn Ḥajar, *Iṣābah*, VII, 163–64.

78. One of the districts of Damascus; see Yāqūt, *Mu'jam*, I, 338. Le Strange, *Palestine*, 32–34.

79. A town south of Aleppo precisely described by Yāqūt, *Mu'jam*, IV, 403; Le Strange, *Palestine*, 486; *EI*², s.v. (Elisséeff).

80. The area south of Damascus, the principal center of which is 'Ammān; see Yāqūt, *Mu'jam*, I, 489; Le Strange, *Palestine*, 34–35.

81. A place that is part of the province of Aleppo; see Yāqūt, *Mu'jam*, V, 155. The same as Ma'arrat Qinnasrīn; see Le Strange, *Palestine*, 39.

82. The maternal uncle of Mu'āwiyah. See Ibn Ḥajar, *Tahdhīb*, XII, 261; Ibn 'Abd Rabbih, *'Iqd*, IV, 398.

83. Ibn Sharāḥīl (d. ca. 103/721), the famous narrator; see Ibn Ḥajar, *Tahdhīb*, V, 65–69, especially 68. See also Ibn Sa'd, *Ṭabaqāt*, V, 341; Rosenthal, *Historiography*, 63, 187, 380.

84. Zayd b. Thābit was a famous Companion, who died in 45/665. See Ibn Ḥajar, *Tahdhīb*, IV, 41–43.

[December 21], 640–December 10, 641.[85] The governor of al-Kūfah was ʿAmmār b. Yāsir, who was also in charge of the police.[86] ʿAbdallāh b. Masʿūd was in charge of the treasury, ʿUthmān b. Ḥunayf of the land tax, and Shurayḥ reportedly held the office of judge.[87]

---

85. It is in fact necessary to go back to the end of the year 17 (638–39) to find the complete list. Cf. Ṭabarī, I, 2570; Translation, XIII, 150.

86. For this meaning of *aḥdāth*, see Dozy, *Supplément*, I, 258, with expressions from Balādhurī. See also Hinds, "Conquests," 50 n. 33; *EI*², s.v. (Cahen).

87. That is, Shurayḥ b. al-Ḥārith al-Kindī, a famous, perhaps "legendary," judge of early Islam (d. 72–99/691–718). See Schacht, *Origins*, 228–29; Translation, XIII, 159 n. 543.

The Events of the Year 22

(NOVEMBER 30, 642–NOVEMBER 19, 643)

Abū Ja'far [al-Ṭabarī] said: In (this year) Azerbaijan was conquered, according to Aḥmad b. Thābit al-Rāzī—someone he mentioned—Isḥāq b. 'Īsā—Abū Ma'shar:[88] Azerbaijan was [conquered] in the year 22, its commander being al-Mughīrah b. Shu'bah. Al-Wāqidī also reported thus.

However, Sayf b. 'Umar said, according to al-Sarī—Shu'ayb: The conquest of Azerbaijan took place in the year 18 of the Hijrah after the conquest of Hamadhān, al-Rayy, and Jurjān and after the ruler of Ṭabaristān[89] had sued for peace with the Muslims. He continued: All this took place in the year 18.[90]

---

88. For Aḥmad and Abū Ma'shar, see Sezgin, *GAS*, I, 292, 796; Translation, I, 6; for Isḥāq (d. 214/829), see *GAS*, 200 n. 245.

89. Yāqūt, *Mu'jam*, IV, 14–15, explains that *isbahbad*, the term used here, is that used in Ṭabaristān as the title of the ruler. See also Morony, *Iraq*, 28.

90. On the question of the date of the conquest of Azerbaijan, see Balādhurī, *Futūḥ*, 326; also Ya'qūbī, *Tārīkh*, 156, who gives only the date 22; Ibn al-Athīr, *Kāmil*, III, 13, under the year 22. For the conquest of Hamadhān, see Balādhurī, *Futūḥ*, 309–11 (in the year 23); Ya'qūbī, *Tārīkh*, II, 157 (also in 23); Ibn al-Athīr, ibid., 10, *sub anno* 22.

(Sayf) continued: The reason for the conquest of Hamadhān, so it was claimed, was [as follows]. Muḥammad, al-Muhallab, Ṭalḥah, ʿAmr, and Saʿīd had informed (Sayf) that al-Nuʿmān was diverted to the two provincial centers [of Nihāwand and al-Dīnawar][91] because the Persians had assembled in Nihāwand. The Kūfans were diverted there too, and they, including Ḥudhayfah, joined up with (al-Nuʿmān). When the Kūfans left Ḥulwān and arrived at Māh,[92] they attacked a castle (*qalʿah*) in a field (*marj*) in which was a body of armed men. They forced them to come down—and this was the first [step] in the con-
[2648] quest—and settled cavalry in their place to keep a hold on the castle. They named their camp after the field, calling it Marj al-Qalʿah. Then they marched from Marj al-Qalʿah in the direction of Nihāwand and reached a[nother] castle containing some men. They left al-Nusayr b. Thawr attacking it with [a group of] ʿIjl and Ḥanīfah,[93] and it was called after him. He took it after the victory of Nihāwand, and thus not one ʿIjlī, or one Ḥanafī, was present at Nihāwand; they remained with al-Nusayr stationed at the castle. Nevertheless, when (the Muslims) made a comprehensive assessment of the immovable booty[94] of Nihāwand and the castles, they gave all of them a share in it, as they had given one another support. From that time on they gave a name according to its characteristics to everything they observed between Marj al-Qalʿah and Nihāwand, [that is,] the area they had already passed through, and what they had observed from al-Marj to it. Some riding camels (*rikāb*) jostled together on one of the mountain roads (sing. *thaniyyah*) of Māh, so it was called al-Rikāb, or Thaniyyat al-Rikāb. They came upon another the

91. That is, the dual of the Persian word *māh* = Arabic *qaṣabah*. The former is south, the latter southwest of Hamadhān. See Yāqūt, *Muʿjam*, V, 48; Le Strange, *Lands*, 196–97; Translation, XIII, 4, 199; *EI*², s.v. "Māh al-Baṣra," "Māh al-Kūfa" (Morony). See also note 2.

92. That is, Nihāwand, see note 91.

93. That is, al-Nusayr b. Daysam b. Thawr al-ʿIjlī, about whom there is no information. ʿIjl here are presumably ʿIjl b. Lujaym b. Ṣaʿb, a tribal division (*baṭn*) of Bakr b. Wāʾil, originally occupying an area between al-Yamāmah and al-Baṣrah; see *EI*², s.v. "ʿIdjl" (Watt). ʿIjl and Ḥanīfah are closely related tribal groups (*EI*², s.v. "Ḥanīfa" [Watt]). See also Ibn Ḥazm, *Jamharah*, 309, 312; Caskel, *Ǧamharat*, I, Tables 141, 156, 157; Kaḥḥālah, *Muʿjam*, I, 312; II, 757.

94. Arabic *fayʾ*. See *EI*², s.v. (Løkkegaard).

track of which went round a rock, so they called it Malwiyyah (twisted). Their original names were obliterated, and they were given names in keeping with their characteristics. (The Muslims) passed by the long mountain overlooking [other] mountains, and one of them said that it was like the tooth of Sumayrah—Sumayrah was a Ḍabbī woman from Banū Muʿāwiyah,[95] one of those who migrated with the Prophet, who had a tooth projecting over her [other] teeth; so this mountain was named after her tooth. Ḥudhayfah had sent Nuʿaym b. Muqarrin and al-Qaʿqāʿ b. ʿAmr[96] in pursuit of the defeated troops of Nihāwand. The two reached Hamadhān, and Khusrawshunūm[97] made peace with them. They left (the Hamadhānīs) and returned; then later he reneged. When ʿUmar's agreement with (Khusrawsunūm) arrived among those dis- [2649] patched by him, (Nuʿaym) bade Ḥudhayfah farewell, and Ḥudhayfah did [likewise], (Nuʿaym) making for Hamadhān, while (Ḥudhayfah) made to return to al-Kūfah. (The latter) appointed as deputy of Nihāwand and al-Dīnawar ʿAmr b. Bilāl b. al-Ḥārith.[98]

ʿUmar's letter to Nuʿaym b. Muqarrin [included the instruction] to march on Hamadhān, dispatch Suwayd b. Muqarrin in charge of his vanguard and Ribʿī b. ʿĀmir and Muhalhil b. Zayd[99]—the latter a Ṭāʾī, the former a Tamīmī—in charge of the wings. So Nuʿaym b. Muqarrin went forth with his [army] in formation. He went down Thaniyyat al-ʿAsal (the Mountain Road of Honey). It had been given this name because of the honey found there after the battle of Nihāwand, where they pursued the defeated troops. [At that time] al-Fayruzān[100] had

---

95. That is, Ḍabbah b. Shihāb b. Muʿāwiyah, rather than the better-known Ḍabbah b. Udd; see Caskel, *Ǧamharat*, I, Table 309.

96. A Tamīmī hero of both Qādisiyyah and Nihāwand, his exploits are much emphasized by Sayf b. ʿUmar. See Ṭabarī, I, 2459–64 and 2626–28; Translation, XIII, passim, in particular 39–43, 209–11; EI^2, s.v. (Zetterstéen).

97. The Persian general; see Morony, *Iraq*, 194.

98. ʿAmr b. Bilāl b. al-Ḥārith is unidentified.

99. Ribʿī b. ʿĀmir is unidentified. Muhalhil b. Zayd al-Khayl al-Ṭāʾī was a hero of the Riddah wars. See Ibn Ḥajar, *Iṣābah*, X, 49.

100. The Persian general in charge of the army defeated at Nihāwand. See Morony, *Iraq*, 192–93, for earlier events in which he played a part.

reached (the road), which was crowded with beasts of burden carrying honey and other things, so he was hemmed in by them until he dismounted. Then he had gone up the mountain. His horse, [being riderless], had gone back down and was pursued and [eventually] taken. When they stopped at Kinkiwar,[101] some of the Muslims' animals were stolen, so it was given the name Qaṣr al-Luṣūṣ (Stronghold of Thieves).

Then Nu'aym went down the mountain road and stopped at the town of Hamadhān. But they had already fortified it against (the Muslims), so he besieged (the Hamdhānīs), taking the area between there and Jarmīdhān.[102] (The Muslims) took control of the whole area of Hamadhān. When the inhabitants of the town realized this, they sued for peace [with the request] that he treat them and those who had [originally] complied [with his demand to surrender] exactly alike. This he did and accepted tribute from them for their protection. He divided up Dastabā[103] among a
[2650] group of Kūfans, [comprising] 'Iṣmah b. 'Abdallāh al-Ḍabbī, Muhalhil b. Zayd al-Ṭā'ī, Simāk b. 'Ubayd al-'Absī,[104] Simāk b. Makhramah al-Asadī,[105] and Simāk b. Kharashah al-Anṣārī.[106] These were the first to be appointed governors over the frontier regions[107] of Dastabā and to fight the Daylam.[108]

But, according to al-Wāqidī: The conquest of Hamadhān and

101. Persian Kangavar, a small town between Hamadhān and Qarmīsīn. See Yāqūt, *Mu'jam*, IV, 484, who mentions Qaṣr al-Luṣūṣ; Spuler, *Iran*, 127 and end maps; Barthold, *Geography*, 195; *EI*², s.v. "Kinkiwar" (Savory). See also Bal'ami, *Chronique*, III, 482.

102. Yāqūt's "A place in al-Jabal; I think it is in the regions of Hamadhān" (II, 129) is not very helpful. This must be a small place, not far from the town of Hamadhān.

103. Dastabā is the extensive area between al-Rayy and Hamadhān, and this is clearly what is meant here. See Yāqūt, *Mu'jam*, II, 454; Le Strange, *Lands*, 220. It is given as a town on Map 1, 60–61, of the *CHIr*, IV.

104. Warrior in the eastern conquests. Lived until the end of the caliphate of Mu'āwiyah. See Ibn Ḥajar, *Iṣābah*, IV, 254; Hill, *Termination*, 125, 129.

105. Died in al-Raqqah in Mu'āwiyah's caliphate. See Ibn Ḥajar, *Iṣābah*, IV, 254; Ibn al-Athīr, *Usd*, II, 353.

106. Fought at al-Qādisiyyah. See Ibn Ḥajar, *Iṣābah*, IV, 253; Ibn al-Athīr, *Usd*, II, 352–53.

107. *Masāliḥ* the eastern equivalents of the western *thughūr*; i.e., the regions on the edge of Muslim control as they pushed eastward.

108. For the land and its people, see *EI*², s.v. (Minorsky). The territory of Daylam is the highlands of Jīlān.

al-Rayy took place in 23 [November 19, 643–November 7, 644]. According to him also: It is said that Qaraẓah b. Ka'b[109] conquered al-Rayy.

Also according to (al-Wāqidī)—Rabī'ah b. 'Uthmān:[110] The conquest of Hamadhān took place in [the month of] Jumādā I, exactly six months after the murder of 'Umar b. al-Khaṭṭāb. Its commander was al-Mughīrah b. Shu'bah.

According to (al-Wāqidī): It is also reported that the conquest of al-Rayy took place two years before the death of 'Umar. It is also said that 'Umar was killed while his armies were [engaged in hostilities] against it.[111]

To return to Sayf's account: While Nu'aym was at the head of 12,000 troops in the town of Hamadhān, engaged in subduing it, the Daylam, the inhabitants of al-Rayy, and those of Azerbaijan entered into correspondence among themselves. Then Mūtā,[112] at the head of the Daylam, went forth and halted at Wāj Rūdh.[113] Al-Zīnabī Abū al-Farrukhān,[114] at the head of the Rayy army, arrived to join him, and Isfandiyādh, brother of Rustam, did the same at the head of the Azerbaijan army.[115] The commanders of the Dastabā frontier regions[116] fortified themselves and sent to Nu'aym, giving him the news. So he ap- [2651]

109. Qaraẓah b. 'Amr b. Ka'b al-Khuzā'ī died in al-Kūfah during the caliphate of Mu'āwiyah. See Ibn Ḥajar, *Iṣābah*, VIII, 151–52.

110. He died in 154/771. See Ibn Ḥajar, *Iṣābah*, III, 266–67; *Tahdhīb*, III, 260; Ibn al-Athīr, *Usd*, 170.

111. Balādhurī, *Futūḥ*, 319, says that the final conquest of al-Rayy was carried out by Qaraẓah b. Ka'b al-Anṣārī during the governorship of Abū Mūsā over al-Kūfah on behalf of 'Uthmān; see Zarrīnkūb, "Conquest," p. 23, erroneously Qurẓat. Ya'qūbī, *Tārīkh*, II, 157, agrees, this statement coming under the year 23. Cf. Ibn al-Athīr, *Kāmil*, III, 11–12, who, as always, follows Ṭabarī, mentioning without authority Qaraẓah as conqueror. He mentions too a date of 21 for the conquest. Cf. Ibn al-Athīr, *Usd*, II, 170; *Kāmil*, III, 9. 'Umar died from his wounds on Dhū al-Ḥijjah 3, 23/October 13, 644.

112. This Daylamī leader appears as Mūthā in Yāqūt, *Mu'jam*, V, 341.

113. Wāj (al-)Rūdh is situated between Hamadhān and Qazwīn. Yāqūt, *Mu'jam*, V, 341, gives the date of the battle as 29.

114. I vocalize this Persian proper name thus after reference to Justi, *Namenbuch*, 386. But see cf. Bal'ami *Chronique*, III, 489, al-Zīnbī; and Hill, *Termination*, 128, etc., al-Zaynabī.

115. Isfandiyādh was the brother of Rustam b. Farrukhzādh, the Persian general defeated at al-Qādisiyyah. See Zarrīnkūb, "Conquest," 10.

116. That is, 'Iṣmah, Muhalhil, and the three Simāks; see above.

pointed Yazīd b. Qays[117] as his deputy and went to do battle against (the Persians) at the head of his army, coming down upon them at Wāj al-Rūdh. They fought together there vehemently; it was a great battle like Nihāwand, not at all inferior. Great, incalculable numbers were killed, and the bloody struggle between them was no less then [other] great battles. They had already written to ʿUmar of the amassing [of forces] against them. He was disturbed at this [assembly of troops at Wāj al-Rūdh] and was worried about the [outcome of the] battle. He expected [news] of them coming through and was taken by surprise only by the message bearing the good news [of the victory]. He said, "Is that someone bearing good news (*bashīr*)?" The reply was, "[No], it is ʿUrwah!"[118] When he repeated his question, (ʿUrwah) understood and replied, "[Yes], good news (*bashīr*)!" ʿUmar asked if it was the envoy of Nuʿaym and was told it was. He asked for the news and was told the good news of the conquest and victory. He gave him [all] the news. (ʿUmar) praised God and ordered the letter to be read out to the people, and they too praised God. Then Simāk b. Makhramah, Simāk b. ʿUbayd, and Simāk b. Kharashah arrived at the head of the delegations of the Kūfans with the fifths [of booty for the state treasury] to see ʿUmar. He asked them their lineage and all three Simāks told him. He said: "God bless you! O God, raise up (*usmuk*)[119] Islam through them and strengthen them through Islam!"

Dastabā and its frontier regions as far as [the town of] Hamadhān were [treated as] part of [the province of] Hamadhān until the envoy returned to Nuʿaym b. Muqarrin with the reply from ʿUmar b. al-Khaṭṭāb. [In it he instructed him] to appoint a deputy over Hamadhān, reinforce Bukayr b. ʿAbdallāh [in Azerbaijan] by means of Simāk b. Kharashah, proceed to al-Rayy,

117. A Yemeni Arḥabī from Hamdān; see below. See also Madʿaj, *Yemen*, 124, 141, etc.

118. ʿUmar actually said, "*A-bashīr*?" which can mean either "Is that someone bearing good news?" or "Is that Bashīr?" the latter being a man's name. ʿUrwah, the messenger, interpreted the question in the latter meaning; hence his reply.

119. ʿUmar makes a pun on their name, Simāk. Cf. Balʿami, *Chronique*, III, 488.

face their army in battle, and remain there, as it was the most central and unified part of this territory for his purposes. So Nu'aym established Yazīd b. Qays al-Hamdānī in charge of Hamadhān and marched out from Wāj al-Rūdh with his army to al-Rayy. [2652]

Nu'aym recited the following concerning Wāj al-Rūdh:[120]

When I heard that Mūtā[121] and his tribe,
Banū Bāsil,[122] had driven on their Persian armies,[123]
I roused up my armies against them, competing in glory,
that I might deny them with my swords my protection.[124]
We brought upon them our steel [armor]—'twas as if we
were mountains looming up through the branches of the *qalāsim* trees.[125]
When we met them in battle at [Wāj al-Rūdh, the valley] wide and abundant in trees,
they having already begun to rear up to fight like a champion,
We repelled them at Wāj Rūdh with our force
on the morning we inflicted upon (the Persians) one of the great calamities.[126]
They could not endure for any time at all, as death hovered,
against our sharp spears[127] and cutting swords.
When their forces scattered, they were like
a wall the baked brick of which has crumbled with destroying blows.

---

120. Meter *ṭawīl*. Yāqūt, *Mu'jam*, V, 341, quotes lines 1, 5, 6, 8, and 10.

121. Yāqūt, *Mu'jam*, V, 341, Mūthā; i.e., the ruler of Daylam.

122. This is the claim that the Daylamites are decended from Bāsil b. Ḍabbah. See Ibn Ḥazm, *Jamharah*, 203 ("*wa-Bāsilu bnu Ḍabbah, yuqālu inna al-Daylama min waladi-h*"); Caskel, *Ǧamharat*, I, Table 89.

123. Yāqūt, *Mu'jam*, has *khuyūl* for *junūd*, "their Persian cavalry."

124. Nu'aym is here saying that he intends to slay them all and thus will not have to make arrangements for their protection (*dhimmah*) after the battle.

125. "Mountains" to signify the strength and bulk of the Muslim forces. I am unable to identify *qalāsim*, nor indeed find this species of tree in the lexica at my disposal.

126. That is, after the defeats of al-Qādisiyyah and Nihāwand, now Wāj (al)-Rūdh.

127. Yāqūt, *Mu'jam*, reads *bi-ḥaddi* for *li-ḥaddi*.

We killed Mūtā there and his army around him;[128]
there was booty there quickly distributed.[129]
[2653] We pursued them until they took refuge in their side wadis,
slaughtering them as fierce dogs would!
'Twas as if they in Wāj Rūdh and in its wide valley
were sheep killed by the gaping wounds from our spears.[130]

Simāk b. Makhramah's name was given to the mosque of Simāk.[131]

Nuʿaym repeated the Hamadhān peace document in their case. He left as his deputy in charge of (Hamadhān) Yazīd b. Qays al-Hamdānī. (Nuʿaym) himself marched with his armies and reached al-Rayy. The first Daylamites were [descended] from the Arabs, but Nuʿaym disputed (this opinion) with them.[132]

The Conquest of al-Rayy[133]

They report [also]: Nuʿaym b. Muqarrin left Wāj Rūdh, having laid it waste, at the head of the army [and made] for Dastabā. He departed thence for al-Rayy when (its inhabitants) had assembled together to [stand against] him. Al-Zīnabī Abū al-Farrukhān came out and met him at a place called Qihā[134] to make peace with him in defiance of the ruler of al-Rayy, once he had seen what the Muslims were like, [comparing their attitude] with the envy of Siyāwakhsh and his family. So (al-Zīnabī) came, together with Nuʿaym, while the ruler at that time in
[2654] al-Rayy was [this] Siyāwakhsh b. Mihrān b. Bahrām Shūbīn.[135]

---

128. Yāqūt reads *liffa-hu* for *jamʿa-hu*.

129. Yāqūt reads *ghānimi* for *ʿātimi*.

130. Yāqūt reads *wa-jarri-hi* for *wa-jawwi-hi* in the first hemistich. The second hemistich is fraught with difficulties and the translation tentative: *ḍaʾīnun aṣābat-hā furūju al-makhārimi*. Yāqūt reads *aghānat-hā* for *aṣābat-hā*.

131. Masjid Simāk was in al-Kūfah. See Balādhuri, *Futūḥ*, 284; Iṣfahānī, *Aghānī*, X, 85; Yāqūt, *Muʿjam*, V, 125.

132. This is how I interpret *wa-kāna awwalu nasli al-Daylami min al-ʿArab wa-qāwala-hum fī-hi Nuʿaym*.

133. Cf. Balādhurī, *Futūḥ*, 317ff.; Ibn al-Athīr, *Kāmil*, III, 11; Balʿami, *Chronique*, III, 489.

134. A large village between al-Rayy and Qazwīn; see Yāqūt, *Muʿjam*, IV, 417.

135. For the man and his ancestors, see Spuler, *Iran*, 16; Nöldeke, *Geschichte*, 139 n. 3; Zarrīnkūb, "Conquest," 19; *EIr*, s.v. (Shahbazi).

(Siyāwakhsh) asked the people of Dunbāwand,[136] Ṭabaristān, Qūmis, and Jurjān for their help, saying, "You are already aware that, once these (Muslim troops) have occupied al-Rayy, there will be no place for you." So they [all] mustered to support (Siyāwakhsh). Siyāwakhsh made to attack (al-Zīnabī). They met at the foot of the mountain of al-Rayy to one side of the town and did battle there. Al-Zīnabī had said to Nu'aym: "The enemy is numerous, whereas you are at the head of a small army. Send some cavalry with me. I shall take them into their town, [al-Rayy], by a way in that [even] (the locals) do not know. You attack them, for if (the cavalry) [with me also] comes out against them, they will not stand firm against you." So Nu'aym despatched some cavalry with him by night under the command of his nephew, al-Mundhir b. 'Amr.[137] Al-Zīnabī took them into the town without the enemy's knowing, and Nu'aym launched a surprise attack on (the latter) by night and distracted them away from [the defense of] their town. Battle was joined, and (the enemy) stood firm against (Nu'aym) until they heard the cry [of the cavalry], "God is great," behind them. Then they were put to flight and were killed in such numbers as to be reckoned in fathoms.[138] God gave the Muslims at al-Rayy about the same amount of spoils as those at al-Madā'in. Al-Zīnabī made peace
with (Nu'aym) for the inhabitants of al-Rayy, and (Nu'aym) [2655]
appointed him governor (*marzaba-hu*) over them. The honor of al-Rayy continued to be greatest among the family of al-Zīnabī, including Shahrām and Farrukhān.[139] The family of Bahrām[140] fell from grace, and Nu'aym destroyed their town, which was called al-'Atīqah (the Old Town); that is, the town of al-Rayy. Al-Zīnabī gave orders for the building of the new town of al-Rayy.

Nu'aym wrote to 'Umar about the victory that God had

---

136. The great mountain that dominates Ṭabaristān and a small town, modern Damāvand, to the south of the mountain. See Yāqūt, *Mu'jam*, II, 475; Le Strange, *Lands*, 371.

137. Al-Mundhir b. 'Amr was an early military leader who had fought with the Prophet. See Ibn al-Athīr, *Usd*, III, 418–19.

138. Arabic *qaṣab*. See Dozy, *Supplément*, II, 353; *Glossarium*, CDXXIV.

139. The two sons of al-Zīnabī; see Justi, *Namenbuch*, 276.

140. See note 135.

given him, [dispatching the letter] with al-Muḍārib al-ʿIjlī.[141] He also sent the fifth parts [of the booty for the state treasury] with ʿUtaybah b. al-Nahhās[142] and Abū Mufazzir,[143] along with some Kūfan notables. (ʿUmar) sent Simāk b. Kharashah al-Anṣārī to reinforce Bukayr b. ʿAbdallāh after al-Rayy had been conquered. So Simāk marched off to Azerbaijan as reinforcement for Bukayr. Nuʿaym wrote a document for the inhabitants of al-Rayy:

> In the name of God, the Compassionate, the Merciful. The following is what Nuʿaym b. Muqarrin has granted to al-Zīnabī b. Qūlah. He has granted him security for the people of al-Rayy and those others with them on [payment of] tribute, as much as each one who has reached puberty can provide annually. They must give good advice and guidance and must not act treacherously or steal. They must provide hospitality to the Muslims for a whole day and a night and show them respect. Anyone who abuses a Muslim or holds him in contempt will be severely punished. Anyone who physically abuses him will be killed. If anyone of them reneges and is not handed over intact, your [whole] community [is deemed to] have reneged.

He wrote [it], and it was witnessed.

[2656] (Nuʿaym) was sent messages by the ruler [of Dunbāwand][144] on the subject of peace, offering what would keep him free of (the Muslims), without (Nuʿaym's) demanding from him any aid and protection.[145] (Nuʿaym) accepted this and drew up a document between the two of them, without any aid [on the part of the people of Dunbāwand] or any assistance against anyone [being made obligatory]. So they got what they asked for as follows.

---

141. Al-Muḍārib al-ʿIjlī was a Companion or Follower, who has brief entries in Ibn Ḥajar, *Tahdhīb*, X, 166–67; Ibn al-Athīr, *Usd*, III, 371.

142. Little information appears to be available on ʿUtaybah. See Donner, *Conquests*, 383; Ibn ʿAbd Rabbih, *ʿIqd*, I, 283; Iṣfahānī, *Aghānī*, II, 47–48.

143. That is, al-Aswad b. Quṭbah, a poet and warrior who was present at al-Qādisiyyah; see Ibn Ḥajar, *Iṣābah*, I, 171; Translation, XIII, 11.

144. The title *maṣmughān* has a religious connotation; see *CHIr*, 199.

145. Arabic, *"fī al-sulḥi ʿalā shay'in yaftadī bi-hi min-hum min ghayri an yas'ala-hu al-naṣra wa-al-manʿah."*

> In the name of God, the Compassionate, the Merciful. This is a document from Nuʿaym b. Muqarrin to Mardānshāh, ruler of Dunbāwand and the people of Dunbāwand, al-Khuwār,[146] al-Lāriz,[147] and al-Shirriz.[148] You and those who enter [into this agreement] with you will be secure on condition you refrain [from hostile acts] and on condition that you restrain the people of your territory. You will insure yourself [against military action being taken against you] by [paying] 200,000 dirhams, the weight of seven,[149] annually to whoever is governor of your region. You will not be attacked, nor will you be approached save by permission, as long as you remain within these [conditions] [and] unless you renege. If anyone reneges, he will not [be covered by] any agreement, nor will he who does not hand him over.

He wrote [the document] and it was witnessed.

The Conquest of Qūmis[150]

They reported [also]: When Nuʿaym wrote of the conquest of al-Rayy, [despatching the news] with al-Muḍārib al-ʿIjlī, and when he submitted the fifths [of booty for the state treasury], ʿUmar replied to him that he should send Suwayd b. Muqarrin in advance to Qūmis, posting in charge of his vanguard Simāk b. Makhramah, of his flanks ʿUtaybah b. al-Nahhās and Hind b. [2657]
ʿAmr al-Jamalī.[151] Suwayd b. Muqarrin mobilized (his army) and moved from al-Rayy on Qūmis. No one showed him any

146. The westernmost town of Qūmis and the first important place east of al-Rayy. See Yāqūt, *Muʿjam*, II, 394, with no definite article; Le Strange, *Lands*, 367.

147. The MSS are far from clear here, and these place names are doubtful. Al-Khuwār is possible; see note 146, above. I can find no reference to a place called al-Lāriz in the sources at my disposal. But see *EI*², s.v.v. "Lār" and "Lārijān" (Calmard).

148. Yāqūt, *Mu*ʿjam, III, 334, has a Shirriz, without the article, but this is a mountain in al-Daylam.

149. That is, every 10 dirhams weighing seven *mithqāls*. See Sauvaire, "Matériaux," 460; see also Hinz, *Masse*, 1ff.

150. See Balādhurī, *Futūḥ*, 317ff.

151. An unidentified military leader.

hostility, so he took it peacefully and encamped there. When (his army) drank from a river belonging (to the people of Qūmis) called Malādh,[152] they began to suffer from stiff necks, so Suwayd told them to change their [source of] water until they got used to it like the local inhabitants. They did so and found (the new supply) healthy. Those of [the locals] who had taken refuge in Ṭabaristān and those who had sought safe refuges sent (Suwayd) communications. So he called on them to make peace and [pay] tribute, writing to them as follows:

> In the name of God, the Compassionate, the Merciful. This is the guarantee of safety that Suwayd b. Muqarrin has granted to the people of Qūmis and to their followers, for their persons, their religion, and their possessions, on condition that they pay tribute directly,[153] every one of them who has reached puberty according to his capacity [to pay]; also on condition that they give good, not bad, advice, guide [the Muslims], and give hospitality to any Muslims who settle among them for a period of one day and one night with their ordinary food.[154] If they renege and hold their agreement in contempt, then the convenant no longer applics to them.

He wrote [the document] and it was witnessed.

The Conquest of Jurjān[155]

They reported [also]: Suwayd b. Muqarrin encamped at Bisṭām.[156]
[2658] He wrote to the ruler of Jurjān, Ruzbān Ṣūl.[157] (Suwayd) marched

---

152. I cannot identify River Malādh, but it must be in Qūmis.

153. Arabic, "*'an yadin.*" See Qur'ān, IX:29. That is, directly without involving a third party. A number of interpretations are possible as well as the one given here: "willingly," "by ready money," or "in token of subjection." See Bayḍāwī, *Commentarius*, in ibid.; Penrice, *Dictionary*, 164–65. See also Cahen, "Coran IX-29," passim, and Kister "*'An yadin*," passim.

154. See Qur'ān, V:89.

155. Cf. Balādhurī, *Futūḥ*, 334ff.

156. A town less than 50 miles northeast of the capital of Qūmis, Dāmghān, it is the second town of the province. See Yāqūt, *Mu'jam*, I, 421–22; Le Strange, *Lands*, 364–65 and Map V, opposite 185.

157. Ruzbān Ṣūl himself is not further identified. For Ṣūl, see Translation, XXXIII, 44 n. 148.

on (Jurjān) and Ruzbān Ṣūl entered into correspondence with him. (Ruzbān Ṣūl) hastened to make peace with him, [with the provision] that he should pay tribute and that he would save (Suwayd) the trouble of making war on Jurjān; if (Suwayd) were being defeated, (Ruzbān Ṣūl) would give him assistance. (Suwayd) accepted his terms. He was met by Ruzbān Ṣūl before he entered Jurjān, and he went in with him. He encamped there until the collection of the taxes had been carried out and until he had specified [the various] frontier regions (of Jurjān) by name.[158] He allocated the Turks of Dihistān,[159] [to look after] them, removing the tribute from those who remained to defend them and taking taxes from the remainder of the people of (Jurjān). He drew up a document between them and himself as follows:

> In the name of God, the Compassionate, the Merciful. This is a document from Suwayd b. Muqarrin to Ruzbān Ṣūl b. Ruzbān and the people of Dihistān and all of those of Jurjān. You have our covenant, while it is our duty to protect [you], on condition that you pay tribute annually according to your capacity, everyone who has reached the age of puberty. Any one of you whose help we seek shall pay his tribute in the form of assistance he renders instead of his [regular] tribute. The guarantee of safety covers their persons, their possessions, and their religion and laws. Nothing of all this can be broken; it remains in force for them as long as they pay [their dues], guide the traveler, give good advice, provide hospitality to the

---

158. I translate the Arabic *kharāj* "taxes." This term and the word *jizyah*, which alone of the two has appeared in the text so far, were undoubtedly synonymous in early Islam, with the meaning of tribute. The terms were later refined in Islamic law and *kharāj* took on the technical meaning of land tax. It should be noted, however, that here both terms are to be found in the same paragraph (and are perhaps not synonymous at all) and that, when it comes to the actual document, only *jizyah* is used. Here, however, Suwayd not only collected the *kharāj*, but also busied himself with the assessment of the frontier regions (*furūj*) of Jurjān, as if for the purpose of levying some sort of tax based on the land. For the two terms, see *EI*², s.v.v. "djizya" and "kharadj" (Cahen); Ben Shemesh, *Taxation*, 19–20.

159. An area to the north of Jurjān is clearly meant here, although the name is given several locations in Yāqūt. See *Muʿjam*, II, 492; Le Strange, *Lands*, 379–81.

> Muslims, and perpetrate no theft or any treacherous act. He who stays among them has similar rights to theirs. He who leaves remains in safety until he reaches "his place of safety."[160] There is also the condition that anyone abusing a Muslim will be dealt with very severely. Anyone physically abusing him may be killed.[161]

[2659] It was witnessed by Sawād b. Quṭbah,[162] Hind b. ʿAmr, Simāk b. Makhramah and ʿUtaybah b. al-Nahhās. It was drawn up in the year 18 [January 12, 639–January 2, 640].

But al-Madāʾinī[163] reported on the authority of Abū Zayd:[164] Jurjān was conquered in the time of ʿUthmān in the year 30 [September 4, 650–August 24, 651].

The Conquest of Ṭabaristān[165]

(The same sources) continued: The ruler [of Ṭabaristān] sent messages to Suwayd on the subject of a peace on the understanding that they make a formal pact and that (Suwayd) propose terms to him without his being obliged to render help or assistance against anyone. (Suwayd) accepted these terms and gave (the people of Ṭabaristān) what they wanted. He wrote him a document [as follows]:

> In the name of God, the Compassonate, the Merciful. This is a document from Suwayd b. Muqarrin addressed to al-Farrukhān, ruler of Khurāsān in authority over Ṭabaristān and to the ruler (*jīl*) of Jīlān,[166] our [previous] enemy. You will be secure in God's safekeeping on condition that you restrain your robbers and the people

---

160. Qurʾān, IX:6.
161. Arabic, "*ḥalla damu-h.*"
162. Sawād b. Quṭbah al-Tamīmī has a brief entry in Ibn al-Athīr, *Usd*, II, 375, where these events are mentioned.
163. The famous historian ʿAlī b. Muhammad (d. ca. 225/839). See Duri, *Rise*, 48ff.; Rosenthal, *Historiography*, 69ff.; Sezgin, *GAS*, I, 314ff.
164. An unidentified narrator.
165. See Balādhurī, *Futūḥ*, 334ff.
166. See *EI*[1], s.v. "Māzyār" (Minorsky). Jīlān was a small province at the west end of the southern Caspian shore. See Yāqūt, *Muʿjam*, II, 201; Le Strange, *Lands*, 172 and Map 5, opposite 185.

> on the borders of your territory. You will harbor nobody or nothing we are seeking and you will insure yourself [against military action against you] by [paying] anyone governing your border territory 500,000 dirhams, those [in use] in your territory. If you carry [all] this out, none of us will have a right to attack you, or to invade your territory, or [even] to approach you without your permission. Our way to you, provided that we obtain your permission, will be in safety, just as yours [to us] will be. Do not harbor anybody or anything we are seeking. Do not steal what is ours, [as if acting] against an enemy, or carry out any treacherous act. If you do, there will be no pact between us.

It was witnessed by Sawād b. Quṭbah al-Tamīmī, Hind b. ʿAmr
al-Murādī, Simāk b. Makhramah al-Asadī, Simāk b. ʿUbayd [2660]
al-ʿAnsī and ʿUtaybah b. al-Nahhās al-Bakrī. It was drawn up in the year 18 [January 12, 639–January 2, 640].

The Conquest of Azerbaijan[167]

(The same sources) made [the following] report. When Nuʿaym conquered Hamadhān for a second time and marched on al-Rayy from Wāj Rūdh, ʿUmar wrote to him, [instructing] him to despatch Simāk b. Kharashah al-Anṣārī to reinforce Bukayr b. ʿAbdallāh in Azerbaijan. But (Nuʿaym) delayed [the implementation of] this [instruction] until he had taken al-Rayy. Then (Nuʿaym) sent (Simāk) from al-Rayy and he marched to join Bukayr in Azerbaijan. Now Simāk b. Kharashah and ʿUtbah b. Farqad were two rich Arabs, having [originally] brought their wealth to al-Kūfah. Bukayr had already set off, when he was sent to (Azerbaijan), but, when he came up opposite Jarmīdhāh b. al-Farrukhzādh, fleeing from Wāj Rūdh, advanced on him (and his men). [This] was the first fighting (Bukayr) encountered in Azerbaijan. They fought and God put (Isfandiyādh's) army to flight; Bukayr took him prisoner. Isfandiyādh asked him whether he preferred peace or war. He replied that he preferred

---

167. See Balādhurī, *Futūḥ*, 325ff; Balʿami, *Chronique*, III, 494; *CHIr*, 20.

peace. (Isfandiyādh) said, "Keep me with you, for if I make no peace treaty involving the people of Azerbaijan, nor join [them], they will not stand up to you, but will disperse into the surrounding Caucasus mountains and those of Asia Minor (*min al-Qabj wa-al-Rūm*). Those who can fortify themselves [there] will do so for some time." So (Bukayr) held (Isfandiyādh) with him, keeping him in his control. [All] the area fell to him except
[2661] what was fortified. Simāk b. Kharashah joined him as reinforcement, whereas Isfandiyādh [remained] in (Bukayr's) custody, having taken the regions near him, while ʿUtbah b. Farqad had taken those near him. Bukayr said to Simāk, when the latter came to him, joking with him, "What am I to do with you and ʿUtbah, with two such rich men?! If I obey my instincts, I shall advance and leave you two behind as deputies. But you can remain with me if you so wish, or you can join ʿUtbah if you so wish. I give you a free hand, as I see no alternative but to leave you both and go after something more unpleasant than this!"[168] So (Bukayr) sought permission of ʿUmar to be excused, and he wrote to (Bukayr), permitting him to advance on al-Bāb[169] and ordering him to appoint a deputy over his province, [Azerbaijan]. So he appointed ʿUtbah deputy over the regions he had conquered. (Bukayr) advanced, having handed over Isfandiyādh to ʿUtbah, who took him into his entourage. ʿUtbah also appointed Simāk b. Kharashah—not Abū Dujānah[170]—over [that part of] Bukayr's province that he had conquered. ʿUmar united the whole of Azerbaijan under ʿUtbah b. Farqad.

(The same sources) report [as follows]. Now Bahrām b. al-Farrukhzādh[171] had taken the route to be used by ʿUtbah b. Farqad, and he waited for him at the head of his troops until ʿUtbah arrived. Battle was joined and ʿUtbah defeated (Bahrām) who fled. When the news reached Isfandiyādh, who was in the custody of Bukayr, of Bahrām's defeat and flight, he said, "Now

168. That is, the enemy.

169. That is, Bāb al-Abwāb or simply al-Abwāb, Darband on the west coast of the Caspian. See Yāqūt, *Muʿjam*, I, 303–6; Le Strange, *Lands*, 180.

170. That is, not the Abū Dujānah Simāk who appears first in Ṭabarī, I, 1395, under the year 3 and several times afterward.

171. An unidentified Azerbaijani ruler.

the peace is complete and war has been brought to an end." So (Bukayr) made peace with (Isfandyādh), and all (the people of Azerbaijan) agreed to this. The country returned to a state of peace. Bukayr and ʿUtbah wrote to inform ʿUmar of this and sent the fifth of what booty God had granted them. They also [2662] sent out delegations with this news. Bukayr had conquered the regions near him before ʿUtbah and peace was [only] complete after ʿUtbah's defeat of Bahrām. ʿUtbah drew up a document between himself and the people of Azerbaijan in which Bukayr's province was united with his own:

> In the name of God, the Compassionate, the Merciful. This is what ʿUtbah b. Farqad, the governor of ʿUmar b. al-Khaṭṭāb, Commander of the Faithful, has granted to the people of Azerbaijan, mountains and plains, borders and frontiers, all people of whatever religion, viz., security for their persons, their possessions, their religion and laws, on condition that they pay the tribute according to their capacity [to do so]. There is no [such] obligation for minors, or women, or the chronically poor who have nothing of the present world, or religious devotees remaining in isolation who have nothing of the present world. All this [is granted] to them and to those who live with them. But they are obliged to give hospitality to Muslim soldiers for the period of a day and a night and to guide them. Those who are recruited for military service[172] in any one year are exempt the tribute of that year. He who remains [from now on] shall be granted the same [concessions] and have [the same obligations] as he who has remained [permanently], whereas he who leaves has safe-conduct until he finds his place of refuge.

Jundub[173] wrote down [the document], which was witnessed by Bukayr b. ʿAbdallāh al-Laythī and Simāk b. Kharashah al-Anṣārī.

---

172. Arabic, "*wa-man ḥushira min-hum fī sanatin.*" It might also be rendered "Those who suffer distress"; that is, drought, crop failure, etc.

173. Jundub is unidentified.

[The document] was drafted in the year 18 [January 12, 639–January 2, 640].

(The same sources) relate [as follows]. In this year also [22; November 30, 642–November 19, 643] ʿUtbah brought ʿUmar some sweet date mix that he gave him as a gift. Now ʿUmar used to require his governors every year to perform the pilgrimage, thereby restraining them from any [act of] tyranny and preventing them from [doing any such thing].

[2663] In this same year [22; November 30, 642–November 19, 643] [the following] took place.

The Conquest of al-Bāb[174]

According to Sayf, they, that is, those whose names I have previously mentioned, reported [as follows]. ʿUmar sent Abū Mūsā back to al-Baṣrah and Surāqah b. ʿAmr, known as Dhū al-Nūr,[175] to al-Bāb. He appointed over his vanguard ʿAbd al-Raḥmān b. Rabīʿah who was also known as Dhū al-Nūr. He appointed over one of the wings Ḥudhayfah b. Asīd al-Ghifārī and named for the other Bukayr b. ʿAbdallāh al-Laythī, who was already facing al-Bāb before Surāqah b. ʿAmr reached him. (ʿUmar) wrote to (Surāqah), [instructing] him to join up with (Bukayr). (ʿUmar) also appointed Salmān b. Rabīʿah in charge of the division of the spoils. Surāqah placed ʿAbd al-Raḥmān b. Rabīʿah in the van and set out immediately behind him. When he had left Azerbaijan on his way to al-Bāb, he came upon Bukayr at the approaches to al-Bāb. He proceeded slowly with him and entered the region of al-Bāb, as ʿUmar had planned it. ʿUmar sent him Ḥabīb b. Maslamah[176] as reinforcement, having diverted him from al-Jazīrah. He also sent Ziyād b. Ḥanẓalah in (Ḥabīb's) place in charge of al-Jazīrah. When ʿAbd al-Raḥmān b. Rabīʿah approached the ruler in al-Bāb (he being at that time

---

174. See Ibn al-Athīr, *Kāmil*; *CHIr*, 226.

175. Mentioned in Ṭabarī only in the context of the conquest of al-Bāb. See Ibn Ḥajar, *Iṣābah*, IV, 127; Ibn al-Athīr, *Usd*, II, 264.

176. Al-Fihrī, a Companion who figures quite prominently in military matters in later years under ʿUthmān and who supported the first Umayyad caliph, Muʿāwiyah. He died in 42/662. See Ṭabarī, I, 2808, 2893–94, 3062; Ibn Ḥajar, *Iṣābah*, II, 208–9; *Tahdhīb*, II, 190–91; Ibn al-Athīr, *Usd*, I, 373.

Shahrbarāz, a Persian who was in control of this frontier area and whose origins were from the family of Shahrbarāz, the ruler who had routed the Israelites and driven them out of al-Shām),[177] Shahrbarāz sent him messages and sought safe-conduct to come to him. ('Abd al-Raḥmān) agreed, and he came [2664] and said, "I am facing a rabid enemy and different communities who are not of noble descent. It is not fitting for the noble and intelligent to assist such people or to ask their help against those of noble descent and origins. Noblemen [stick] close to noblemen, wherever they are. I am certainly not a Caucasian or an Armenian. You have conquered my land and my community. Now I am one of you; I am completely with you and my inclinations are the same as yours. God bless us and you! Our tribute to you will be the military assistance we render you and our carrying out whatever you desire. But do not humiliate us with tribute, so that you render us weak against your enemy." 'Abd al-Raḥmān replied, "There is someone superior to me who has already taken you into his protection; go to him." So he passed him over to Surāqah. When (Shahrbarāz) came to him, he found a similar attitude on his part. Surāqah said, "I accept this for your followers in this enterprise, as long as they continue to be so engaged. But anyone remaining and not moving off [elsewhere] must pay the tribute." (Shahrbarāz) accepted this, and it became the practice for those polytheists who made war on the enemy and for those who had to provide no tribute other than to be ready to fight and were thus exempt from the tribute [altogether] of that particular year.[178] Surāqah wrote to 'Umar [2665] b. al-Khaṭṭāb on this (point of practice), and he gave him his permission to carry it out and [expressed] his approval of it.

Those territories in the mountainous zone comprised only high ground in which the Armenians remained in readiness for a speedy departure. They were only inhabitants from the immediate vicinity or from more distant parts whose high ground

177. Shahrbarāz, the Persian military commander in question is unidentified. For his ancestors, see Nöldeke, *Geschichte*, 290–92, 294ff., 299ff. I am unable to provide further information on the incident mentioned in the text.

178. Arabic, *wa-fī-man lam yakun 'inda-hu al-jizā'u illā an yustanfarū fa-tūḍa'u 'an-hu jizā'u tilka al-sanah*. That is, whether they actually fight or not is immaterial. If they stand ready to fight, they are exempt the tribute.

had been removed from them by raids from lowlanders.[179] The mountain folk among them took to their refuges in their mountains and pulled out of their lowland territories. So only the military and those supporting them or doing business with them remained there. (The Armenians) received a document from Surāqah b. ʿAmr [as follows].

> In the name of God, the Compassionate, the Merciful. This is the safe-conduct Surāqah b. ʿAmr, governor of the Commander of the Faithful, ʿUmar b. al-Khaṭṭāb, has granted to Shahrbarāz, the inhabitants of Armenia, and the Armenians [in al-Bāb]. [He grants] them safe-conduct for their persons, their possessions, and their religion lest they be harmed and so that nothing be taken from them. [The following is imposed] upon the people of Armenia and al-Abwāb, those coming from distant parts and those who are local and those around them who have joined them: that they should participate in any military expedition, and carry out any task, actual or potential, that the governor considers to be for the good,[180] providing that those who agree to this are exempt from tribute but [perform] military service. Military service shall be instead of their paying tribute. But those of them who are not needed for military service and who remain inactive have similar tribute obligations to the people of Azerbaijan [in general]. [These include] guiding and showing hospitality for a whole day. If they perform military service, they are exempt from [all] this.
> [2666] If they abandon [the agreement], they will be punished.

179. The translation of these two difficult, and seemingly corrupt, sentences is tentative. The Arabic reads: *wa-laysa li-tilka al-bilādi allatī fī sāḥati tilka al-jibāli nabakun lam yuqim al-Armanu bi-hā illā ʿala awfāzin wa-innamā hum sukkānun mimman ḥawla-hā wa-min al-ṭurrāʾi istaʾṣalat al-ghāratu nabaka-hā min ahli al-qarār.*

180. Arabic, *an yanfirū li-kulli ghāratin wa-yanfudhū li-kulli amrin nāba aw lam yanubʾ raʾā-hu al-wālī ṣalāḥan.*

ʿAbd al-Raḥmān b. Rabīʿah, Salmān b. Rabīʿah and Bukayr b. ʿAbdallāh were witnesses. Marḍī b. Muqarrin[181] drafted it and was a witness.

Thereafter Surāqah despatched Bukayr b. ʿAbdallāh, Ḥabīb b. Maslamah, Ḥudhayfah b. Asīd, and Salmān b. Rabīʿah to the people of those mountains surrounding Armenia. He also despatched Bukayr to Mūqān,[182] Ḥabīb to Tiflīs,[183] Ḥudhayfah b. Asīd to the people of the mountains of Allān,[184] and Salmān b. Rabīʿah to the other side. Surāqah wrote to ʿUmar b. al-Khaṭṭāb of the conquest and of the circumstances in which he despatched these people. So ʿUmar learned of something that he did not think would be accomplished for him so quickly and without trouble. It was a vast frontier region in which there were large numbers of [enemy] military, and the Persians were waiting to see what (the Muslims) would do and then would cease fighting or carry it on [further]. When they had settled down and come to appreciate the fairness of Islam, Surāqah died, leaving ʿAbd al-Raḥmān b. Rabīʿah as his successor, as all the leaders whom Surāqah had despatched had passed on [to other areas] and none of them had conquered what he had been sent to conquer, with the exception of Bukayr. He had scattered [the people of] Mūqān and then they returned, gradually [agreeing to the payment] of tribute. (Bukayr) drew up a document for them [as follows]:

> In the name of God, the Compassionate, the Merciful. This is what Bukayr b. ʿAbdallāh has granted to the

---

181. This secretary is mentioned only here in the text. He is the brother of Nuʿaym and Suwayd. See Ibn Ḥajar, *Iṣābah*, IX, 168, with a reference to this document.

182. Or Mūghān/Mūghkān. The great plain that extends south of the River Aras along the west coast of the Caspian. See Yāqūt, *Muʿjam*, V, 225; Le Strange, *Lands*, 175–76 and Map 3, 87.

183. Capital of Georgia (Jurjistān) on the upper reaches of the River Kur. See Yāqūt, *Muʿjam*, II, 35–37; Le Strange, *Lands*, 181.

184. Allān is one of the districts of the Khazars, north of Georgia. Yāqūt simply says that it is an extensive area on the edge of Armenia, near al-Bāb, its people bordering the land of the Khazars. Yāqūt, *Muʿjam*, V, 8–9; Le Strange, *Lands*, 179.

> people of Mūqān in the Caucasus Mountains: safe-conduct for their possessions, their persons, their religion, and their laws on the payment of tribute, a dinar or its equivalent on every male who has reached puberty. [He must give] sound advice, guidance, and hospitality for a day and a night to the Muslim. They shall have safe-conduct as long as they submit themselves [to these conditions] and give good advice. We also must carry out
> [2667] [our obligations] in full, and God's help is to be sought. But, if they abandon this [agreement] and their perfidy becomes evident, they shall have no safe-conduct, unless they hand over every one of those who act perfidiously; otherwise they are [all] aiding and abetting one another.

Al-Shammākh b. Ḍirār,[185] al-Rusāris b. Junādib,[186] and Ḥamalah b. Juwayyah[187] were witnesses. It was drafted in the year 21 [December 10, 641–November 30, 642].

(The same sources) have reported [as follows]. When 'Umar heard of the death of Surāqah and that he had made 'Abd al-Raḥmān b. Rabī'ah his successor, he confirmed the latter in charge of the frontier region of al-Bāb, ordering him also to attack the Turks. So 'Abd al-Raḥmān set out with his army and passed through al-Bāb. Shahrbarāz asked him what he intended to accomplish, and he replied that he intended [to take] Balanjar.[188] [Shahrbarāz] said, "We are indeed happy that (the people of Balanjar) leave us with al-Bāb." But ('Abd al-Raḥmān) replied, "But we are not happy with this [situation] in our dealings with them until we get at them in their own territory. We have with us men with whose help, if our commander were to allow us to persevere, I would push on to the rampart."[189]

---

185. The famous Qaysī poet. See Iṣfahānī, *Aghānī*, VIII, 101–8.

186. This unidentified witness features only in this place in the text.

187. A Kinānī mentioned only on one other occasion in the text under the year 14; see Ṭabarī, I, 2236.

188. A town in the territory of the Khazars, north of the River Aras. See Yāqūt, *Mu'jam*, I, 489–90.

189. I take this to refer to the great wall—reportedly built by Anūshirvān in the sixth century A.D.—which ran westward from the town of al-Bāb over the mountains to keep out the warring tribes to the north. See Yāqūt, *Mu'jam*, I, 303; Le Strange, *Lands*, 180; Barthold, *Historical Geography*, 229.

(Shahrbarāz) asked who they were, and ('Abd al-Raḥmān) told him they were men who had accompained the Messenger of God and who had intentionally become involved in this enterprise.[190] Before Islam they were men of good conduct and honor, and both qualities had [since] increased. They were still so involved; victory was still theirs until some conqueror could change them and until they could be deflected from their attitude by someone changing them. So ('Abd al-Raḥmān) made one attack on Balanjar in the time of 'Umar, during which no woman was widowed and no child orphaned. During the attack on it his cavalry reached as far as al-Bayḍā', no nearer than 200 [2668] parasangs from Balanjar.[191] Then he attacked [again] and survived. Later, in the time of 'Uthmān, he made many attacks. 'Abd al-Raḥmān was killed when the Kufans rebelled during the time 'Uthmān was Commander of the Faithful, because (the latter) appointed as governors former apostates in order to seek to reform them. But this did not reform them; rather they became more disobedient, led as they were by those seeking [only] this present world. They caused a great deal of trouble for 'Uthmān, and he used [the following verse] as an example [of their obstructive behavior]:[192]

I, with regard to 'Amr, was like a man who fattened up his dog,
but he was [nevertheless bitten] by its canine teeth and scratched by its claws!

According to al-Sarī—Shu'ayb—Sayf—al-Ghuṣn b. al-Qāsim[193] —a man of B. Kinānah[194]—Salmān b. Rabī'ah: When 'Abd al-

---

190. The "enterprise" I take to mean Islam itself, although it might refer to the conquests being undertaken by the Muslims.

191. Al-Bayḍā' must be a place name here, although I can trace no further reference to it. A parasang is generally reckoned to be 3 miles, see Hinz, *Masse*, 62, about 6 kilometers.

192. The meter is *ṭawīl*.

193. Al-Kinānī. He first appears as a narrator in the year 11; see Ṭabarī, I, 1977.

194. I here include the editorial addition from the Leiden *apparatus criticus*, because al-Ghuṣn b. al-Qāsim was from Banū Kinānah himself and other similar chains of authority include the added phrase. Banū Kinānah is Kinānah b. Khuzaymah, a large tribal confederation of 'Adnān living in the Hejaz. See Kaḥḥālah, *Mu'jam*, III, 996–97.

Raḥmān b. Rabīʿah penetrated [their ranks], God prevented the Turks from attacking him. They remarked, "This man has dared to attack us only because the angels are with them protecting them from death!" So they retired and fortified themselves against him. But he came back with the spoils and victory, and this was during the time ʿUmar was Commander of the Faithful. Then he made several attacks on them during the time of ʿUthmān; he was victorious, as he had been [previously]. Then the Kufans rebelled because ʿUthmān appointed as governors former apostates. After this he attacked them. The Turks blamed one another, one saying to another, "They are not dying!"; he replied that they should keep watch. They did so and lay in ambush for them in the thickets. One of them shot at a Muslim unexpectedly and killed him, upon which his men fled. So [the Muslims] attacked him at that point, and battle was joined. (The Muslims) fought hard and somebody cried out into the
[2669] air, "Stand fast, men of ʿAbd al-Raḥmān; you are promised paradise!" ʿAbd al-Raḥmān fought until he was killed and the two sides stood apart.[195] But then Salmān b. Rabīʿah took up the standard and fought with it. Someone shouted out into the air, "Stand fast, men of Salmān b. Rabīʿah!" Salmān retorted, "Can you see any lack of resolve?!" Then he went forth with the army. Salmān and Abū Hurayrah al-Dawsī[196] attacked Jīlān and passed through it to arrive in Jurjān. The Turks showed their daring after this and felt no restraint in taking up the body of ʿAbd al-Raḥmān, using his (name) until now to seek rain.[197]

According to ʿAmr b. Maʿdī Karib—Maṭar b. Thalj al-Tamīmī:[198] I went in to see ʿAbd al-Raḥmān b. Rabīʿah in al-Bāb, when Shahrbarāz was with him. A man in a state of fatigue

---

195. Arabic, "*wa-inkashafa al-nās.*" I take this difficult phrase to indicate a temporary lull in the fighting after ʿAbd al-Raḥmān's death. For this meaning of the Arabic verb, see Dozy, *Supplément*, II, 470.

196. Famous in particular as a narrator (d. ca. 58/677). See Ibn Ḥajar, *Tahdhīb*, XII, 262–67; EI^2, s.v. (Robson); Rosenthal, *Historiography*, 334.

197. It is a common practice even to this day throughout the Middle East to pray for rain in times of drought. These non-Muslim Turks presumably had some kind of rain-seeking ceremony during which ʿAbd al-Raḥmān's name was invoked. See EI^2, s.v. "istisḳāʾ" (Fahd).

198. Maṭar b. Thalj al-Tamīmī, an unidentified narrator. The name means Rain, son of Snow! He appears only in this context in the text.

and emaciation arrived and came in to see ʿAbd al-Raḥmān. He sat down next to Shahrbarāz. Now Maṭar was wearing a cloak of striped Yemeni cloth with a reddish ground and black figuring or reddish figuring and a black ground. (The man and Shahrbarāz) questioned one another. Then Shahrbarāz said (to ʿAbd al-Raḥmān), "Commander, do you know where this man has come from? I sent him some years ago to the wall[199] to examine what it and the people on the other side of it were like. I gave him great wealth and wrote on his behalf to those [in authority] in [2670]
the territories adjoining mine, presenting each with a gift and asking him to write on (my envoy's) behalf to the next one. I gave him a gift for each ruler, and he carried all this out in the case of every ruler until he finally reached the one in whose own land the wall was situated. So (the ruler) wrote on (the envoy's) behalf to his governor of this area, and (the envoy) reached (the governor). (The latter) sent with him his austringer, carrying his eagle, and (the envoy) gave him a piece of silk." (The envoy) reported, "The austringer thanked me, and we eventually arrived at two mountains with a wall in between them that was level with them and even went higher. In front of the wall was a ditch, blacker than night because it was so deep. I looked at all of this and examined it carefully. Then I made to go away. The austringer told me to wait and he would recompense me and that no successive ruler [in this land] ever failed to draw closer to God by bringing with him the best of what he had of this present world and casting it down into this narrow defile. So he cut up a lump of meat that he had with him and threw it into this empty space. The eagle swooped down after it, and he said, 'If she takes it before it falls [to the bottom], there is no [bottom]! But, if she does not, then there is a [bottom there].' The eagle emerged and came to us carrying the meat in her talons. Inside there was a precious stone, which he gave me—and this is it." Shahrbarāz took it, a ruby, and handed it over to ʿAbd al-Raḥmān. He looked at it, then returned it to Shahrbarāz, [2671]
who said, "This is indeed worth more than this town, al-Bāb. I swear by God, I would rather you be in power than the family of

199. See note 189.

the Persian emperor. Were I in their power and then they heard news of (the ruby), they would snatch it away from me. I swear by God, nothing will stand in your way as long as you remain true to your word and your great ruler does likewise."[200] ʿAbd al-Raḥmān turned to the envoy and said, "What was this rampart like?" He replied that [it was like] the garment this man was wearing. And (Maṭar) said, "And he looked at my garment." Maṭar b. Thalj said to ʿAbd al-Raḥmān b. Rabīʿah; "The man has certainly told the truth! He has been and seen for himself." He replied, "Yes indeed, he has given a description of iron and brass," and he recited "Bring me pieces of iron" right to the end of the verse.[201] ʿAbd al-Raḥmān said to Shahrbarāz, "How much was your gift worth?" He replied, "The value of 100,000 in my own country and 3,000,000 or more in these parts."

Al-Wāqidī claimed that Muʿāwiyah launched a summer campaign this year and penetrated into Byzantine territory at the head of 10,000 Muslims.

Some authorities report that the death of Khālid b. al-Walīd took place this year.

In [this year] Yazīd b. Muʿāwiyah[202] and ʿAbd al-Malik b. Marwān[203] were born.

During this year ʿUmar b. al-Khaṭṭāb led the pilgrimage. His
[2672] governor of Mecca was ʿAttāb b. Asīd.[204] Yaʿlā b. Umayyah[205]
[was governor] of the Yemen. Those who were his governors in the previous year whom we have already mentioned [remained] in charge of the rest of the Muslim garrison towns.

---

200. That is, the caliph himself, ʿUmar b. al-Khaṭṭāb.

201. See Qur'ān, XVIII:94–97. This is the story of Dhū al-Qarnayn (*EI*², s.v. "al-Iskandar" [Watt]), who keeps out Gog and Magog by building between two mountains a wall made of iron and molten brass. The words *sadd* and *radm* used here in the text are both found in this passage in the Qur'ān.

202. The second Umayyad caliph (60–64/680–683).

203. The famous fifth Umayyad caliph (65–86/685–705). See *EI*², s.v. (Gibb).

204. It would seem that ʿAttāb b. Asīd b. Abī al-ʿĪṣ b. Umayyah b. ʿAbd Shams remained governor of Mecca from its conquest by the Prophet in 8/629 right through to this year, 22. See Ibn Hishām, *Sīrah*, II, 440 (Guillaume, *Life*, 568); Wāqidī, *Maghāzī*, III, 889; *EI*², s.v. (ed.).

205. Yaʿlā b. Umayyah/Munyah al-Tamīmī died at Ṣiffīn in 37/657 after twenty-four years as governor in the Yemen. See Ibn Ḥajar, *Tahdhīb*, XI, 399; Rāzī, *Ṣanʿāʾ*, 69–70; Madʿaj, *Yemen*, 141 and table 4, 148. See also note 781, below.

During this year ʿUmar equalized [the material benefits of] thc conquests carried out by the Kufans and Basrans.

Information on [ʿUmar's Division of the Conquered Lands]

According to al-Sarī—Shuʿayb—Sayf—Muḥammad, Ṭalḥah, al-Muhallab, ʿAmr and Saʿīd: ʿAmmār b. Yāsir remained as governor of al-Kūfah for a whole year and part of another during the caliphate of ʿUmar. ʿUmar b. Surāqah, at that time governor of al-Baṣrah, wrote to ʿUmar b. al-Khaṭṭāb, indicating to him how large the population of al-Baṣrah was and how little land tax they received and requesting that he add one of the two Māhs or Māsabadhān to them [as a source of land tax].[206] News of this reached the Kufans, and they asked ʿAmmār to write on their behalf to ʿUmar, [proposing] that Rāmahurmuz[207] and Īdhaj[208] become theirs [for the purpose of land tax] to the exclusion of (the Basrans), who did not assist them in any way in [fighting against] these two places and who did not join them until they had already conquered them. But ʿAmmār replied that he could do nothing about the whole matter. ʿUṭārid[209] said to him, "Why do you not give us [the revenue from] our immovable booty, you slave with the mutilated ear!" He replied, "Now you abuse my good ear!"[210] and he [refused to] write concerning this matter. He was therefore hated by them. When the Kufans were adamant that they should [continue] the dispute concerning the two (places) with the Basrans, certain people gave evidence to (the Basrans) that Abū Mūsā had granted the people of

206. The two Māhs are Nihāwand and Dīnawar. See Yāqūt, *Muʿjam*, V, 48; Le Strange, *Lands*, 189, 197. Māsabadhān is that part of the Jibāl province due south of Kurdistān. See Le Strange, *Lands*, 202 and Map 5, opposite 185.

207. A town a little east of al-Ahwāz in Khūzistān. See Yāqūt, *Muʿjam*, III, 17–18; Le Strange, *Lands*, 243.

208. A town a little north of Rāmahurmuz in Khūzistān. See Yāqūt, *Muʿjam*, I, 288–89; Le Strange, *Lands*, 245 and Map 2, opposite 25.

209. ʿUṭārid b. Ḥājib b. Zurārah b. ʿUdas/ʿUdus, a leader of Banū Tamīm. He was a member of the Tamīmī delegation to the Prophet in 9/630. See Ṭabarī, I, 1710–11; Ibn Hishām, *Sīrah*, II, 560–61 (Guillaume, *Life*, 628); Wāqidī, *Maghāzī*, III, 975.

210. Arabic *la-qad sababta aḥabba udhunayya ilayya*. That is, "I don't want to hear any more of this!" ʿAmmār had lost an ear at the battle of al-Yamāmah; see *EI*², s.v. "ʿAmmār" (Reckendorf).

[2673] Rāmahurmuz and Īdhaj safe-conduct and that the Kufans and the army of al-Nu'mān [b. Muqarrin] had corresponded with them while they were [enjoying this] safe-conduct. 'Umar permitted them to do this to them and for the benefit of the Basrans had his authorization duly witnessed. The Basrans laid claim to certain settlements in Iṣfahān that Abū Mūsā had conquered on this side of Jayy when 'Umar had sent (the Basrans) as reinforcements to (the Kufans) under the command of 'Abdallāh b. 'Abdallāh b. 'Itbān. The Kufans said: "You came to us as reinforcements when we had already conquered the area, but we shared the spoils with you. The covenant is ours; the land is ours." 'Umar confirmed that they were right. Then the Basrans who had taken part in the battles and who were at al-Qādisiyyah took up another matter, saying, "Let them give us our share of their main body of cultivated land and that on its periphery in which we participated with them." 'Umar asked them if they would be satisfied with Māh,[211] at the same time asking the Kufans if they would approve his granting (the Basrans) one of the two Māhs. [212] They replied that he should do as he thought fitting. So he granted them Māh Dīnār[213] with its share for those of them who had taken part in the battles and who were at al-Qādisiyyah as far as the district of al-Baṣrah and Mihrajānqadhaq.[214] All this was for those Basrans who took part in the battles and who were at al-Qādisiyyah. Mu'āwiyah [when he was governor of Syria] was the one who garrisoned Qinnasrīn with a military force from the Iraqs that had refused [to serve 'Alī further] in the latter's time.[215] Qinnasrīn was simply one of the rural districts of Ḥimṣ until Mu'āwiyah made it into a garrison town and garrisoned it with those who had left al-Kūfah and al-Baṣrah at that time and he took for them, as their share for the conquests of Iraq, Azerbaijan, Mosul, and al-Bāb, and brought them all together. The population of al-Jazīrah and
[2674] Mosul were at that time floating, mixed with all those of the

---

211. That is, Nihāwand, also known as Māh al-Baṣrah.

212. That is, Nihāwand and Dīnawar. See note 206, above.

213. Māh Dīnār is Nihāwand. See Yāqūt, *Mu'jam*, V, 49.

214. Mihrajānqadhaq is the second of the two parts of the Jibāl province due south of Kurdistān. See Le Strange, *Lands*, 202 and Map V, opposite 185.

215. *Rāfiḍah* is not to be taken here in its later meaning; viz., a term of abuse used by the Sunnīs of the Shī'īs.

two areas [al-Baṣrah and al-Kūfah] who had not emigrated [to participate in the conquests]. Al-Bāb, Azerbaijan, al-Jazīrah, and Mosul were conquered by the Kufans.[216] When Mu'āwiyah b. Abī Sufyān was appointed governor [of Syria], all this was transferred to those of them who had moved to Syria in the time of 'Alī and to those with whom al-Jazīrah and Mosul were populated who had not emigrated [to participate in the conquests] in the time of 'Alī.

At the time of Mu'āwiyah['s governorship of Syria] the people of Armenia were unbelievers.[217] (Mu'āwiyah) had made Ḥabīb b. Maslamah commander of al-Bāb, he being at that time in Jurzān.[218] He entered into correspondence with the inhabitants of Tiflīs and those mountain areas, but then he fought against them until they indicated their obedience [to him] and obtained an agreement from him. After he had corresponded with them, he wrote to them [as follows]:

> In the name of God, the Compassionate, the Merciful. From Ḥabīb b. Maslamah to the people of Tiflīs in Jurzān, the land of al-Hurmuz.[219] You are at peace. I commend God to you. There is no other god than He. Your envoy, Taflī, has come to us, has brought your message, and has delivered [the gifts] you sent. Taflī has mentioned that, according to your reckoning, we used not to be one community, and indeed we were not thus until God gave us guidance in the form of Muḥammad and strengthened us with Islam after we had been few, lowly, and ignorant. Taflī has mentioned that you desire [2675]
> to be at peace with us, and those who believe with me and I are not averse to this. I send you 'Abd al-

216. Ṭabarī presents the temporal clause (Arabic, *wa-lammā waliya Mu'āwiyatu bnu Sufyān*), which I have relegated in translation to the following sentence, before the three previous sentences that are explanatory material in parenthesis.

217. Although there had been earlier attacks on Armenia by the Muslim forces, it is clear that the major onslaught, led by Ḥabīb came in 24/645 or 31/652 during the caliphate of 'Uthmān. See Ṭabarī, I, 2808, 2871; Translation, XV, 10–11, 78; Balādhurī, *Futūḥ*, 197.

218. Georgia, regarded by Yāqūt as that part of Armenia the chief town of which is Tiflīs. See Yāqūt, *Mu'jam*, II, 125; Le Strange, *Lands*, Map III, opposite 87; Minorsky, *Studies*, map, 79.

219. That is, the local ruler.

Raḥmān b. Jaz' al-Sulamī,[220] who is one of our most knowledgeable religious and Qur'anic scholars. With him I send my document granting you safe-conduct. If you agree, he will hand it over to you; if you do not, he will "declare war" on you "fairly; God does not love the treacherous."[221]

[The document:]

In the name of God, the Compassionate, the Merciful. This is a document from Ḥabīb b. Maslamah to the people of Tiflīs in Jurzān, the land of al-Hurmuz, [granting you] safe-conduct for your persons, your possessions, your religious buildings (*ṣawāmi'*), your places of worship, and your prayers, with the imposition of a small tribute, a whole dinar on every household. We [in turn shall have] your good counsel, your help against God's and our enemy, your hospitality for one night for the passerby, [providing] the permitted food and drink of the People of the Book, and guidance along the way insofar as none of you thereby comes to any harm. If you become Muslims, pray, and pay alms; then we shall [all] be brethren within Islam, and [you will be] our clients. But he who turns his back on God, His apostles, His books, and His partisans, we shall "declare war" on you "fairly; God does not love the treacherous."

'Abd al-Raḥmān b. Khālid,[222] al-Ḥajjāj,[223] and 'Iyāḍ[224] were witnesses, and Rabāḥ[225] wrote, "And I call God, His angels, and

220. This scholar remains unidentified, and there is no other mention of him in the text.

221. Qur'ān, VIII:58.

222. That is, 'Abd al-Raḥmān b. Khālid b. al-Walīd al-Makhzūmī, son of the famous early Muslim general, Khālid b. al-Walīd. He died in 46/666, supposedly poisoned at the instruction of a jealous Mu'āwiyah. See Ṭabarī, II, 82–83; Translation, XVIII, 88–89.

223. An unidentified witness.

224. Both the Leiden and Cairo indexes indicate that this is 'Iyāḍ b. Ghanm al-Fihrī, later governor in the Jazīrah and Muslim leader in Syria, who died after 31/651. See Ṭabarī, I, 2505, 2865–66; Translation, XIII, 86; Translation, XV, 72–73. Ibn al-Athīr (*Usd*, IV, 164–66), however, and Ibn Sa'd (*Ṭabaqāt*, IV, 269; VII, 398) insist that 'Iyāḍ died in 20/641.

225. A witness mentioned only here in the text.

those who believe to witness; 'God is sufficient as a witness.'"[226]

In this year [22; November 30, 642–November 19, 643] 'Umar b. al-Khaṭṭāb reportedly removed 'Ammār from al-Kūfah and appointed Abū Mūsā governor. We have, however, already mentioned above what al-Wāqidī had to say on this subject.[227] [2676]

The Reason for [the Dismissal of 'Ammār]

I have already mentioned part of the reason for his dismissal, and [now] I shall report on the remainder. According to al-Sarī—Shu'ayb—Sayf—those of his shaykhs I have already mentioned:[228] The people of al-Kūfah, this 'Uṭārid, and others with him wrote to 'Umar about 'Ammār, "He is no commander and cannot cope with the situation in which he finds himself." The Kufans put pressure on him, so 'Umar wrote to 'Ammār, [telling him to] present himself. He set out with a delegation of Kufans, taking with him [only] those whom he considered to be his supporters. But they were more against him than those left behind. He became worried and was asked. "What is worrying you, Abū al-Yaqẓān?" He admitted it was something that he was not proud of, but he had indeed been so afflicted.[229] Now Sa'd b. Mas'ūd al-Thaqafī,[230] the uncle of al-Mukhtār, and Jarīr b. 'Abdallāh[231] were with him, and they spread rumors about him and told 'Umar things [about him] of which he disapproved. So 'Umar dismissed him and gave him no [other] governorship.

According to al-Sarī—Shu'ayb—Sayf—al-Walīd b. Jumay'[232]

---

226. Qur'ān, IV:79 and XLVIII:28.

227. See above, note 23.

228. That is, Muḥammad, Ṭalḥah, al-Muhallab, 'Amr, and Sa'īd. See note 4, above.

229. Arabic, *fa-jazi'a fa-qīla la-hu yā Abā al-Yaqẓān mā hādhā al-jaza'u fa-qāla wa-Allāhi mā uḥmidu nafsī 'alay-hi wa-laqad ubtulītu bi-h.*

230. See Ibn al-Athīr, *Usd*, II, 295. Al-Mukhtār is al-Mukhtār b. Abī 'Ubayd b. Mas'ūd al-Thaqafī, born in the first year of the Hijrah (Ṭabarī, I, 1264; Translation, VII, 10) and leader of the Alid movement in al-Kūfah in 64/683 (Ṭabarī, II, 520ff.; Translation, XX, 105ff.).

231. Al-Bajalī, died ca. 54/674. See Ibn Ḥajar, *Iṣābah*, II, 76–77; *Tahdhīb*, II, 73–75; Ibn al-Athīr, *Usd*, I, 279–80; Hill, *Termination*, 103ff.

232. An unidentified narrator.

—Abū al-Ṭufayl:[233] ʿAmmār was asked if he was displeased by his dismissal. He replied that he had not in any way been pleased when he was appointed governor, but he was displeased when he was dismissed.

[2677] According to al-Sarī—Shuʿayb—Sayf—Ismāʿīl b. Abī Khālid[234] and Mujālid[235]—al-Shaʿbī: ʿUmar asked the Kufans which of their two settlements they liked better, that is, al-Kūfah or al-Madāʾin. He added, "I am asking you, but I can indeed see in your faces which one of them is preferred." Jarīr replied that the nearer settlement of theirs, [al-Madāʾin], was closer to the [fertile] Sawād land, whereas the other was [a place, as if] by the sea, of exhausting, intense heat, with mosquitoes. ʿAmmār retorted that he was lying, but ʿUmar told him he was a bigger liar than (Jarīr). (ʿUmar) also asked them what they thought of their commander, ʿAmmār. Jarīr answered that he was indeed inadequate and deficient, with no knowledge of management.

According to al-Sarī—Shuʿayb—Sayf—Zakariyyāʾ b. Siyāh[236]—Hishām b. ʿAbd al-Raḥmān al-Thaqafī:[237] Saʿd b. Masʿūd said, "You, [ʿAmmār], have no idea of what [territories] you are governor!" ʿUmar asked (ʿAmmār) of what [territories] he had made him governor. ʿAmmār replied "Of al-Ḥīrah and its region."[238] (ʿUmar) said that he had heard of al-Ḥīrah from merchants going frequently to and from there. (ʿUmar) asked of what [else he was governor]. (ʿAmmār) replied, "Of Babylon and its region."[239] (ʿUmar) said, "You have heard mention of it in the Qurʾān!" (ʿUmar) further asked of what [else he was governor]. "Of al-Madāʾin and its surrounding areas," (ʿAmmār) replied. (ʿUmar) asked him if this was the Ctesiphon of the Sasanian emperor, and he replied that it was. (ʿUmar) asked

233. ʿĀmir b. Wāthilah, a narrator who died in the early second/eighth century. See Ibn Ḥajar, *Tahdhīb*, V, 82–84.

234. D. 146/763. See Ibn Ḥajar, *Tahdhīb*, I, 291ff.

235. Mujālid b. Saʿīd b. ʿUmayr (d. 144/762). See Ibn Ḥajar, *Tahdhīb*, X, 39–41.

236. An unidentified narrator.

237. An unidentified narrator.

238. A settlement near al-Kūfah, capital of the Lakhmids and dating from pre-Islamic times. See Yāqūt, *Muʿjam* II, 328ff.; Le Strange, *Lands*, 75 and Map 2, 25; *EI*[2], s.v. (Shahid).

239. About 50 miles south of Baghdad in Iraq; Arabic, Bābil. See Yāqūt, *Muʿjam*, I, 309ff.; Le Strange, *Lands*, 72; *EI*[2], s.v. "Bābil" (Awad).

him of what [else he was governor]. ('Ammār) replied, "Of Mihrajānqadhaq and its region."[240] (Sa'd and his companions) said, "We have already told you that he does not know of what [territories] you have sent him [as governor]. So ('Umar) dismissed ('Ammār). He later summoned him and asked him if he had been displeased when he had dismissed him. ('Ammār) replied that he had been in no way happy when he sent him [as governor], but that he was indeed displeased when he dismissed him. ('Umar) commented, "I knew you were not a governor, but [2678] I gave meaning [to the following]: "We wished to show favor to those who were considered weak on earth, make them examples, and make them the inheritors."[241]

According to al-Sarī—Shu'ayb—Sayf—Khulayd b. Dhafarah al-Namarī[242]—his father with an account similar to this and more: ('Umar) asked ('Ammār) if he was inviting approval of himself because of his knowledge of those with whom he had been dealing since his arrival. He added, "You will stop at no limit, 'Ammār, with the result that [this] puts you in a weak position; indeed, if age comes upon you, you will certainly grow weak, and if you are weak, you will indeed be sorely tested. Then ask God for death." Then ('Umar) turned to the Kufans and asked them whom they wanted. They replied, "Abū Mūsā." So ('Umar) appointed him their commander after 'Ammār. He remained their governor for a year. But his servant sold fodder and al-Walīd b. 'Abd Shams[243] heard (Abū Mūsā) say, "I have never kept company with any people without honoring them. Only my association with the witnesses of al-Baṣrah has prevented me from calling them liars.[244] If I befriend you, I shall certainly bring you goodness." Al-Walīd said, "No one other than you has taken away our land; you will certainly not [continue] as our governor." So he and others with him left [al-Kūfah], saying that they had no need of Abū Mūsā. ('Umar)

---

240. 'Umar had in fact given Mibrajānqadhaq to the Basrans; see p. 44 and note 213, above.

241. Qur'ān, II:102. See p. 44, note 213, above.

242. An unidentified narrator.

243. Al-Walīd b. 'Abd Shams, a Qurashī noble, has brief notices in Ibn al-Athīr, *Usd*, V, 90, and Ibn Ḥajar, *Iṣābah*, X, 311.

244. I am unable to clarify this obscure remark.

asked [them] why. They replied, "He has a servant who deals in the fruits of our land!" So ('Umar) dismissed him and sent him
[2679] to al-Baṣrah. He also sent 'Umar b. Surāqah to al-Jazīrah. He said to the Kufan followers of Abū Mūsā who went with him when he was dismissed, "Do you prefer someone strong and tough or someone weak, but a believer?" But he got no response from them. So ('Umar) went off on his own to a part of the mosque and went to sleep. Al-Mughīrah b. Shu'bah came to him and stood watch over him until he woke up. Then he said, "You have acted in this way, Commander of the Faithful, only because of something very serious. Has some disaster overtaken you?" He replied, "What is happening is more disastrous than 100,000 who are not pleased with a commander, when he is not pleased with them." And he went on for some time on this subject. (Al-Kūfah was originally founded for 100,000 troops.) ('Umar's) followers came to him and asked him what was on his mind. He told them it was the Kufans whose problem was causing him some distress. 'Umar repeated his request for advice from them as before, and al-Mughīrah gave him his answer. He said, "The weak Muslim's weakness is not in your interests, nor in those of the other Muslims [as well as his own]. His excellence [by being a Muslim] is [only] in his own interests. The strong, tough man's strength is in your interests and those of the other Muslims [as well as his own], whereas his toughness works both against him and in his favor." So ('Umar) sent (al-Mughīrah) [as governor] over (the Kufans).

According to al-Sarī—Shu'ayb—Sayf—Muḥammad b. 'Abdallāh—Sa'īd b. 'Amr:[245] 'Umar, before appointing al-Mughīrah governor, asked what his opinion was of making someone
[2680] governor who was weak, but a Muslim, as opposed to someone strong and tough. Al-Mughīrah replied, "The faith of a weak Muslim works [only] in his own interests, whereas his weakness works against your interests. The toughness of a strong, tough man will work in his own interests and his strength in those of the Muslims." ('Umar) told him he was sending him [as governor to al-Kūfah]. Al-Mughīrah was in this

245. Sa'īd b. 'Amr b. Sa'īd b. al-'Āṣ, a Qurashī scholar in al-Kūfah. See Ibn Ḥajar, *Tahdhīb*, IV, 68.

position until 'Umar died, that is something more than two years. When al-Mughīrah was taking his leave (of 'Umar) to go to al-Kūfah, he said to him, "Let the pious trust you and the wicked fear you, Mughīrah." Later 'Umar wanted to send Sa'd [b. Abī Waqqāṣ] as governor in place of al-Mughīrah, but he was killed before he could do this, leaving the recommendation [that Sa'd should become governor]. Now it was 'Umar's practice and habit to require his governors to make the pilgrimage every year; [this was] for the purpose of good management, to isolate them in this way from their subjects and to provide a time for their subjects to complain and an objective that they could thus accomplish.

In this year [22; November 30, 642–November 19, 643] according to some reports, al-Aḥnaf b. Qays attacked Khurāsān and made war on Yazdajird. Sayf, however, reported that al-Aḥnaf moved against Khurāsān in the year 18 [January 12, 639–January 2, 640].

Yazdajird's Journey to Khurāsān and the Reason for It

Historians (*ahl al-siyar*) differ in the reason [they give] for this and how the whole affair happened. There is Sayf's account of this on the authority of his [previous] authorities. Al-Sarī wrote to me on the matter—Shu'ayb—Sayf—Muḥammad, Ṭalḥah, al-Muhallab and 'Amr: Yazdajird b. Shahriyār b. Kisrā, who was at that time ruler of Persia, made for al-Rayy when the [2681]
forces at Jalūlā'[246] were defeated. A single litter that could fit on to the back of his camel was provided for him, so as the journey progressed, he could sleep and he did not [need to] camp with his army. While he was asleep in his litter, they brought him to a ford. They woke him up so that he might be aware [of what was happening] and not be afraid when the camel forded over, [as he would be] if he were awakened from sleep. But he

246. A town about 70 miles east of Sāmarrā, on the route from Baghdad to Ḥulwān. See Yāqūt, *Mu'jam*, II, 156; Le Strange, *Lands*, 62 and Map II, opposite 25. The defeat here referred to is that of the Persians at the hands of the Muslim forces under Sa'd b. Abī Waqqāṣ in 16/637. See Balādhurī, *Futūḥ*, 264ff.; Ṭabarī, I, 2456ff. (Translation, XIII, 36ff.); Zarrīnkūb, "Conquest," 13.

reproached (his men), saying, "You were wrong to do this! If you had left me alone, I would have found out how long this [Islamic] community will last. I saw in a dream Muḥammad and myself speaking together alone in the presence of God. (God) told (Muḥammad) that he would give them 100 years' power. He asked for more and (God) made it 110 years. (Again Muḥammad) asked for more and (God) made it 120 years. (Again Muḥammad) asked for more and (God) granted it, but then you woke me up. If you had left me alone, I would have found out how long this community will last!"

When he finally reached al-Rayy, where Ābān Jādhawayh was governor, (the latter) seized him and took him prisoner. (Yazdajird) accused him of acting treacherously toward him. He replied, "No, rather you have abandoned your empire, and it has fallen into the hands of someone else. I [only] want to record everything that is mine and nothing more." He took Yazdajird's seal, produced some parchment and made some written statements and records of every thing he wanted. Then he placed the seal on them and returned it. Later he approached Sa'd, and (the latter) returned to him everything [listed] in his document. When Ābān Jādhawayh treated Yazdajird in this way, the latter
[2682] left al-Rayy for Iṣfahān, expressing a hatred for Ābān Jādhawayh as he fled from him and not trusting him. He decided to go to Kirmān, taking his fire[247] and intending to install it there. Later he decided to make for Khurāsān. He arrived in Marw[248] and settled there, having also brought his fire, for which he erected a building. He set up a cultivated area and built a passage 2 parasangs long from Marw. It was exactly 2 parasangs. He felt secure within himself and secure from approach. From Marw he corresponded with those Persians remaining in those areas not conquered by the Muslims. They expressed their obedience to him, and finally he induced the people of Fārs and followers of

247. Arabic simply reads *nār*, fire. I take this to be some kind of sacred flame used in his practice of Zoroastrianism.

248. A famous town about 240 miles due north of Herat, one of the capitals of the Khurāsān province and standing on the River Murghāb. See Yāqūt, *Mu'jam*, Marw al-Shāhijān, V, 112ff.; Le Strange, *Lands*, 398ff.; *EI*², s.v. (Bosworth).

al-Hurmuzān to rebel [against the Muslims], and the people of al-Jibāl and the followers of al-Fayruzān did likewise. This it was that induced 'Umar to permit the Muslims to penetrate farther. The armies of al-Baṣrah and al-Kūfah pushed on farther with the result that they decisively conquered the whole area.

Al-Aḥnaf left for Khurāsān, took Mihrajānqadhaq, then left for Iṣfahān, while the Kufans were besieging Jayy. He entered Khurāsān from al-Ṭabasayn[249] and took Herat[250] by force. He appointed as his deputy there Ṣuḥār b. Fulān al-'Abdī,[251] then marched on Marw al-Shāhijān. He dispatched to Naysābūr,[252] there being no intervening battle, Muṭarrif b. 'Abdallāh b. al-Shikhkhīr,[253] and to Sarakhs[254] al-Ḥārith b. Ḥassān.[255] When al-Aḥnaf drew near to Marw al-Shāhijān, Yazdajird left it for [2683]
Marw al-Rūdh[256] and remained there, while al-Aḥnaf remained

249. For the conquest of Khurāsān, see Balādhurī, *Futūḥ*, 403ff. Al-Aḥnaf was approaching from the southwest. The dual form, al-Ṭabasayn, is not infrequently used for one of the two towns called Ṭabas, Ṭabas al-Tamr and Ṭabas al-'Unnāb. The two are about 200 miles apart, al-Tamr in the west, al-'Unnāb in the southwest of Qūhistān. Assuming he could march through the Great Desert, more or less as the crow flies, al-Aḥnaf would have passed through Ṭabas al-Tamr on his way from Iṣfahān to Herat. See Yāqūt, *Mu'jam*, IV, 20; Le Strange, *Lands*, 359ff. and Map 8, opposite 335.

250. The famous town in present-day Afghanistan. The town sits on the River Herat in the southwest of the province of Khurāsān and was chief town of one of its quarters. See Yāqūt, *Mu'jam*, V, 396–97; Le Strange, *Lands*, 407–9, 429–31; EI^2, s.v. (Frye).

251. That is, from 'Abd al-Qays. Perhaps his father's name was Ṣakhr, see the Leiden *apparatus criticus*, Ṭabarī, I, 2682, note o. He figures as a narrator under the year 17, Ṭabarī, I, 2537, and later *sub anno* 23, I, 2707, delivering the fifths to the caliph from Makrān. There is brief mention of Ṣuḥār b. Ṣakhr in Ibn Ḥajar, *Iṣābah*, V, 126.

252. In the west of Khurāsān and a chief town of one of its quarters. See Yāqūt, *Mu'jam*, V, 331–33; Le Strange, *Lands*, 382ff. and Map VIII, opposite 335.

253. Al-Ḥarashī. If this is the Basran jurist who died ca. 86/705, he must have been very young at this time. See Ibn Ḥajar, *Tahdhīb*, X, 173–74; Ibn Ḥazm, *Jamharah*, 288.

254. A town on the River Herat in Khurāsān, situated about 100 miles east of Naysābūr. See Yāqūt, *Mu'jam*, III, 208–9; Le Strange, *Lands*, 395ff. and Map 8, opposite 335.

255. Al-Dhuhlī. A Muslim leader who is reported as assuming various military tasks during the conquests. See Ṭabarī, I, 2475, 2477 etc.; Ibn al-Athīr, *Usd*, I, 323–25; Ibn Ḥajar, *Iṣābah*, II, 152–53; *Tahdhīb*, 139.

256. About 150 miles south of Marw on the River Murghāb in Khurāsān. See Yāqūt, *Mu'jam*, V, 112; Le Strange, *Lands*, 397ff. and Map VIII, opposite 335.

in Marw al-Shāhijān. While he was in Marw al-Rūdh, Yazdajird wrote to the ruler of the Turks (*khāqān*)[257] asking for reinforcements and to the ruler of Soghdia[258] for the same reason. His two envoys to ruler of the Turks and the ruler of Soghdia departed, and he wrote also to the ruler of China asking for assistance. Al-Aḥnaf, when Kufan reinforcements had joined him under the command of four commanders, ʿAlqamah b. al-Naḍr al-Naḍrī, Ribʿī b. ʿĀmir al-Tamīmī, ʿAbdallāh b. Abī ʿUqayl al-Thaqafī, and Ibn Umm Ghazāl al-Hamdānī,[259] departed from Marw al-Shāhijān, leaving Ḥātim b. al-Nuʿmān al-Bāhilī[260] as his deputy there. He marched on Marw al-Rūdh. However, when Yazdajird heard of this, he left for Balkh.[261] Al-Aḥnaf stayed in Marw al-Rūdh, sending the Kufans on to Balkh. Al-Aḥnaf followed on after them; and the Kufans and Yazdajird met in battle in Balkh, and God defeated the latter, who made for the river at the head of his Persian army and crossed it. Al-Aḥnaf joined up with the Kufans, when God had already given them victory. So Balkh was one of the victories of the Kufans.

The combatants of Khurāsān between Naysābūr and Ṭukhāristān,[262] in what used to be the territory of the Persian emperor, followed one after the other to make peace, those who had fled and those who had made fortified positions. Al-Aḥnaf returned to Marw al-Rūdh where he remained, having made Ribʿī b. ʿĀmir his deputy in charge of Ṭukhāristān. It is he

257. For the title *khāqān*, see *EI*², s.v. (Boyle).

258. May be taken in the wider sense to cover the area between the rivers Oxus and Jaxartes, of which Bukhārā and Samarqand were the chief towns, or more narrowly the district around Samarqand. See Yāqūt, *Muʿjam*, III, 409–10; Le Strange, *Lands*, 460ff. and Map IX, opposite 433.

259. Four Muslims leaders sent in 17/638 by ʿUmar to reinforce al-Aḥnaf on the eastern front. See Ṭabarī, I, 2569.

260. A Muslim leader who appears in various military roles later in the text. See Ṭabarī, I, 2886–88 etc.

261. Chief town of the fourth quarter of Khurāsān. See Yāqūt, *Muʿjam*, I, 479–80; Le Strange, *Lands*, 420ff. and Map VIII, opposite 335.

262. A large district of Khurāsān stretching to the east of Balkh on the south side of the River Oxus. Cf. Yāqūt, *Muʿjam*, IV, 23; Le Strange, *Lands*, 426–27 and Map 8, opposite 335.

about whom al-Najāshī recited the following, linking his name with his mother who was a noble Arab:[263]

Oh, many's the one who is called a young brave who is not really so! [2684]
Oh, Rib'ī b. Ka's is a real young brave![264]
[Standing] tall [above them], when those sitting in the yard of his house
have taken their fill of what is left in his bowl, he gives them to drink.

Al-Aḥnaf wrote to 'Umar of the conquest of Khurāsān and ('Umar) said, "I wish I had not sent an army there. I wish there were a sea of fire between us."[265] 'Alī asked him why and he replied, "The people (of Khurāsān) will burst forth from it on three occasions and they will be destroyed on the third. I prefer that this should happen to its own people rather than to the Muslims!"

According to al-Sarī—Shu'ayb—Sayf—Abū 'Abd al-Raḥmān al-Fazārī—Abū al-Janūb al-Yashkurī[266]—'Alī b. Abī Ṭālib: When 'Umar heard of the conquest of Khurāsān, he said, "I wish there were a sea of fire between us." 'Alī asked him why he was so distressed by its conquest, when it was a joyful occasion. 'Umar said, "Yes, but I . . ." and so on until the end of [2685]
the [preceding] account.

According to al-Sarī—Shu'ayb—Sayf—'Īsā b. al-Mughīrah[267] and a member of Bakr b. Wā'il called al-Wāzi' b. Zayd b. Khulaydah:[268] When 'Umar heard of al-Aḥnaf's conquest of the

263. Al-Najashī is Qays b. 'Amr; see Iṣfahānī, *Aghānī*, XII, 73, 76. The meter is *ṭawīl*.

264. Ka's is not only the name of Rib'ī's mother, but, because it means "cup" or "goblet," a pun is intended; he is generous in entertaining his guests with drink.

265. Perhaps a reference to the Zoroastrian religion and its fire worship practiced in pre-Islamic Iran.

266. Two narrators mentioned only here in the text. Abū al-Janūb 'Uqbah b. 'Alqamah al-Yashkurī has a brief notice in Ibn Ḥajar, *Tahdhīb*, VII, 247.

267. A narrator mentioned only here in the text and who has only a brief notice in Ibn Ḥajar, *Tahdhīb*, VIII, 231–32.

268. A narrator mentioned only here in the text. Bakr b. Wā'il is a large tribal confederation of 'Adnān, the northern Arabs. See Ibn Ḥazm, *Jamharah*, 307ff., 469; Kaḥḥālah, *Mu'jam*, I, 93ff.; *EI*², s.v. (Caskel).

two Marws and Balkh, he said, "He is al-Aḥnaf! He is the lord of the people of the east called by something other than his name!"[269] 'Umar wrote to al-Aḥnaf as follows, "To continue. On no account go beyond the river;[270] keep to this side. You know how you made an entry into Khurāsān, so keep to this method and victory will continue to be yours. Beware of crossing over and dispersing."

When the envoys of Yazdajird reached the ruler of the Turks and Ghūrak,[271] it was not a straightforward matter to give him assistance until he had actually crossed over the river in defeat to meet them. Then it became so, and the ruler of the Turks gave him assistance—for rulers see it as an obligation to assist one another. He came forward at the head of the Turks, assembled the army of Farghānah[272] and Soghdia, and marched them out. Yazdajird returned to Khurāsān and crossed over to Balkh, the ruler of the Turks crossing with him. The Kufan army mustered at Marw al-Rūdh under al-Aḥnaf, and the polytheists left Balkh and fell upon him there. When al-Aḥnaf heard that
[2686] the ruler of the Turks had crossed the River Balkh with the Soghdians to attack him, he went out at night among his troops to see if he could pick up any useful ideas. As he passed by two men who were cleaning fodder, either straw or barley, one of them was saying to the other, "If only the commander would send us up into this mountain, with the river forming a ditch between us and the enemy, the mountain at our backs to prevent our being approached from behind and the fighting thus being on one front, I would hope that God would give us victory!" So (al-Aḥnaf) returned, content at (what he had heard). This was one dark night. In the morning he assembled the army and said, "You are few, whereas your enemy are many. Let them not strike terror into you. 'How often a company that is few in number has overcome a company that is many by God's leave;

269. Al-Aḥnaf's name was Ṣakhr. See note 45, above.

270. That is, the River Oxus.

271. The text reads Ghūzak, but see Barthold, *Turkestan*. 96 etc., "the *ikhshīd* of Soghd."

272. The province of Farghānah stretched for more than 200 miles along the upper stream of the River Jaxartes. See Yāqūt, *Mu'jam*, IV, 253; Le Strange, *Lands*, 476–77 and Map IX, opposite 433.

God is with those who show patience'.[273] Go from here and up this mountain. Place it at your backs; place the river between you and your enemy, and fight them on one front." They did all this, preparing everything that would give them an advantage, (al-Aḥnaf) being at the head of 10,000 Basrans, while there was a similar number of Kufans. The Turks advanced, together with those whom they had collected together, and fell upon (the Muslim forces), attacking them morning and evening and withdrawing at night; this went on for some time while al-Aḥnaf sought intelligence of their nocturnal position. After he had discovered this, he went out one night, acting as a scout for his men until he came close to the camp of the ruler of [2687]
the Turks and halted. At the first light of dawn a Turkish cavalryman came forth, wearing his horsetail and beating his drum. Then he positioned himself where someone of his rank positions himself in relation to the troops. Al-Aḥnaf attacked him and the two exchanged spear thrusts. Al-Aḥnaf pierced him and killed him, as he recited the following in the *rajaz* meter:

Every chief has a duty to
    dye his spear [with blood] or [to fight until] it break;
We have a leader here who was made to face up to
    the sword of Abū Ḥafṣ[274] that remains [intact].

Then he stood where the Turk had stood and took his horsetail. Another Turk came out, did exactly as his colleague had done, then stood near him. Al-Aḥnaf attacked him and they exchanged spear thrusts. Al-Aḥnaf pierced him and killed him, as he recited the following in the *rajaz* meter:

The chief takes a high, lofty position,
    keeping away herdsmen if they let [their beasts] pasture.[275]

Then he stood where the second Turk had stood and took his horsetail. A third Turk came out, did exactly the same as the other two had done, then stood near [where] the second [had

273. Qur'ān, II: 250.
274. Abū Ḥafṣ is the *kunyah* of 'Umar b. al-Khaṭṭāb.
275. *Khullā'*, herdsmen, is the plural of *khālin*; see *Glossarium*, CCXXXII. The hemistitch reads, *wa-yamna'u l-khullā'a immā arba'ū*. Perhaps "let [their beasts] come to water"?

been]. Al-Aḥnaf attacked him and they exchanged spear thrusts. Al-Aḥnaf pierced him and killed him, as he recited the following in *rajaz* meter:

> [He ran forward] like al-Shamūs, ready to respond to anything,
> running at full speed, bad tempered.[276]

[2688] Then al-Aḥnaf went off back to camp. Not one of (his troops) knew anything about this until he returned there and prepared himself [for war].

It was in the nature of the Turks that they did not go out [for battle] until three of their cavalrymen had come forward like these, each one beating his drum. Then, after the third one, they would [all] go out [to do battle]. So on that night the Turks went out after the third horseman had done so, and they came across [all three of] them slaughtered. So the ruler of the Turks found this a bad omen and said, "We have been [here] too long and these men have been killed in a situation such as no one has ever been killed before. There can be no good for us in fighting these men. Let us all retire." So their leaders withdrew. When day broke, the Muslims could see nothing, and news came to them that the ruler of the Turks had retired to Balkh. Yazdajird b. Shahriyār b. Kisrā had originally left the ruler of the Turks in Marw al-Rūdh and departed for Marw al-Shāhijān. Ḥātim b. al-Nuʿmān and his followers fortified their positions against (Yazdajird), but he besieged them, removing his treasures from where they were kept, while the ruler of the Turks was in Balkh waiting for him. The Muslims suggested to al-Aḥnaf that they should pursue them, but he told them to remain in their position and leave them alone. When Yazdajird had collected together those of his possessions left in Marw, he did not have enough time to collect them all. He intended to make himself the sole possessor (of the treasures), because they were a large

---

276. Al-Shamūs is the name of the horse of ʿAbdallāh b. ʿĀmir al-Qurashī. Of an animal the word means "recalcitrant." See Ibn Manẓūr, *Lisān*, VI, 113–14; Fīrūzābādī, *Qāmūs*, II, 232; Zabīdī, *Tāj*, XVI, 175; Lane, *Lexicon*, VIII, 2770. The expression *nājizun bi-nājiz* originates in the commercial world, meaning, "ready [merchandise] for ready [money]". I translate "ready to respond to anything." For the meaning of *mushāriz*, "bad tempered," "hostile," "quarrelsome," see Fīrūzābādī, *Qāmūs*, II, 185; Zabīdī, *Tāj*, V, 361.

part of [all] the treasures of the Persians. He also intended to join the ruler of the Turks, and the Persians asked him what he intended to do. He replied that he wanted to join the ruler of the Turks and remain with him or [go] to China. They told him to tread warily, for this was a bad idea, going to a people in their [2689] own country, while abandoning his own land and people. [They told him] he should take them back to (the Muslims), so that they could make peace with them. (The Muslims) were completely faithful, men of religion and in control of (the Persians') land. An enemy ruling over Persians in their own land was a better political arrangement than an enemy ruling over them in his own land, who moreover had no religion, nor would they know how faithful (his people) would be. But he refused [to accept their argument] and they refused [to give in to him]. They told him to leave their treasures alone and they would return them to their own territory and to its ruler. He should not remove them from their land. He [again] refused [to accept their argument]. They told him they would not let him go. They drew on one side and left him alone with his followers. They did battle together and they put him to flight, taking the treasures and assuming complete control over them, abandoning him completely. The (Persian) polytheists wrote to al-Aḥnaf, giving him the news, so the Muslims intercepted them, while the polytheists were in Marw resisting (Yazdajird). They fought (Yazdajird) and caught up with him at the rear of the army, rushing him away from his treasures (*athqāl*). He went off to seek refuge, crossed the river to Farghānah and the Turks. (Yazdajird) remained throughout the time of ʿUmar corresponding with (the Persians), and they with him, or at least some of them. So the people of Khurāsān rebelled during the time of ʿUthman['s caliphate].

The Persians came to al-Aḥnaf and made peace with him, exchanging agreements with him and handing over the treasures and monies [mentioned above]. They gradually returned to their lands and wealth in as good a state as they had been at the time of the Sasanian emperors. It was as if they were [still] under their rule except for the fact that the Muslims were more worthy of their confidence and acted more justly toward them. So they rejoiced in their condition and were the object of envy. [The

share of the booty that] came to the cavalryman in the battle
[2690] against Yazdajird was like that of the cavalryman at the battle of al-Qādisiyyah.[277]

When the Khurāsānīs threw off their allegiance in the time of 'Uthmān, Yazdajird went and settled in Marw. When he, together with his followers, and the Khurāsānīs fell into disagreement, he took refuge in a mill. (The Khurāsānīs) found him eating from a field around the mill and killed him, throwing him into the river.

When Yazdajird was killed in Marw—he was on that day in hiding in a mill seeking to reach Kirmān—the Muslims and polytheists took possession of his immovable booty. Al-Aḥnaf got to hear of this and left immediately at the head of his army for Balkh, making for the ruler of the Turks and arranging for the dependents and family of Yazdajird to follow with both Muslims and non-Muslims of the Persians, while the ruler of the Turks and the Turks [remained] in Balkh. When (the ruler of the Turks) heard of what had happened to Yazdajird and of the Muslims' departure from Marw al-Rūdh with al-Aḥnaf in his direction, he left Balkh and crossed the river. Al-Aḥnaf arrived and remained in Balkh and the Kufans also settled in the four regions (of Khurāsān).[278] Then he returned to Marw al-Rūdh and remained there, writing to 'Umar of the defeat of the ruler of the Turks and Yazdajird. He also sent the fifths to him, and the [official] delegations [from Khurāsān] reached him.

(The same sources) reported as follows. When the ruler of the Turks, together with the dependents of the family of the Persian emperor or those of them who had made their way with Yazdajird to Balkh, had crossed over the river, they met the messenger of Yazdajird, whom he had sent to the ruler of China

277. The famous battle that took place in 16/637 and a decisive victory for the Muslim forces over the Persians.

278. I here take the Arabic *kuwar* to indicate the four divisions of Khurāsān. It is true that they were officially known as *arbā'*, the plural of *rub'*, and that these quarters were a later development. My explanation would be that suggesting there were such quarters at this early date is an anachronism and that all that is really meant is that the Kufans settled throughout Khurāsān. For the four quarters of Khurāsān and their chief towns of Balkh, Naysābūr, Marw, and Herat, see Le Strange, *Lands*, 382–83.

and with whom he had sent gifts and who was bringing back a reply to his letter from the ruler of China. They asked him what [2691] had happened to him. He replied that, when he delivered the letter and the gifts to [the ruler], he had presented him in return with what they could see—and he showed them the present he [was carrying]. [The ruler of China] responded to Yazdajird by writing him the following letter, [but only] after he had addressed (the messenger) as follows. "I know that in truth rulers must give aid to [other] rulers against those who overcome them. So describe these people who drove you out of your land to me. I notice that you mention they are few and you are many. Such a small number will not affect you in this way with your great numbers. They can do this only if they are good and you evil." (The messenger) suggested that he ask him whatever he wanted. So he asked him if they kept to their agreement and he replied that they did. (The ruler) asked what they said to them before they made war on them. (The messenger) replied that they called upon us to choose one of three things: [to accept] their faith—and if we do, they treat us as themselves—or [to pay] tribute and [enter] their protection or to be subjected to open warfare. (The ruler) asked about how obedient they were to their leaders. (The messenger) replied that no one was more obedient to him leading them. (The ruler) asked what they permitted and what they forbade, and (the messenger) told him. He asked if they ever forbade what was permitted to them or permitted what was forbidden them. [When] (the messenger) replied that they did not, (the ruler) remarked that they would never perish until they permitted what was forbidden and forbade what was permitted to them. He then asked about their clothes, and (the messenger) told him. [He asked] about their riding animals, and (the messenger) mentioned their pure Arabian horses and described them [to him]. "What fine horses they are!" exclaimed (the ruler). [The messenger then] described camels to him, how they kneel down and go forth to carry [loads]. (The ruler's response was that this was the description of long-necked beasts!) (The ruler of China) sent a letter to Yazdajird with (the messenger) as follows. "I am not prevented from dispatching an [2692] army to you stretching from Marw to China by my not knowing what is proper for me. But if these people described to me by your messenger were to try, they could demolish mountains; if nothing were to stand in their way, they would wipe me out, as long as they are as described! Make your peace with them therefore and accept some modus vivendi with them. Do not stir them up, as long as they do not stir you up." Yazdajird and the royal family remained in Farghānah in [formal] agreement with the ruler of the Turks.

When the messenger brought to ʿUmar b. al-Khaṭṭāb [news of] the conquest and the delegation [other] news, carrying the booty with them on behalf of al-Aḥnaf, (ʿUmar) assembled the people and addressed them. He also ordered the conquest document to be read out to them. In his own address, he spoke as follows:

> God, ever blessed and almighty, has mentioned His Apostle and the guidance He sent with him. He promised, for anyone following Him, immediate and future reward [comprising] the goodness of this world and the next. He said, "He it is who sent His Apostle with the guidance and the true religion that He might make it prevail over any [other] religion, even though the polytheists were averse."[279] Praise be to God who has fulfilled His promise and granted His army victory. Yes indeed, God has destroyed the rule of the Magians and disunited them. They do not possess one single span of their territory that can bring harm to a Muslim. Yes indeed, God "has made you heirs to their land, houses,
> [2693] wealth and sons" "in order to see how they behave."[280] Yes indeed, the distance between the garrison towns [of al-Kūfah and al-Baṣrah] and the border areas (of Persia) is now the same as [that between] you and the two towns in the past, now that (our armies) have penetrated into the land. "God brings His command to pass"[281] fulfills His promise right through to the last. So apply yourselves and He will carry out His agreement with you in full and fulfill His promise to you. Do not rebel, lest

279. Qur'ān, IX:33 and LXI:9.
280. Qur'ān, X:14 and XXX:27.
281. Qur'ān, LXV:3.

God substitute others for you. My only fear for this community is that it will be put in danger by you.

Abū Ja'far [al-Ṭabarī] reported [as follows]. Then the Khurāsānīs from far and near came out in opposition in the time of 'Uthmān b. 'Affān, two years into his caliphate. We shall mention the remainder of the news of their break-away movement in its [proper] place, God willing, together with the killing of Yazdajird.[282]

'Umar b. al-Khaṭṭāb led the people on pilgrimage in this year. His governors of the garrison towns then were the same as those in the year 21 [December 10, 641–November 30, 642] except for al-Kūfah and al-Baṣrah. His governor of al-Kūfah and [official] in charge of the police was al-Mughīrah b. Shu'bah and his governor of al-Baṣrah was Abū Mūsā al-Ash'arī.

---

282. See Ṭabarī, I, 2872ff.; Translation, XV, 78ff.

The Events of the Year 23

(November 19, 643–November 7, 644)

The conquest of Iṣṭakhr[283] took place in [this year] according to the report of Abū Ma'shar. According to Aḥmad b. Thābit al-Rāzī—someone else—Isḥāq b. 'Īsā—Abū Ma'shar: The first (campaign of) Iṣṭakhr and [that of] Hamadhān were in the year 23 [643–644]. Al-Wāqidī made a similar report, whereas Sayf said that the conquest of Iṣṭakhr came after the second (campaign of) Tawwaj.[284]

The Conquest of Tawwaj[285]

According to al-Sarī—Shu'ayb—Sayf—Muḥammad, Ṭalḥah, al-Muhallab and 'Amr: The Basran army went forth, those

---

283. The ancient town of Persepolis on the River Pulvar in Fārs province. The district of Iṣṭakhr covered the whole of the northern part of Fārs. See Yāqūt, *Mu'jam*, I, 211–12; Le Strange, *Lands*, 275ff. and Map 6, opposite 249.

284. A commercial town in Fārs on or near the River Shāpūr only about 40 miles from the Gulf coast. See Yāqūt, *Mu'jam*, II, 56–57; Le Strange, *Lands*, 259–60.

285. See Balādhurī, *Futūḥ*, 386–87; Bal'ami, *Chronique*, III, 511.

(troops) dispatched to Fārs as commanders there, accompanied by Sāriyah b. Zunaym,[286] and those sent with them beyond, while the army of Fārs was assembled at Tawwaj. But (the Basrans) did not face the army (of Fārs) directly with their own forces; rather each district commander made for his own command and the district to which he had been assigned. This [intelligence] reached the army of Fārs, so they dispersed to their [different] areas—just as the Muslims themselves had done—to defend them. This brought about the defeat of the Fārsīs and the complete dispersal of their forces. The [Fārsī] polytheists regarded all this as a bad omen and it was as if they were staring fate in the face. Mujāshi' b. Mas'ūd[287] headed for Sābūr[288] and Ardashīr Khurrah,[289] at the head of his Muslim followers. They and the army of Fārs met at Tawwaj and fought for a long time. God brought about the defeat for the Muslims of those [who [2695]
fought] at Tawwaj and gave the Muslims authority over them. They killed them in every conceivable manner, doing with them whatever they wished. (God) gave (the Muslims) everything in their camp as booty, and they took possession of it. This was the last [battle of] Tawwaj; it never had such military strength after this. The first was that in which the troops of al-'Alā' at the time of [the battle of] Ṭāwūs were rescued, the battle during which they fought together.[290] The first and last battles rival

---

286. Al-Kinānī, governor and Muslim military leader active in Fārs. See also Ṭabarī, I, 2569; Ibn al-Athīr, *Usd*, II, 244; Ibn Ḥajar, *Iṣābah*, IV, 96–98.

287. Al-Sulamī, Companion and Muslim military leader who died in 36/656. See Ibn al-Athīr, *Usd*, IV, 300; Ibn Ḥajar, *Iṣābah*, IX, 87; *Tahdhīb*, X, 38.

288. The Persian Shāpūr or Bīshāpūr, the district of Fārs within the basin of the upper reaches of River Shāpūr. The town is about 40 miles northeast of Tawwaj. See Yāqūt, *Mu'jam*, III, 167–68; Le Strange, *Lands*, 262 and Map VI, opposite 249.

289. One of the five districts of Fārs, of which the chief town is Shīrāz. See Yāqūt, *Mu'jam*, I, 146; Le Strange, *Lands*, 248 and Map VI, opposite 249.

290. Al-'Alā' was governor of Bahrain under the Prophet and the early caliphs and a participant in the Riddah wars. In 17/638 he took a force from Bahrain over to Fārs, and, although launching a successful raid, his ships were lost and he was cut off and had to be rescued. 'Umar dismissed him for this unauthorized attack. See Wāqidī, *Maghāzī*, II, 782; Ibn Hishām, *Sīrah*, II, 576, 600, 607; Donner, *Conquests*, 86, 327; Zarrīnkūb, "Conquest," 21. The battles with the Fārsīs (Ṭabarī, I, 2546ff.) were fought in Ṭāwūs, a place described by Yāqūt (*Mu'jam*, IV, 8) as being situated in the coastal region of Fārs.

each other [in importance]. Then (the inhabitants of Tawwaj) were summoned [to pay] tribute and [to make] a compact. So they came back and settled. Mujāshi' divided out the fifth of the spoils and sent them [to 'Umar], sending out a delegation [to him also]. Those bringing the good news [of the victory] and the delegations were provided with gifts[291] and their needs catered for according to a practice instituted by the Messenger of God.

Al-Sarī—Shu'ayb—Sayf—Muḥammad b. Sūqah[292]—'Āṣim b. Kulayb[293]—his father: We left with Mujāshi' b. Mas'ūd to attack Tawwaj. We besieged it and fought (their army) for a long time. We conquered it, seized much booty and killed a great number. I was wearing a torn shirt, so I took a needle and thread and began to mend my shirt.[294] Then I caught sight of a man among the dead who had on a shirt, so I took it, brought it to some water, beat it between two stones until the dirt was
[2696] removed, and put it on. When the spoils had been collected together, Mujāshi' got up to address [us]. He praised and extolled God and said, "Men, do not take what is not yours; anyone who steals will bring what he has stolen on the Day of Resurrection. Return [anything you have stolen], be it only a needle!" When I heard this, I took the shirt off and threw it among the fifth parts [of the booty].

The Conquest of Iṣṭakhr

(The source) continued: 'Uthmān b. Abī al-'Āṣ[295] made for Iṣṭakhr. He and the army of Iṣṭakhr met at Jūr[296] and fought a

291. Arabic, "*yujāzūna.*" It might mean "were given sufficient water."

292. An unidentified narrator.

293. A narrator who died in 137/754. See Ibn Ḥajar, *Tahdhīb*, V, 53ff.

294. For these last two sentences the Arabic reads, "*fa-lammā iftataḥnā-hā . . . fa-akhadhtu.*" I have done away with the temporal clause in translation.

295. Al-Thaqafī, a Muslim military leader and one-time governor of al-Ṭā'if, Bahrain and Oman. He died in ca. 55/675. See Ibn al-Athīr, *Usd*, III, 372–74; Ibn Ḥajar, *Tahdhīd*, VII, 128–29; Ṭabarī, I, 2570, 2830 etc.; Hill, *Termination*, passim.

296. The earlier name for Fīrūzābād, the chief town of the district of Ardashīr Khurrah. See Yāqūt, *Mu'jam*, II, 181–82; Le Strange, *Lands*, 255 and Map VI, opposite 249.

long battle. Then God granted them Jūr as a conquest, and the Muslims [also] conquered Iṣṭakhr, having killed a great many of [the enemy] and taken what they wanted, though some [of the enemy] fled. Then ʿUthmān called upon the people to [pay] tribute and to [make] a compact. They therefore sent messages to him, and he to them. Their religious leader[297] and all those who had fled or left responded favorably to his [call]. They gradually came back and yielded to [the payment of] tribute. Now when the enemy fled, ʿUthmān collected together all the booty God had granted them and took out a fifth, sending it to ʿUmar, and distributing four-fifths of the booty among the army. They abstained from plundering and delivered up what was in their care, considering this lower world to be of little importance. ʿUthmān mustered them to him and rose to speak. He told them that things would continue to advance and that everyone would remain safe and sound from anything distasteful as long as they did not take what was not theirs. If they did, they would experience something unpleasant, and the much they might have had then would not go as far as the little [2697] they had now.

According to al-Sarī—Shuʿayb—Sayf—Abū Sufyān[298]—al-Ḥasan: ʿUthmān b. Abī al-ʿĀṣ said on the day Iṣṭakhr [was conquered], "When God wishes a people to prosper, He restrains them and increases their trustworthiness. Hold on to it, for the first thing you lose of your faith is trustworthiness. Once you do lose it, every day something new will be lost to you."

[A Persian called] Shahrak[299] threw off [his allegiance] at the end of ʿUmar's caliphate or at the beginning of ʿUthmān's. He roused up the people of Fārs, calling upon them to break [the peace agreement]. So ʿUthmān b. Abī al-ʿĀṣ was dispatched against him for a second time, accompanied by reinforcements under the command of ʿUbaydallāh b. Maʿmar[300] and Shibl b.

---

297. *Hirbadh,* actually a functionary of the Zoroastrian fire temple. See Christensen, *L'Iran,* 144; Morony, *Iraq,* 531.

298. An unidentified narrator.

299. The Perisan governor (*marzbān*) of Fārs. See Zarrīnkūb, "Conquest," 21.

300. Al-Taymī, Companion and Muslim military leader who died in 29/649. See Ibn al-Athīr, *Usd,* III, 345.

Ma'bad al-Bajalī.[301] (The Muslim forces and the Fārsīs) met in battle in Fārs. On the battlefield 3 parasangs away from one of their settlements called Rīshahr[302] and 12 from their headquarters, Shahrak said to his son, "Son, where will our lunch be, here or in Rīshahr"? He replied, "Father, if (the Fārsīs) leave us alone, our lunch will be neither here, nor in Rīshahr! It can only be at home.[303] But I certainly do not think they will leave us alone." The two were still talking when the Muslims launched
[2698] their attack. They fought together vehemently. Shahrak and his son were both killed in [the battle] and God caused great slaughter, al-Ḥakam b. [Abī] al-'Āṣ b. Bishr b. Duhmān,[304] the brother of 'Uthmān, being entrusted with the killing of Shahrak.

It was Abū Ma'shar who reported that the first [campaign] for Fārs and the last for Iṣṭakhr took place in the year 28 [September 25, 648–September 14, 649]. He also said that the last [campaign] for Fārs and [that of] Jūr took place in the year 29 [September 14, 649–September 4, 650]. This was also according to Aḥmad b. Thābit al-Rāzī—someone who heard Isḥāq b. 'Īsā mention this [same report]—Abū Ma'shar.

According to 'Abdallāh b. Aḥmad b. Shabbawayh al-Marwazī[305]—his father—Sulaymān b. Ṣāliḥ[306]—'Ubaydallāh[307]—

301. A Muslim military leader, possibly a Muzanī rather than a Bajalī. See Ibn al-Athīr, *Usd*, II, 385.

302. There are two places with this name in Fārs. One near Būshahr (Bushire), the other in the north of the province, just south of the River Ṭāb. It is impossible to know for sure which is meant here. Yāqūt (*Mu'jam*, III, 112–13), however, mentions only the latter and recounts the story of the death of Shahrak, whom he calls Suhrak. Cf. Le Strange, *Lands*, 261, 271 and Map 6, opposite 249.

303. Arabic, *fa-qāla yā abati in tarakū-nā fa-lā yakūnu ghadā'u-nā hāhunā wa-lā bi-Rīshahra wa-lā yakūnanna illā fī al-manzil.*

304. Al-Thaqafī. 'Uthmān employed his brother in a senior military role mainly in the area of Fārs. Ibn Ḥajar, *Iṣābah*, II, 271, gives his full name as Ibn al-'Āṣ b. Nasr b. 'Abd b. Duhmān. Ibn al-Athīr, *Usd*, II, 35, gives Ibn Abī al-'Āṣ b. Bashīr b. Duhmān. Cf. Balādhurī, *Futūḥ*, 362, 386–87; Hill, *Termination*, 122, 135.

305. An unidentified narrator.

306. Sulaymān b. Ṣāliḥ al-Laythī died before 110/728. See Ibn Ḥajar, *Tahdhīb*, IV, 199–200.

307. 'Ubaydallāh is impossible to identify. 'Ubayd, rather than the 'Abd of the Leiden text is from the Cairo edition and the Leiden *Addenda*. It must be

'Ubaydallāh b. Sulaymān:[308] 'Uthmān b. Abī al-'Āṣ was sent to Bahrain, so he dispatched his brother, al-Ḥakam b. Abī al-'Āṣ at the head of 2,000 [men] to Tawwaj. The Persian emperor had already fled from al-Madā'in and had reached Jūr in Fārs.

(The source) continued: According to Ziyād, the client of al-Ḥakam b. Abī al-'Āṣ—al-Ḥakam b. Abī al-'Āṣ: Shahrak came at me. 'Ubayd[309] added that he had been sent by the Persian emperor. Al-Ḥakam continued: He came up against me at the head of his troops. Then they came down a mountain road, having donned their armor. I was afraid that my men [2699] would be blinded [by the reflection of the sun off their armor]; so I had the order shouted out that all those wearing a turban should wrap it over their eyes and all those not wearing a turban should close their eyes. I called out that they should dismount, and when he saw this, Shahrak did the same. Then I called out that [my men] should mount, and we stationed ourselves in ranks against (Shahrak's men). (The latter) also mounted and I put al-Jārūd al-'Abdī[310] in command of the right wing and Abū Ṣufrah of the left; that is, the father of al-Muhallab. (The enemy) attacked the Muslims, but (the latter) put them to flight; I could not hear a single sound from them. Al-Jārūd informed me that the army had disappeared. But I replied that he would see what would happen. Their horses soon returned, riderless, whereas the Muslims were pursuing (the enemy) and killing them. Heads were scattered around in front of me. Now I had with me one of their rulers, called al-Muka'bir,[311] who had deserted the emperor and joined me. I was brought a huge head, and al-Muka'bir told me it was that of al-Azdahāq, meaning

---

asked if the text is corrupt here and whether this 'Ubaydallāh and 'Ubaydallāh b. Sulaymān are not one and the same. See next note.

308. Perhaps more correctly 'Ubayd b. Sulaymān. See Ibn Ḥajar, *Tahdhīd*, VII, 67; Translation, I, 227 n. 402.

309. That is, the same authority as the 'Ubaydallāh b. Sulaymān above in the text; see preceding note.

310. That is, Abū al-Mundhir al-Jārūd b. 'Amr b. Ḥanash b. al-Mu'allā al-'Abdī was a convert from Christianity and a leader of 'Abd al-Qays. Ibn Ḥajar, *Iṣābah*, II, 51, says he died in 21/642, or at Nihāwand, or in 'Uthmān's caliphate. See also Ibn al-Athīr, *Usd*, II, 260–61; Ibn Ḥajar, *Tahdhīb*, II, 53–54.

311. Al-Muka'bir was Āzādh Furūz b. Jushnas. See Justi, *Namenbuch*, 53.

Shahrak.[312] [Finally] they were besieged in the town of Sābūr and (al-Ḥakam) made peace with them. Their ruler was Ādharbiyān[313] and al-Ḥakam asked his assistance in the fight against the army of Iṣṭakhr. [At this point] ʿUmar died and ʿUthmān sent ʿUbaydallāh b. Maʿmar in place of (al-Ḥakam) [as commander]. ʿUbaydallāh heard that Ādharbiyān was intending to betray them, so he told him he wanted him to prepare some food for his men and slaughter a head of cattle for
[2700] them, putting its bones on the bowl next to [ʿUbaydallāh]. [The latter further] told him that he wanted to suck out the marrow from the bones. (Ādharbiyān) did this and (ʿUbaydallāh)—one of the strongest of all men—took hold of a bone that could be chopped up only by means of an axe and broke it in his hand to suck out the marrow. The ruler, [Ādharbiyān], got up, seized his foot and said, "This is the position of one seeking refuge!" So (ʿUbaydallāh) granted him a [peace] agreement. ʿUbaydallāh was wounded by a mangonel, but [before he died] predicted to them that they would conquer this town, God willing. [He also urged them] to kill (the enemy) there for a while for his sake. (The Muslims) did this and killed many men.

ʿUthmān b. Abī al-ʿĀṣ had joined al-Ḥakam, after he had defeated Shahrak, and he wrote to ʿUmar informing him that there was a breach between him and al-Kūfah and that he was afraid that the enemy would attack him through it. The lord of al-Kūfah wrote a similar letter that there was a breach between him and such and such a place. The two letters reached (ʿUmar) at the same time, so he dispatched Abū Mūsā at the head of 700 [men] and settled them in al-Baṣrah.

The Conquest of Fasā and Darābjird[314]

According to al-Sarī—Shuʿayb—Sayf—Muḥammad, Ṭalḥah, al-Muhallab and ʿAmr: Sāriyah b. Zunaym made in the direction

---

312. In Persian mythology Azhd Dahāk was the tyrant who overthrew Jamshād and ruled for 1,000 years. He was the personification of evil. See *CHIr*, III, especially pp. 426–27.

313. For Ādharbiyān, see Justi, *Namenbuch*, 42, Arzanbān.

314. Darābjird is the easternmost district of Fārs, and the chief town has the same name. Fasā is a town in the district less than 60 miles west of the town of

of Fasā and Darābjird and finally reached the camp of their (army). He positioned himself against them and besieged them for some time. They then sought reinforcements, themselves rallying together, and the Kurds of Fārs joined them. The Muslims were unexpectedly faced with a serious situation [in the form of] a huge army. On the very eve [of these events], ʿUmar saw in a dream (the Muslims') battle and the [large] number [of enemy forces] at a particular hour of the day. The next day he gave the call for congregational prayers. When the hour arrived that he had noted in his dream, he came out to the (people). The Muslims had been shown to him in a desert area; if they remained there, they would be surrounded. If they retreated to a mountain behind them, they could be attacked only on one front. (ʿUmar) then stood up and told his people that he had seen these two armies and described their situation. He then declared, "[To] the mountain, [to] the mountain, Sāriyah!" Turning to the (people), he said, "God has armies; perhaps one of them will bring them the message [of my dream]!" When this particular hour did actually arrive on the day, Sāriyah and the Muslims all agreed to make for the mountain. This they did and fought the enemy on one front [only]. God routed (the enemy) for (the Muslims) and they wrote to ʿUmar [informing] him of all this, of their capture of the region, of the call of its people [to accept an agreement] and their [consequent] pacification. [2701]

Al-Sarī—Shuʿayb—Sayf—Abū ʿUmar Dithār b. Abī Shabīb[315]—Abū ʿUthmān[316] and Abū ʿAmr b. al-ʿAlāʾ[317]—a member of B. Māzin:[318] ʿUmar sent Sāriyah b. Zunaym al-Duʾalī to Fasā and Darābjird. He besieged [the inhabitants], but they later prepared themselves for war and sought him out in the desert

---

Darābjird. See Yāqūt, *Muʿjam*, II, 446; IV, 260–61; Le Strange, *Lands*, 288ff. and Map VI, opposite 249. For the conquests in Balādhurī, see *Futūḥ*, 388–90.

315. An unidentified narrator.

316. Al-Nahdī, famous figure in early Islam who died about 100/718. See Ibn Ḥajar, *Tahdhīb*, VI, 277ff.

317. Abū ʿAmr b. al-ʿAlāʾ was himself of Māzin of Tamīm. He died in 57/677. See Ibn Ḥajar, *Tahdhīb*, XII, 178–80.

318. That is, Māzin b. Mālik of Tamīm. See Kaḥḥālah, *Muʿjam*, III, 1023–24. Cf. preceding note.

area [where he was], outnumbering him and coming against him on every side. ʿUmar proclaimed, as he gave the address one Friday, "[To] the mountain, [to] the mountain, Sāriyah b. Zunaym!" When that day came, the Muslims had a mountain to one side; if they took refuge in it, they could be attacked only on
[2702] one front. So they did so. Then (the Muslims) fought them and defeated them. (Sāriyah) took the spoils from them, including a casket containing a precious stone. He asked the Muslims' permission to hand it over to ʿUmar as a gift and they agreed, so he sent it off with a man who also [announced news of] the conquest. (Now the envoys and delegations were given gifts and [all] their needs were catered for.) Sāriyah said to (the man), "Borrow what will enable you to reach [ʿUmar] and what you can leave behind for your family against the gift you [will get from ʿUmar]." So the man arrived in al-Baṣrah and did this. Then he left [al-Baṣrah] and came to ʿUmar [in Medina]. He found him feeding the people carrying the stick that he used to drive his camel. (The messenger) went toward him, and he turned toward him with (the stick) and told him to sit down. So he sat down and when the people had eaten, ʿUmar went off. (The messenger) got up and followed him, so ʿUmar thought he was somebody who had not had his fill. He told him, when he had finally got to the door of his house, to come in, already having ordered the baker to take the food tray to where the baking was done for the Muslims. So when he sat down in the house, some lunch was brought for him, bread, olive oil, and coarsely ground salt, and put down. (ʿUmar) asked [his wife] whether she would come out and eat [with them]. She replied, "I can hear the voice of a man!" He said, "Yes, indeed," to which she replied, "Had you wanted me to show myself off in front of men, you would have bought me another dress!" He said, "Are you not pleased that people say, 'Umm Kulthūm is the daughter of ʿAlī and the wife of ʿUmar!'" She replied, "A lot of good that does me!" Then ʿUmar told the man to come near and eat. "If she were in a good mood, (the food) would be better than what you can see!" So they both ate [together], and when he had finished, the messenger of Sāriyah b. Zunaym exclaimed, "O
[2703] Commander of the Faithful!" He replied that he was very welcome. He then brought him close until their knees were

touching and asked him about the Muslims [in Fārs], then about Sāriyah b. Zunaym. He gave ('Umar) the information. Then he told him of the story of the casket, but ('Umar) took one look at it and shouted at him, "No, I'll give you nothing[319] until you return to this army and make a [fair] distribution among them." And he dismissed him. But he told the Commander of the Faithful, that he had exhausted his camels and borrowed against a gift from him. He asked him to give him what would satisfy him. He would not leave ('Umar) alone until he exchanged his own camel for one of the camels given as alms, and he took his camel and put it with the alms camels. The messenger set off back, an object of anger and denied any gift. He came to al-Baṣrah and [onward to the army and finally] carried out 'Umar's order. [While he was in Medina], people asked him about Sāriyah, about the conquest and whether they had heard anything on the day of the battle. He replied that they had heard, "[To] the mountain, Sāriyah." [He added] that they were almost done for, so they took refuge on it and God granted them the conquest.

Al-Sarī—Shu'ayb—Sayf—al-Mujālid—al-Sha'bī gave an account similar to that of 'Amr.

The Conquest of Kirmān[320]

According to al-Sarī—Shu'ayb—Sayf—Muḥammad, Ṭalḥah, al-Muhallab and 'Amr: Suhayl b. 'Adī made for Kirmān and was joined by 'Abdallāh b. 'Abdallāh b. 'Itbān. In charge of the vanguard of Suhayl b. 'Adī was al-Nusayr b. 'Amr al-'Ijlī.[321] [2704]
Now the Kirmānīs had massed against (Suhayl), they having sought assistance in the [region of] the Qufs.[322] They fought (the Muslims) just within their own territory, but God scattered them. (The Muslims) seized the road against them and al-Nusayr killed the [local] governor (*marzbān*). Suhayl advanced along

319. Arabic, *lā wa-lā karāmata.*

320. See Balādhurī, *Futūḥ*, especially 391–92, in which Suhayl b. 'Adī does not feature; Bal'ami, *Chronique*, III, 516–17.

321. An unidentified military leader.

322. An extensive mountain area to the southeast of Jīraft (see next note). See Yāqūt, *Mu'jam*, IV, 380–82; Le Strange, *Lands*, 317 and Map VI, opposite 249; *EI2*, s.v. "Ḳufṣ" (Bosworth).

what is today the settlement road as far as Jīraft,[323] while ʿAbdallāh b. ʿAbdallāh [came] from the desert region of Shīr.[324] They seized what camels and ewes they wished, putting a value on the camels and sheep and dividing them up among themselves according to the prices (they would fetch), because the Bactrians were bigger than the Arabians and they did not want to value [them] too highly.[325] They wrote to ʿUmar and he replied to them that the Arabian could be valued only according to the amount of meat, (the Bactrian) being [treated] in the same way. [He added that], if they were of the opinion that the Bactrians had more meat, then they should value them more highly, for [prices] can be only in accordance with value.

According to al-Madāʾinī—ʿAlī b. Mujāhid[326]—Ḥanbal b. Abī Ḥarīdah, judge of Qūhistān[327]—the governor of Qūhistān: ʿAbdallāh b. Budayl b. Warqāʾ al-Khuzāʿī[328] conquered Kirmān during the caliphate of ʿUmar b. al-Khaṭṭāb. He then went on to al-Ṭabasayn from Kirmān, then came to ʿUmar. He said that he
[2705] had conquered al-Ṭabasayn and asked that it be granted to him as a land concession.[329] (ʿUmar) was willing to do this, but was told it was an important district. He therefore did not grant it to (ʿAbdallāh) as a land concession. It is [in fact] the gateway [from Kirmān] to Khurāsān.

---

323. I take the Arabic *qurā* here to mean the settlements of the Kirmānīs and translate accordingly. There might, however, be a place named al-Qurā, in which case the translation would need amendation to "Suhayl advanced along what is today the road to al-Qurā as far as Jīraft." There is no reference to such a toponym in the geographical sources at my disposal. Jīraft is spelled Jīruft by Le Strange. The town is situated south of the town of Kirmān, and its district was the whole of southern Kirmān province. See Yāqūt, *Muʿjam*, II, 198; Le Strange, *Lands*, 314ff. and Map VI, opposite 249.

324. An unidentified place.

325. That is, instead of the usual division of the animals as spoils by numbers.

326. D. ca. 182/789. See Ibn Ḥajar, *Tahdhīb*, VII, 377ff.; Sezgin, *GAS*, I, 312.

327. Ḥanbal b. Abī Ḥarīdah is unidentified. Qūhistān is the province to the southwest and west of Khurāsān. See Le Strange, *Lands*, 352ff. and Map VIII, opposite 335.

328. Ibn Budayl must in fact have been only ten years old in the year 23; see note 22, above.

329. Arabic verb *aqṭaʿa*; see *EI*², s.v. "Iḳṭāʿ" (Cahen). For al-Ṭabasayn, see note 249, above.

The Conquest of Sijistān[330]

[The same sources] reported as follows: 'Āṣim b. 'Amr[331] made for Sijistān and was joined by 'Abdallāh b. 'Umayr.[332] The people of Sijistān met them, and they joined battle just within their own territory. (The Muslims) defeated them, then pursued them and besieged them in Zaranj,[333] crossing through the region of Sijistān at will. (The Sijistānīs) then sought a peace treaty covering Zaranj and [all] the lands (the Muslims) had taken. This they were granted. (The Muslims) also stipulated in the peace treaty they made (with the Sijistānīs) that the desert regions of [Sijistān] should be out of bounds [to the Muslims]. When the latter went out anywhere, they would warn each other for fear they encroach on any of (these desert regions) and so break the [peace agreement]. So the Sijistānīs paid the land tax and the Muslims granted [them what they had requested].[334]

[The districts] of Sijistān were greater and spread further afield than [those of] Khurāsān. (The Muslims) made war [there] against Kandahar,[335] the Turks, and many [different] communities. (Sijistān) covered the whole area between Sind and the river of Balkh.[336] It remained the greater of the two provinces, the more difficult and larger in terms of numbers and fighting men of the

330. For the conquest, see Balādhurī, *Futūḥ*, 392ff.; Bal'ami, *Chronique*, III, 517ff. Sijistān is the province to the south of Khurāsān. See Yāqūt, *Mu'jam*, III, 1902; Le Strange, *Lands*, 334ff. and Maps VII and VIII.

331. Al-Tamīmī, a Muslim military leader renowned for his courage, the brother of al-Qa'qā'. See Ṭabarī, I, 2433ff. etc.

332. An unidentified narrator.

333. The capital of Sijistān, E of Lake Zarah. Cf. Yāqūt, Mu'jam, III, 138; Le Strange, Lands, 335ff. and Maps VII and VIII. Cf. also Bosworth, *Sīstān* and map, in the district of al-Rukhkhaj.

334. This sentence and the first two of the following paragraph read in Arabic, *fa-tamma ahlu Sijistāna 'alā al-kharāji wa-al-Muslimūna 'alā al-'aṭā' fa-kānat Sijistānu a'ẓama min Khurāsāna wa-ab'ada furūjan yuqātilūna al-Qandahār.* The translation might therefore be, "So the Sijistānīs paid the land tax, while the Muslims on stipends ([the districts] of Sijistān were greater and spread further afield than [those of] Khurāsān), were making war on Kandahar, . . ."

335. Arabic al-Qandahār, east of Zaranj. See Yāqūt, *Mu'jam*, IV, 402–3; Le Strange, *Lands*, 347 and Map VIII, opposite 335; Bosworth, *Sīstān*, map.

336. Something of an exaggeration, as a glance at the map in the *CHIr*, 60–61, shows! "The river of Balkh" must be the Oxus, which is in fact north of the town.

[2706] two frontier districts until Muʿāwiyah's time. At that time the ruler (*shāh*) fled from his brother, who was called Zunbīl,[337] to an area called Āmul,[338] and (he and his followers) paid allegiance to Salm b. Ziyād,[339] at that time governor of Sijistān. (The latter) was pleased with this [development], made a pact with (the ruler and his followers), and allowed them to settle in this area. He wrote to Muʿāwiyah about this, indicating that it had been conquered. But Muʿāwiyah replied that his cousin might be pleased, but that he was not and that it was not indeed proper that (his cousin) should be pleased. Muʿāwiyah was asked why this was and replied it was because the area between Āmul and Zaranj was where there were difficulties and trouble. These were people who were wily and treacherous, so there would be discord in future. The very least they would do would be to take over the whole region of Āmul. But Ibn Ziyād concluded an agreement with them. After Muʿāwiyah's death when there was civil war, the ruler rebelled and conquered Āmul. Zunbīl was afraid of the ruler, so he took refuge from him in a particular place in which he remains to this day. But he did not take kindly to this, when the people just ignored him, and he began to covet Zaranj. So he attacked (the town) and besieged (its inhabitants) until reinforcements arrived from al-Baṣrah. Zunbīl and all those who came with him and settled in this area became "a bone in the throat" that has remained unremoved to this day. This region had been subdued until Muʿāwiyah died.

---

337. The text has Rutbīl, but cf. Bosworth, *Sīstān*, 34–36. Cf. Balʿami, *Chronique*, III, 518.

338. This place must be in or near Sijistān and cannot be either the Āmul in Ṭabaristān or that between Marw and Bukhārā on the Oxus. Perhaps Kābul to the northeast of Sijistān is meant. See Balādhurī, *Futūḥ*, 397 and *Addenda*, DCXXIII.

339. Salm, according to Ṭabarī elsewhere (Ṭabarī, II, 391), was appointed governor of Sijistān in 61/680 by Yazīd b. Muʿāwiyah (reigned 60–64/680–683), after Muʿāwiyah's death. Yazīd too would have been Salm's cousin, whereas Muʿāwiyah would have been his uncle. It seems we should read Yazīd throughout this passage rather than Muʿāwiyah. Another possible explanation is that Salm's brother, ʿAbbād, was appointed governor of Sijistān by Muʿāwiyah about the year 59/679 (Ṭabarī, II, 189), and perhaps he is meant rather than Salm. See also Bosworth, *Sīstān*, 44–45.

The Conquest of Makrān[340]

(The same sources) reported as follows: Al-Ḥakam b. ʿAmr al-Taghlibī[341] made for Makrān and finally arrived there. He was [2707] joined by Shihāb b. al-Mukhāriq b. Shihāb[342] and reinforced by Suhayl b. ʿAdī and ʿAbdallāh b. ʿAbdallāh b. ʿItbān themselves. They came to a point just this side of the river[343] where the Makrān army had assembled, halted on its bank, and made camp. Rāsil, their ruler,[344] had the ruler of Sind cross over toward (the Muslims), and he drew near with (his men), facing the Muslims. So they met and fought together at a place on the Makrān side, some days' journey from the river, after the advanced party of (the Makrān army) had arrived and camped there to allow the rest to catch up. God defeated Rāsil and took spoils from him. He permitted the Muslims to despoil his camp. In the battle they killed many and pursued (the remainder), killing them off for some days until they finally reached the river. Then (the Muslims) returned and remained in Makrān. Al-Ḥakam wrote to ʿUmar of the conquest and sent the fifths with Ṣuḥār al-ʿAbdī, also asking (ʿUmar's) instruction concerning the elephants [that they had captured]. Suḥār brought ʿUmar the news and the spoils and ʿUmar asked him about Makrān, [for] no one came to him without his enquiring of him about the area from which he was coming. He replied, "Commander of the Faithful, it is a land whose plains are mountains (*jabal*); whose water is scarce (*washal*); whose [only] fruit is poor quality dates (*daqal*); whose enemies are heroes (*baṭal*); whose prosperity is little (*qalīl*); whose evil is long-lasting (*ṭawīl*); what is much there is little; what is little there is nothing; as for what lies beyond, [2708] it is even worse!" "Are you a rhymed prose reciter or someone

340. Brief mention is made of Makrān in Balādhurī, *Futūḥ*, 433ff.; Balʿami, *Chronique*, III, 518. Makrān or Mukrān is the large coastal province, mainly arid and economically poor, situated between Kirmān in the west and Sind in the east. See Yāqūt, *Muʿjam*, V, 179–80; Le Strange, *Lands*, 329ff. and Map VII, opposite 323.

341. An unidentified military leader.

342. An unidentified military leader.

343. It is not clear which river is here meant, but it is likely it is the Indus.

344. For Rāsil b. Basāyah, see Balādhurī, *Futūḥ*, 438; Lambrick, *Sind*, 158–59; *Fatḥnamah*, 118–19, 124–26.

bringing [accurate] information?!" retorted ʿUmar.[345] He said he was really bringing [accurate] information, so ʿUmar insisted that not one of his armies should attack (Makrān), as long as he remained in authority. He wrote to al-Ḥakam b. ʿAmr and Suhayl, [forbidding] any of their armies from passing beyond Makrān. [He ordered them] to restrict themselves to (territory) on this side of the river and al-Ḥakam to sell the elephants within Muslim territory and distribute the price obtained among all those to whom God had granted the booty of Makrān.

Al-Ḥakam b. ʿAmr composed the following on this subject:[346]

Without boasting, those whose provisions were exhausted had
their fill of booty brought to them from Mukkurān.[347]
It came to them after total exhaustion and effort, when there
was no food to cook during the winter.
The army can place no blame on what I did; nor can my sword
or my lance tip be blamed,
On the morn when I had their diverse troops[348] pushed back
into extensive Sind and the neighboring regions.
We had a body of troops, in what we wanted obedient, not
allowing their [horses'] bridles to be slack.[349]
Were it not for my Commander's veto,[350] we would have passed
over to (those) ample[-bodied] whores![351]

Bayrūdh in al-Ahwāz[352]

(The same sources) report: When the [Muslim] cavalry dispersed throughout the various districts, a large force of Kurds and

345. As the Arabic terms given in the text indicate, Ṣuḥār gave ʿUmar his description of Makrān in rhymed prose.

346. The meter of the poem is *wāfir.*

347. A variant spelling of Makrān used to fit the metre of the poem.

348. It should be recalled that the forces opposing the Muslims were a mixture of Makrānīs and Sindīs.

349. That is, they kept their horses and, by implication, themselves under complete control.

350. A reference to ʿUmar's express order that the Muslims should penetrate no farther than Makrān.

351. Arabic, *al-bududi 'l-zawānī,* that is, feminine plural, hence the translation. It is a reference to Sind where perhaps the women had such a reputation.

352. A town in the northwest of Khūzistān, north of al-Ahwāz, variously spelled Bayrūdh by Yāqūt (*Muʿjam,* I, 526) and Bayrūt and Bīrūdh by Le Strange

others assembled in Bayrūdh. Now ʿUmar had already ordered Abū Mūsā, when the (Muslim) armies had left for the outlying areas, to march out to [the areas of] those in compact with al-Baṣrah, so that the Muslims could not be attacked in the [2709] rear. (ʿUmar) was also afraid that some of his armies might be completely surrounded, or others cut off, or left behind. What (ʿUmar) was afraid of happened with the assembly of the army of Bayrūdh, when Abū Mūsā had been slow [to act] until they had actually mustered. He then marched out, finally stopping in Ramaḍān in Bayrūdh [to face] the army that had collected there. They met in battle between Nahr Tīrā[353] and Manādhir,[354] when the powerful Persian and Kurdish troops had all come together there, with the purpose of laying traps for the Muslims and effecting a breach in their ranks—(the former coalition) never doubting [that at least] one of the two eventualities [would come to pass]. Al-Muhājir b. Ziyād,[355] having perfumed himself and expressed his willingness to die, rose and said to Abū Mūsā, "Get everyone who is fasting to swear that he will return [from the battle] and break his fast." So (al-Muhājir's) brother returned with others and carried out the provision of the oath. By this he intended simply to distract his brother away from him so that he would not prevent him from exposing himself to death. (Al-Muhājir) advanced and fought until he was killed. God weakened the polytheists, and reduced to a small number and humiliated, they fortified themselves. (Al-Muhājir's) brother, al-Rabīʿ,[356] arrived and, his grief intense, exclaimed [to himself], "O you addicted to this lower world!" Abū Mūsā felt compassion for al-Rabīʿ because of the effect of his brother's tragic death. So he left him behind at the head of an army in authority over (the habitants). Abū Mūsā [himself] left for Iṣfahān, where he found

(*Lands*, 241). See also Le Strange, *Lands*, Map 2, opposite 25. For the battle, Balʿami, *Chronique*, III, 520.

353. A town standing on the canal of the same name, northwest of al-Ahwāz. See Yāqūt, *Muʿjam*, II, 66; Le Strange, *Lands*, 241 and Map II, opposite 25.

354. Strictly speaking, two towns lying in the fertile regions of al-Ahwāz, just north of the town of al-Ahwāz. See, Yāqūt, *Muʿjam* V, 199; Le Strange, *Lands*, 239 and Map II, opposite 25.

355. He has a brief entry in Ibn al-Athīr, *Usd*, IV, 423.

356. He was later governor of Sijistān. See Ibn al-Athīr, *Usd*, II, 164.

[2710] the Kufan armies besieging Jayy. Then he made off for al-Baṣrah after the victory of the (Muslim) troops and when God had given victory to al-Rabīʿ b. Ziyād over the army of Bayrūdh in Nahr Tīrā and (Abū Mūsā) had taken the captives that they had. Abū Mūsā chose some of them for whom there would be a ransom, as a ransom was more profitable to the Muslims than [holding captive] their prominent leaders and their value [in themselves]. He sent delegations and the fifths [to ʿUmar]. A man of ʿAnazah[357] stood up and asked him to send him in the delegation, but (Abū Mūsā) refused. But (the man) left [nevertheless], charging (Abū Mūsā) falsely, and ʿUmar asked (Abū Mūsā) to present himself. (ʿUmar) brought them together, finding that Abū Mūsā had an excuse except in the matter of his servant.[358] He lessened his authority, but sent him back to his post. But the other he charged with unrighteousness and ordered him not to do such a thing again.

Al-Sarī—Shuʿayb—Sayf—Muḥammad, Ṭalḥah, al-Muhallab and ʿAmr: When Abū Mūsā returned from Iṣfahān after the [Muslim] armies had gone out into the various provinces and al-Rabīʿ had defeated the army of Bayrūdh and (Abū Mūsā) had collected together the captives and their possessions, (the latter) came out next morning to sixty young sons of village headmen,[359] whom he had selected and sent them back in return [for their ransom]. He sent news of the conquest to ʿUmar, choosing a delegation [to take it]. A ʿAnazī came to him and asked him to write down his name [for inclusion] in the delegation. (Abū Mūsā) replied that he had already registered [names of] those who were more worthy [of participation in the delegation] than he was. So (the ʿAnazī) withdrew in anger. Abū Mūsā wrote to ʿUmar about the matter of a ʿAnazī called Ḍabbah b. Miḥṣan[360]—and he told him all about him. When the letter [brought by] the delegation [with the news of] the

357. This in all probability refers to Banū ʿAnazah b. Asad, a large tribal group in central Arabia. See Ibn Ḥazm, *Jamharah*, 294; Caskel, *Ǧamharat*, I, Table 172; Kaḥḥālah, *Muʿjam*, III, 846–47; *EI*^{2}, s.v. (Graf).

358. A reference to the slave girl, ʿAqīlah, mentioned, page 81, below.

359. The text has *dihqān*. See *EI*^{2}, s.v. (Lambton). For this anecdote, see Ṭanṭāwī, *Akhbār*, 179ff.

360. The text at last gives us the name of this ʿAnazī bedouin.

conquest reached ʿUmar, the ʿAnazī arrived. He came to ʿUmar and greeted him. "Who are you?" (ʿUmar) asked; and the (ʿAnazī) told him. (ʿUmar) told him there was no welcome for him there, to which he replied, "A welcome comes from God! And there is certainly no family [here]!"[361] He returned to (ʿUmar) on three occasions, (ʿUmar) repeating what he had said to him, and (he) giving him the same response. Finally on the fourth day, he entered and (ʿUmar) said, "What are you accus- [2711] ing your commander, [Abū Mūsā], of?" He replied that he had chosen sixty young sons of landowners for himself, and he also had a slave girl called ʿAqīlah who was given a bowl of food for lunch and supper. "None of us can do this and he also has two measures [of grain][362] and two seals," (the ʿAnazī) added. He further, [said the ʿAnazī], delegated [matters] to Ziyād b. Abī Sufyān,[363] who was governor of al-Baṣrah, and he gave al-Ḥuṭay'ah[364] a gift of a thousand [dirhams].

ʿUmar wrote down everything (the ʿAnazī) said and sent for Abū Mūsā. When he arrived, (ʿUmar) kept him waiting for some days, then summoned him, together with Ḍabbah b. Miḥṣan. He handed the document over to (Ḍabbah), telling him to read what he had written. He read, "He has taken sixty young [captives] for himself." Abū Mūsā replied, "I was shown those who had a ransom [on their head]. I took a ransom for them and divided it out among the Muslims." Ḍabbah agreed that he had not lied, but said that neither had he himself lied. Ḍabbah continued, "He has two measures [of grain]." Abū Mūsā replied, "One for my family with which to feed them and another to give to the Muslims, where they take their provisions." Ḍabbah agreed that he had not lied, but said that neither had he himself lied. When (Ḍabbah) mentioned ʿAqīlah, Abū Mūsā remained silent and made no attempt to justify himself. (ʿUmar) knew that Ḍabbah had told him the truth. (The ʿAnazī) continued that Ziyād was

---

361. ʿUmar says, *lā marḥaban wa-lā ahlan!* The reply reads, *ammā al-marḥabu fa-min Allāh; wa-ammā al-ahlu fa-lā ahla!*

362. Arabic *qafīz*; see Hinz, *Masse*, 49.

363. The famous governor of the Umayyad Muʿāwiyah and often called Ziyād b. Abīhi. See Shaban, *History*, 86–89.

364. Al-Ḥuṭay'ah is the famous poet born before Islam, Abū Mulaykah Jarwal b. Aws. See Iṣfahānī, *Aghānī*, II, 43–62.

in charge of the people's affairs [in al-Baṣrah], but this man did not know what kind of a governor he was. (Abū Mūsā) said, "I found that he was a man of merit and perception, so I handed over responsibility for my governorate to him." "And he gave al-Ḥuṭay'ah a thousand!" (Abū Mūsā) said, "I stuffed his mouth
[2712] with money so he would not revile me!" ('Umar) said, "Now you have done something!"[365] He sent (Abū Mūsā) back [to al-Baṣrah] and told him when he arrived there to send Ziyād and 'Aqīlah to him. This he did. 'Aqīlah arrived before Ziyād, then he came and stood at the door. 'Umar went out while Ziyād was standing at the door, dressed in white linen clothes, and said to him, "What clothes are these?" So he told him. "How much did they cost?" asked ('Umar), and he told him they cost little. ('Umar) believed him and said, "How much is your stipend?" He replied, "Two thousand." ('Umar) asked him what he had done with the first stipend he got. He replied that he had bought his mother and set her free. With the second, [he said], he bought his stepson, a young slave, and set him free. ('Umar) wished him success and questioned him about the ordinances of God, the religious practices and the Qur'ān and found him well versed in religious knowledge. He sent him back, ordering the Basran commanders to follow his advice. He held 'Aqīlah back in Medina. ('Umar) commented, "Indeed Ḍabbah al-'Anazī was angry with Abū Mūsā with some justification, that he came to him, but left him in anger that he received no worldly gain. (Ḍabbah) has told the truth (about Abū Mūsā), but also lied, and his lying has marred his telling the truth. Beware of lying; lying leads [one] into hellfire!"

Now al-Ḥuṭay'ah had met (Abū Mūsā) and he had given him a
[2713] gift during the attack on Bayrūdh. Abū Mūsā had begun to besiege them and attack (the Persians and Kurds), and he finally defeated them. Then he passed on from them, leaving al-Rabī' as his representative among them. Then after the conquest he returned to them and took charge of the division [of the spoils].

According to al-Sarī—Shu'ayb—Sayf—Abū 'Amr[366]—al-

365. Arabic, *fa-qāla qad fa'alta mā fa'alta!*
366. Abū 'Amr was the client of the unidentified Ibrāhīm b. Ṭalḥah. See notes 664 and 665, below.

Ḥasan—Asīd b. al-Mutashammis, nephew of al-Aḥnaf b. Qays: I was present with Abū Mūsā on the day Iṣfahān [was taken] at the conquest of the settlements, in charge of which were 'Abdallāh b. Warqā' al-Riyāḥī and 'Abdallāh b. Warqā' al-Asadī. Then Abū Mūsā was sent to al-Kūfah and 'Umar b. Surāqah al-Makhzūmī[367] was appointed governor of al-Baṣrah. Then Abū Mūsā was reappointed governor of al-Baṣrah, and 'Umar died while he was in charge of prayer there. (His) governorship of (al-Baṣrah) was by turns, not continuous. 'Umar would sometimes summon (Abū Mūsā) to send him as reinforcement to one of the armies, and he would carry out that role.

Salamah b. Qays al-Ashja'ī[368] and the Kurds

According to 'Abdallāh b. Kathīr al-'Abdī[369]—Ja'far b. 'Awn[370]—Abū Janāb[371]—Abū al-Muḥajjal al-Rudaynī[372]—Makhlad al-Bakrī[373] and 'Alqamah b. Marthad[374]—Sulaymān b. Buraydah:[375]
Whenever an army of Believers had been assembled under his [2714]
instructions, the Commander of the Faithful appointed as their commander someone versed in religious knowledge and law. [Now such] an army assembled under his instructions, so he despatched Salamah b. Qays al-Ashja'ī in command. ('Umar) addressed [him as follows]:

> Go forth in God's name and fight in God's cause against all those who do not believe in God. If you meet your polytheist enemy, call upon them to take [one of]

---

367. Following the advice of the Leiden editor, I omit the word *badawī* (or Badrī, according to two MSS), because neither would seem to make sense.

368. Salamah b. Qays al-Asja'ī has a brief notice in Ibn al-Athīr, *Usd*, II, 339.

369. An unidentified narrator.

370. Ja'far b. 'Awn was a narrator who died in 206–207/821–823. See Ibn Ḥajar, *Tahdhīb*, II, 101.

371. An unidentified narrator.

372. An unidentified narrator.

373. An unidentified narrator.

374. 'Alqamah b. Marthad al-Ḥaḍramī has an entry in Ibn Ḥajar, *Tahdhīb*, VII, 272–73.

375. Ibn Ḥajar, *Tahdhīb*, IV, 174–75, says that Sulaymān b. Buraydah b. al-Ḥasīb al-Marwazī died in 105/723. He must, however, have been a contemporary of 'Umar and Salamah.

three courses of action. Summon them to Islam and if they accept, and choose [to remain] in their lands, they will have alms obligations[376] [to be paid] from their own wealth and have no share in the immovable booty [accruing to] the Muslims. If, [having accepted Islam], they choose to join you, they will have similar privileges and obligations to your own. But if they refuse [to accept Islam], then summon them to [pay] the land tax. If they declare that they will pay the land tax, fight their enemy beyond them and leave them free to pay—but do not impose on them more than they have the capacity [to pay]. If they refuse [to pay the land tax], then fight them, for God will be your helper against them. If they fortify themselves against your [attack] in some fortified place and request you to [allow them] to surrender under the terms of God's and His Apostle's judgment, do not allow them to do so, for you do not know what these judgments are as they affect them. If, however, they request you to [allow them] to surrender under the terms of God's and His Apostle's covenant, do not grant them these, but rather grant them your own covenants. If they fight you, do not act unfaithfully or treacherously; do not inflict exemplary punishment [on them] or kill minors.

Salamah reported [as follows]. We marched on and met up
[2715] with our polytheist enemy and summoned them to [act as] the Commander of the Faithful had instructed. But they refused to accept Islam. So we called upon them to [pay] land tax, but they refused to declare [their willingness to pay], so we fought them and God gave us victory over them. We killed their military, but made their children captive. We collected the spoils together. Now Salamah b. Qays spotted an ornament [among the spoils] and said, "You are not interested in this; would you be willing to send it to the Commander of the Faithful? [We] owe [this] to him and [should go to] some trouble for him." They replied that they would be willing. (Salamah) continued: So he put this

376. Arabic *zakāh*; see *SEI*, s.v. (Schacht).

ornament into a casket and sent off one of his men, saying, "Take it and, when you come to al-Baṣrah, against the gifts the Commander of the Faithful [will give you], buy two baggage camels and load them up with provisions for yourself and your young slave. Then make your way to the Commander of the Faithful."

(The messenger) reported as follows: I did this and came to the Commander of the Faithful as he was feeding lunch to the people, leaning on a stick, as a shepherd does, and walking round the huge bowls, saying, "Some more meat for this lot, Yarfa';[377] [2716]
some more bread for these; some more soup for these." When I was pushed [through the crowd] into his presence, he told me to sit down. I did so among those people nearest [to him]. There was some rough food—even the food I had with me was better! When the people had finished, he told Yarfa' to take away his bowls, then he turned away. I followed, and he entered the room of a house. I asked permission to enter and gave my greetings. He gave me permission, and I entered to where he was. He was sitting on a hair cloth leaning against two leather cushions stuffed with palm fibres. He threw one over to me and I sat down on it, [finding myself] in a space inside a vestibule in which there was a compartment with a small curtain. ('Umar) asked [his wife], Umm Kulthūm [to bring us] our lunch. She brought out to him a piece of bread with some olive oil by the side of which was some unground salt. ('Umar) asked Umm Kulthūm to join us and eat some of this [food] with us. She replied, however, that she could hear the voice of a man with [2717]
('Umar). He confirmed that this was true, [adding that] he did not think he was a local.[378] (The messenger) added that this was when he realized that ('Umar) did not know him. (Umm Kulthūm) said, "If you had intended me to come out to join the men, you would have dressed me up, as Ibn Ja'far[379] does his

377. He is 'Umar's personal servant.

378. Implying that she could join the men because the visitor was an outsider and someone who did not know her.

379. 'Abdallāh b. Ja'far b. Abī Ṭālib, the nephew of 'Alī b. Abī Ṭālib died in 80/699 or 85/705. See *EI*², s.v. (Zetersteen).

wife, as al-Zubayr[380] does his wife, and as Ṭalḥah[381] does his wife!" "Is it not enough for you," replied ('Umar), "that you are called Umm Kulthūm, daughter of 'Alī b. Abī Ṭālib and wife of the Commander of the Faithful, 'Umar?!" [To me] he said, "Eat; if she were willing [to join us], she would have given you better food than this!" (The messenger) continued: So I ate a little, but the food I had with me was better than this! He ate, and I have never seen a heartier eater than he. No food stuck to his hand or his mouth! Then he asked for drink, and they brought a bowl of a barley-meal drink. "Give the man a drink," said ('Umar). (The messenger) continued: So I drank a little—the barley-meal drink I had with me was better than this! Then he took hold of it and drank down to the dregs,[382] saying, "Praise be to God who has filled us up with food and quenched our thirst!" I said, "The Commander of the Faithful has eaten and drunk his fill. There is something you can do for me, Commander of the Faithful." He asked what it was. I replied, "I am the envoy of Salamah
[2718] b. Qays." ('Umar) said, "Both Salamah b. Qays and his envoy are welcome. Tell me how the emigrants are."[383] "They are as safe and have conquered as many of their enemies as you would wish, Commander of the Faithful." "What are their prices like?" ('Umar) asked. (The messenger) continued: I said, "The very cheapest." "What about their meat?" he asked, "for this is the mainstay of the Arabs; they will never thrive without their mainstay." I replied, "Beef is such and such a price, mutton such and such. On we went, Commander of the Faithful, and we met up with our polytheist enemy. We called upon them to accept Islam, as you commanded us, but they refused. So we called upon them to [pay] land tax, but they refused, so we fought

---

380. Al-Zubayr b. al-'Awāmm, the famous Companion, was killed by 'Alī at the battle of the Camel in 36/656 after his revolt with Ṭalḥah (see the next note) and the wife of the Prophet, 'Ā'ishah. A member of the electoral council after the assassination of 'Umar. See Shaban, *History*, 71–72; *CHIs*, 70.

381. Ṭalḥah b. 'Ubaydallāh, a Companion also killed with al-Zubayr in 36/656. A member of the electoral council after the assassination of 'Umar. See Shaban, *History*, loc. cit., and *CHIs*, loc, cit. and preceding note.

382. Arabic, *fa-shariba-hu ḥattā qara'a al-qadaḥu jabhata-h*, literally "he drank it until the bowl knocked against his forehead".

383. Arabic, *muhājirūn*. I take this as a euphemism for the Arab troops on the front line.

against them and God gave us victory over them. We killed their military, but took their women captive, and we collected together the spoils. Salamah spotted an ornament among the spoils and said to the men, "You are not interested in this. Are you willing to send it to the Commander of the Faithful?" They replied that they were." I took out my casket. But when he saw the gems, red, yellow and green, he leapt up, put his hand on his waist and said, "May God never, [if I were to accept this,], fill 'Umar's belly again!" (The messenger) continued: The womenfolk thought I was intending to assassinate him, so [2719]
they came to the curtain. He said (to the messenger), "Keep what you brought. Yarfa', strike him on the neck!"[384] So I was [re]arranging my casket, while he was striking me on the neck. I said, "Commander of the Faithful, my camels are exhausted. I need replacements." He replied, "Yarfa', give him two baggage camels from the alms. If you meet anyone who has a greater need of them than you, hand them over to him." I said I would obey his orders. He added, "I swear that, if the Muslims disperse to their winter quarters before this is distributed among them, I shall certainly bring about calamity for you and your master!" (The messenger) continued: "So I left and came to Salamah and said, May God not grant His blessing for what you have done to [2720]
me in this particular case! Distribute this among the men before some calamity befalls us both." So he did. A gem was sold at 5 and 6 dirhams, although it was worth more than 20,000!

According to al-Sarī's version—Shu'ayb—Sayf—Abū Janāb—Sulaymān b. Buraydah: I met the messenger of Salamah b. Qays al-Ashja'ī who said, "When an Arab army assembled under the instructions of 'Umar b. al-Khaṭṭāb, . . . ," and then he reported an account similar to that of 'Abdallāh b. Kathīr on the authority of Ja'far b. 'Awn, except that he said in his report, on the authority of Shu'ayb, on the authority of Sayf [with the following variants], "Grant them your own covenants." He continued, "We met up with our Kurdish enemies, and we called upon them . . ."

(The same source) also reported: We collected the spoils

384. That is, to frighten and scold him.

together and Salamah found two boxes of jewels among them, so he put them in a casket.

He also reported as follows: "Is it not enough for you that you are called Umm Kulthūm, daughter of ʿAlī b. Abī Ṭalib, wife of ʿUmar b. al-Khaṭṭāb?" She replied, "This is of little use to me!" He said [to the messenger], "Eat."

He also reported as follows: They brought a bowl of barley-meal drink. Whenever they moved it, some of its contents fizzed up over (the top). When they left it alone, it was still. Then he told [the messenger] to drink. So I drank a little—my own drink I had with me was better than this! He took the bowl, drinking
[2721] it down to the dregs, then he said, "You are indeed a poor eater and drinker!"

He also reported as follows: I said, "[I am] the messenger of Salamah." He replied, "Welcome, Salamah and his messenger. It is as if you were a product of his loins. Tell me about the emigrants."

He also reported as follows: Then he said, "May God never, [if I were to accept this], fill ʿUmar's belly again!" He continued: The womenfolk thought I had assassinated him, so they drew the curtain. He said, "Strike him on his neck, Yarfa'." So he struck my neck, as I cried out, and exclaimed, "Get out of here and be quick about it!"[385] He continued, "By God, there is no other god but He! If the army disperses to its winter quarters . . . ," and the rest of the account was similar to that of ʿAbdallāh b. Kathīr.

According to al-Rabīʿ b. Sulaymān[386]—Asad b. Mūsā[387]—Shihāb b. Khirāsh al-Ḥawshabī[388]—al-Ḥajjāj b. Dīnār[389]—Manṣūr b. al-Muʿtamir[390]—Shaqīq b. Salamah al-Asadī[391]—the

385. Arabic, "*al-janā'a wa-aẓunnu-ka sa-tubṭi'u.*"

386. An Egyptian narrator who died in 270/884. See Ibn Ḥajar, *Tahdhīb*, III, 245ff.; Rosenthal, *Historiography*, 416.

387. He died in Egypt in 212/827. See Ibn Ḥajar, *Tahdhīb*, I, 260.

388. He has an entry in Ibn Ḥajar, *Tahdhīb*, IV, 366–67.

389. Al-Ḥajjāj b. Dīnār al-Ashjaʿī has an entry in Ibn Ḥajar, *Tahdhīb*, II, 200–1.

390. Abū ʿAttāb Manṣūr b. al-Muʿtamir al-Sulamī died in 132/749. See Ibn Ḥajar, *Tahdhīb*, X, 312–15.

391. Abū Wā'il, who died in 79/698 or 99/717. See Ibn al-Athīr, *Usd*, III, 3; Rosenthal, *Historiography*, 278.

intermediary between 'Umar b. al-Khaṭṭāb and Salamah b. Qays: 'Umar b. al-Khaṭṭāb sent the army to Salamah b. Qays al-Ashja'ī in al-Ḥīrah, saying, "Go forth in God's name . . . ," and he gave an account similar to that of 'Abdallāh b. Kathīr on the authority of Ja'far.

Abū Ja'far [al-Ṭabarī] reported as follows: 'Umar led the wives of the Messenger of God on the pilgrimage this year and this was the last pilgrimage in which he led the people. This is also according to al-Ḥārith[392]—Ibn Sa'd[393]—al-Wāqidī.

('Umar's) death took place during this year, [23; November 19, 643–November 7, 644].

'Umar's Assassination[394] [2722]

According to Salm b. Junādah[395]—Sulaymān b. 'Abd al-'Azīz b. Abī Thābit b. 'Abd al-'Azīz b. 'Umar b. 'Abd al-Raḥmān b. 'Awf[396]—his father—'Abdallāh b. Ja'far[397]—his father—al-Miswar b. Makhramah (whose mother was 'Ātikah, daughter of 'Awf).[398] 'Umar went out one day to wander around the market. He was met by Abū Lu'lu'ah,[399] a young Christian slave of al-Mughīrah b. Shu'bah, who said, "Help me, Commander of the Faithful, against al-Mughīrah b. Shu'bah, for

---

392. Ibn Muḥammad, who died in 282/896. See Rosenthal, *Historiography*, 128; Translation, I, 247.

393. Abū 'Abdallāh Muḥammad b. Sa'd, who died in 230/845, the famous author of the *Ṭabaqāt*. See Ibn Ḥajar, *Tahdhīb*, IX, 182ff.; Duri, *Rise*, 40; Sezgin, *GAS*, I, 300ff.; *EI*[2], s.v. "Ibn Sa'd" (Fück); Translation, I, 215 n. 337.

394. See Ibn al-Athīr, *Kāmil*, III, 24ff.; Mas'ūdī, *Murūj*, IV, 226ff.; Ibn 'Abd Rabbih, *'Iqd*, IV, 272; Bal'ami, *Chronique*, III, 528ff. See also Ṭabarī, *Selection*, which begins at this point in the text.

395. Abū al-Sā'ib Salm b. Junādah died in 254/868. See Ibn Ḥajar, *Tahdhīb*, IV, 128–29.

396. An unidentified narrator.

397. 'Abdallāh b. Ja'far al-Zuhrī died in 170/786. See Ibn Ḥajar, *Tahdhīb*, V, 171.

398. Al-Miswar b. Makhramah died in 64/683. Ibn Ḥajar, *Tahdhīb*, X, 234. 'Ātikah was the sister of 'Abd al-Raḥmān b. 'Awf. See also Ibn Qutaybah, *Ma'ārif*, 429.

399. Abū Lu'lu'ah Fayrūz al-Nihāwandī. He is believed to have originated in Nihāwand, hence his *nisbah*, and to have been captured by the Byzantines during the Perso-Byzantine wars before Islam. He became a Christian when held by the Byzantines. See Ṭabarī, I, 2632.

I pay a great deal of tax." "How much?" enquired ('Umar). "Two dirhams a day," was the reply. "What is your trade?" asked ('Umar). "[I am] a carpenter, stone mason, and smith," he replied. "I do not think your tax is a lot in view of the work you do," ('Umar) said. "I have heard that you claim you could make a mill that will grind by wind power if you wished." He replied that he could. ('Umar) asked him to make him a mill. (Abū Lu'lu'ah) replied, "If you survive, I shall certainly make you a mill that will be the talk of everyone in both East and West!" Then (Abū Lu'lu'ah) left ('Umar), who said [to himself], "[That] slave has just threatened me!" Then he went off home. The next day Ka'b al-Aḥbār[400] came to him and said, "Appoint your successor, Commander of the Faithful, for you are going to die in three days." ('Umar) asked him how he knew this. He replied,
[2723] "I find it in God's book, the Torah." 'Umar said, "Can you actually find 'Umar b. al-Khaṭṭāb in the Torah?" (Ka'b) replied, "Indeed no, but I do find a complete description of you and also that your allotted life span has come to an end." (The source) continued: And 'Umar was experiencing no sickness or pain. Next day Ka'b came to him and said, "One day gone and two to go, Commander of the Faithful!" Then he came to him on the day after that and said, "Two days gone, one and a night to go! You have got until tomorrow morning!" That morning 'Umar went out to prayers; he used to assign certain men to [see to] the lines [of those praying] and when they were straight, he would come and proclaim "God is great!" Abū Lu'lu'ah slipped in among the people, carrying in his hand a dagger with two blades and its haft in the middle. He struck 'Umar six blows, one of which was below his navel, and this was the one which killed him. (Abū Lu'lu'ah) also killed Kulayb b. Abī al-Bukayr al-Laythī,[401] who was behind ('Umar). When ('Umar) felt the heat of the weapon, he fell and said, "Is 'Abd al-Raḥmān b. 'Awf[402]

---

400. Ka'b al-Aḥbār was a Yemenite Jewish scholar who converted to Islam in ca. 17/638. He died ca. 35/655. See *EI*^{2}, s.v. (Schmitz).

401. Kulayb b. Abī al-Bukayr al-Laythī has an entry in Ibn Ḥajar, *Iṣābah*, VIII, minus the Abī, where this event is mentioned.

402. 'Abd al-Raḥmān b. 'Awf was a prominent early Muslim convert and merchant. He died ca. 31/652. See *EI*^{2}, s.v. (Houtsma-Watt).

among the crowd?" They said, "Yes, Commander of the Faithful, he is here." ('Umar) said [to 'Abd al-Raḥmān], "Come forward and lead the people in prayer." So 'Abd al-Raḥmān led the people in prayer, while 'Umar lay prostrate. Then he was carried away and brought into his house. He called for 'Abd al-Raḥmān b. 'Awf and said, "I want to appoint you my successor." He replied, "Indeed, Commander of the Faithful, I accept. If you order me, I shall accept [the appointment] from you." ('Umar) said, "What do you want?" ('Abd al-Raḥmān) said, "I beseech you by God. Do you order me to accept this (appointment)?"
('Umar) replied, "No, indeed." ('Abd al-Raḥmān) said, "I shall [2724]
never have anything to do with [accepting] (the appointment)." ('Umar) said, "Give me some peace and quiet so that I can appoint those who still met with the Messenger of God's approval when he died. Call 'Alī for me, 'Uthmān, al-Zubayr, and Sa'd." [When they had arrived, he said], "Wait for your brother Ṭalḥah for three [nights]. If he does not come, do what you have to do. If you should take authority over the people, 'Alī, I implore you not to bring them under the power of Banū Hāshim.[403] If you should take authority over the people, 'Uthmān, I implore you not to bring them under the power of Banū Abī Mu'ayṭ.[404] If you should take authority over the people, Sa'd, I implore you not to bring them under the power of your relatives.[405] Off you go! Consult together, then do what you have to do. Let Ṣuhayb[406] lead the people in prayer."

Then he called for Abū Ṭalḥah al-Anṣārī[407] and said, "Stand at

---

403. Hāshim b. 'Abd Manāf, a tribal group (*baṭn*) of Quraysh in Mecca to which the Prophet and 'Ali, Muḥammad's cousin and son-in-law, belonged. See Zubayrī, *Quraysh*, 14ff.; Kaḥḥālah, *Mu'jam*, III, 1207; Watt, *Mecca*, 7; *EI*², s.v. (Watt).

404. 'Uthman also belonged to Quraysh, but through 'Abd Shams, a brother of Hāshim, and Umayyah. Abū Mu'ayṭ was Abān b. Abī 'Amr b. Umayyah b. 'Abd Shams. See Ibn Ḥazm, *Jamharah*, 114.

405. Sa'd b. Abī Waqqāṣ was a famous figure in early Islam. He fought at Badr and acted as personal bodyguard to the Prophet. He led the Muslim forces in their defeat of the Persians at al-Qādisiyyah. He died in 51/671. See Ibn Ḥajar, *Tahdhīb*, III, 483–84.

406. Ṣuhayb. b. Sinān was a Byzantine slave emancipated after his move to Mecca. He died in 38/658. See Ibn Ḥajar, *Tahdhīb*, IV, 438–39.

407. Abū Ṭalḥah Zayd b. Sahl al-Anṣārī died in 32/653 or 34/655. See Ibn Ḥajar, *Tahdhīb*, III, 414–15.

their door and do not let anyone enter into their presence. I commend to the caliph after my death the Helpers, 'Who have made their abode in the city [of the Prophet] and in the Faith,'[408] that he do good to him who does good among them and forgive him who does evil among them. I commend to the caliph after my death the Arabs—for they are the very substance of Islam—that what is their due of alms be taken and assigned to their poor. I commend to the caliph after my death the covenant of the Messenger of God that (non-Muslims) be given a compact faithfully fulfilled. O God, have I done what I ought to do?! I leave the caliph after my death in a cleaner [condition] than the palm of the hand.[409] ʿAbdallāh b. ʿUmar,[410] go and find out who has murdered me." He replied, "Commander of the Faithful, you
[2725] have been murdered by Abū Lu'lu'ah, slave of al-Mughīrah b. Shuʿbah." (ʿUmar) exclaimed, "Praise be to God who has never put my fate into the hands of someone who has bowed down to Him on one single occasion![411] Go to ʿĀ'ishah, ʿAbdallāh b. ʿUmar, and ask her to permit me to be buried with the Prophet and Abū Bakr. If the council is divided, ʿAbdallāh b. ʿUmar, you should vote with the majority. If they are [split] three against three, follow the faction that ʿAbd al-Raḥmān supports. Allow the people to enter, ʿAbdallāh." So the Emigrants and the Helpers came in to see him, offering him their greetings. He would ask them if the [assassination] was the result of some conspiracy among them and they would reply, "God protect [us]!" (The source) continued: Kaʿb entered with the others and when he saw him, ʿUmar began to recite the following:[412]

Kaʿb gave me an evil prediction on three distinct occasions;
there can be no doubt that what Kaʿb told me was right.
I am not afraid of death; I shall surely die;

---

408. Qur'ān, LIX:9.
409. That is, with no money in the treasury and not keeping back what was due to the Muslims.
410. The famous son of ʿUmar b. al-Khaṭṭāb who died in 73/692. See Rosenthal, *Historiography*, 287; *EI*², s.v. (Veccia Valgieri).
411. That is, a non-Muslim.
412. The meter is *ṭawīl*. See Ibn al-Athīr, *Kāmil*, III, 25, where we find *tawaʿadda-nī* instead of *fa-awʿada-nī* in line 1.

> but I am afraid of the one transgression followed by another.[413]

(The source) continued: It was suggested to the Commander of the Faithful that he should call a physician. So one from Banū al-Ḥārith b. Kaʿb[414] was summoned and he gave him date wine to drink. But the date wine came back up mixed with blood. (The physican) told [them] to give him milk. (The source) continued: But the milk came back up too, [though] white. It was suggested to the Commander of the Faithful that he should appoint a successor, but he replied that he had already finished [arrangements for this].[415]

He died later, on Tuesday evening, Dhū al-Ḥijjah 27, 23 [November 5, 644]. They took him out early the following day, Wednesday, and he was buried in ʿĀ'ishah's house along with the Prophet and Abū Bakr. Ṣuhayb came forward and prayed over [2726]
him, but before this two of the Companions of the Messenger of God had come forward, ʿAlī and ʿUthmān. One came forward from [his position] at his head, the other from [his position] at his feet. ʿAbd al-Raḥmān exclaimed, "There is no god but God! How eager you both are to get hold of the caliphate! Are you not aware that the Commander of the Faithful left instructions for Ṣuhayb to lead the people in prayer?" Ṣuhayb came forward and performed this task. (The source) added that all five [members of the electoral council] went down into (ʿUmar's) grave.[416]

Abū Jaʿfar [al-Ṭabarī] said that it is also reported that (ʿUmar) died at the beginning of al-Muḥarram, 24 [November 7, 644].

The Sources of [the Conflicting Report of ʿUmar's Death]

According to al-Ḥārith—Muḥammad b. Saʿd—Muḥammad b. ʿUmar [al-Wāqidī]—Abū Bakr b. Ismāʿīl b. Muḥammad b. Saʿd[417]—his father: ʿUmar was stabbed on Wednesday, Dhū al-

---

413. The evil prediction itself followed by the assassination?

414. It would seem to be the Yemenite tribe from the Najrān area in question here. They are a tribal group of Madhḥij. Ibn Rasūl, *Turfah*, 35; Qalqashandī, *Ṣubḥ*. I, 326; Kaḥḥālah, *Muʿjam*, I, 231–32; EI^2, s.v. (Schleifer).

415. That is the appointment of the electoral council (*shūrā*).

416. See page 155, below.

417. An unidentified narrator, the great-grandson of Saʿd b. Abī Waqqāṣ.

Ḥijjah 26, 23 [November 4, 644], and was buried on Sunday morning the beginning of al-Muḥarram, 24 [November 7, 644]. His rule lasted for ten years, five months, and twenty-one nights after the death of Abū Bakr, exactly twenty-two years, nine months, and thirteen days after the Hijrah. The oath of allegiance was given to ʿUthmān b. ʿAffān on Monday, al-Muḥarram 3 [November 9, 644]. (The source) continued: I mentioned this to ʿUthmān al-Akhnasī,[418] but he replied, "I think you are very much mistaken! ʿUmar died on Dhū al-Ḥijjah 26 [November 4, 644] and the oath of allegiance was given to ʿUthmān b. ʿAffān on Dhū al-Ḥijjah 29 [November 7,
[2727] 644]. He began his caliphate on al-Muḥarram, 24."

According to Aḥmad b. Thābit al-Rāzī—a traditionist—Isḥāq b. ʿĪsā[419]—Abū Maʿshar: ʿUmar was killed on Wednesday, Dhū al-Ḥijjah 26, as the year 23 was coming to a close [November 4, 644]. His caliphate lasted ten years, six months, and four days, then the oath of allegiance was given to ʿUthmān b. ʿAffān.

Abū Jaʿfar [al-Ṭabarī] said: According to al-Madāʾinī's version—ʿUmar [b. Shabbah]—Sharīk[420]—al-Aʿmash[421] (or Jābir al-Juʿfī)[422]—ʿAwf b. Mālik al-Ashjaʿī[423] and ʿĀmir b. Abī Muḥammad[424]—some *shaykhs* of his people, and ʿUthmān b. ʿAbd al-Raḥmān[425]—Ibn Shihāb al-Zuhrī:[426] ʿUmar was stabbed on Wednesday, Dhū al-Ḥijjah 23 [November 1, 644]. (The source) continued: Others say that it was Dhū al-Ḥijjah 24 [November 2, 644].

---

418. ʿUthmān b. Muḥammad al-Akhnasī has a brief notice in Ibn Ḥajar, *Tahdhīb*, VII, 153–54.

419. An unidentified narrator.

420. Ibn ʿAbdallāh al-Nakhaʿī, who died ca. 178/793. See Ibn Ḥajar, *Tahdhīb*, IV, 333–37.

421. Sulaymān b. Mihrān, who died ca. 148/765. See Ibn Ḥajar, *Tahdhīb*, IV, 222–26.

422. Ibn Yazīd, who died in 128/745. See Rosenthal, *Historiography*, 517.

423. ʿAwf b. Mālik al-Ashjaʿī died in Damascus in 73/692. See Ibn al-Athīr, *Usd*, IV, 156.

424. An unidentified narrator.

425. ʿUthmān b. ʿAbd al-Raḥmān. Several persons of this name are listed in the biographical dictionaries, and it is not possible to identify the one in question with any certainty.

426. The famous historian Muḥammad b. Muslim b. Shihāb, who died ca. 125/743. Cf. Ibn Ḥajar, *Tahdhīb*, IX, 445–51; Sezgin, *GAS*, I, 280–83; Duri, *Rise*, especially 98ff., 118–19, and passim.

According to Sayf's version—al-Sarī—Shu'ayb—Khulayd b. Dhafarah and Mujālid: 'Uthmān became caliph on al-Muḥarram 3, 24 [November 9, 644]. He went out and led the people in the early evening prayer. He increased [stipends] and sent out envoys, and that practice was thereby established.

According to al-Sarī—Shu'ayb—Sayf—'Amr—al-Sha'bī: The members of the electoral council agreed upon 'Uthmān on al-Muḥarram 3 [November 9, 644] when the time of early evening prayer had begun and after the call to prayer had been given by [2728] Ṣuhayb's muezzin. They reached agreement between the first and second calls to prayer.[427] ('Uthmān) went out and led the people in prayer and provided them with an extra 100 [dirhams]. He also sent out delegations to the garrison towns, treating them with generosity. He was the first one to do this.

According to [the same source]—Hishām b. Muḥammad:[428] 'Umar was killed on Dhū al-Ḥijjah 27, 23 [November 5, 644]. His caliphate lasted ten years, six months, and four days.

'Umar's Genealogy[429]

According to Ibn Ḥumayd—Salamah—Muḥammad b. Isḥāq; according to al-Ḥārith—Ibn Sa'd—Muḥammad b. 'Umar and Hishām b. Muḥammad; according to 'Umar [b. Shabbah]—'Alī b. Muḥammad [al-Madā'inī]:[430] They all agreed that 'Umar's genealogy was as follows: 'Umar b. al-Khaṭṭāb b. Nufayl b. 'Abd al-'Uzzā b. Riyāḥ b. 'Abdallāh b. Qurṭ b. Razāḥ b. 'Adī b. Ka'b b. Lu'ayy. His *kunyah* was Abū Ḥafṣ and his mother was Ḥantamah bt. Hāshim b. al-Mughīrah b. 'Abdallāh b. 'Umar b. Makhzūm.

Abū Ja'far [al-Ṭabarī] said: ('Umar) was called al-Fārūq.[431]

---

427. The *iqāmah* is the second call to prayer, after the *adhān*, given by the muezzin and it marks the beginning of the prayer proper. See *SEI*, s.v. "Iḳāma" (Juynboll).

428. Abū al-Mundhir Hishām b. Muḥammad b. al-Sā' ib al-Kalbī, the famous historian who died ca. 206/822. See Sezgin, *GAS*, I, 268–71; Duri, *Rise*, 51ff. and passim; EI^2, s.v. (Atallah).

429. See Ibn al-Athīr, *Kāmil*, III, 26; Mas'ūdī, *Murūj*, IV, 192ff.; Bal'ami, *Chronique*, III, 533.

430. That is there are three separate chains of authority.

431. Meaning "he who distinguishes between truth and falsehood."

Preceding generations were in dispute about who called him by this name. Some of them have reported that the Messenger of God gave him this name.

The Sources of [the Report that Muḥammad First Called ʿUmar al-Fārūq]

[2729] According to al-Ḥārith—Ibn Saʿd—Muḥammad b. ʿUmar—Abū Ḥazrah Yaʿqūb b. Mujāhid[432]—Muḥammad b. Ibrāhīm[433]—Abū ʿAmr Dhakwān:[434] I asked ʿĀʾishah who gave ʿUmar the name al-Fārūq. She replied that it was the Prophet.

Some people reported that the first to call (ʿUmar) by this name were the People of the Book.

The Sources of [the Report that the People of the Book Did That]

According to al-Ḥārith—Ibn Saʿd—Yaʿqūb b. Ibrāhīm b. Saʿd[435]—his father—Ṣāliḥ b. Kaysān[436]—Ibn Shihāb: We heard that the People of the Book were the first to call ʿUmar al-Fārūq. The Muslims did relate this in their reports, but we have never heard that the Messenger of God made any such reference.

A Description of ʿUmar

According to Hannād b. al-Sarī[437]—Wakīʿ[438]—Sufyān[439]—ʿĀṣim b. Abī al-Najjūd[440]—Zirr b. Ḥubaysh:[441] ʿUmar went out one

---

432. He died ca. 150/767. See Ibn Ḥajar, *Tahdhīb*, XI, 394–95.

433. He died in 120/738. See Ibn Ḥajar, *Tahdhīb*, IX, 5–7.

434. Abū ʿAmr Dhakwān was ʿĀʾishah's client who died in 63/682. See Ibn Ḥajar, *Tahdhīb*, III, 220.

435. He died 208/823. See Ibn Ḥajar, *Tahdhīb*, XI, 380–81.

436. He died after 140/757. See Ibn Ḥajar, *Tahdhīb*, IV, 399–401.

437. Hannād b. al-Sarī b. Muṣʿab b. Abī Bakr who died 243/857. See Ibn Ḥajar, *Tahdhīb*, XI, 70ff.

438. Wakīʿ b. al-Jarrāḥ b. Malīḥ who died in 197/812. See Ibn Ḥajar, *Tahdhīb*, XI, 123–31; Sezgin, *GAS*, I, 96ff.

439. Probably Sufyān b. Saʿīd al-Thawrī, died 161/778 (Ibn Ḥajar, *Tahdhīb*, IV, 111–15); Sezgin, *GAS*, I, 96.

440. ʿĀṣim b. Abī al-Najjūd al-Muqrī, a Kufan Qurʾān reader who died ca. 128/746. See Ibn Ḥajar, *Tahdhīb*, V, 38–40; Sezgin, *GAS*, I, 7.

441. He died ca. 83/702. See Ibn Ḥajar, *Tahdhīb*, III, 321–22.

festival day or to the funeral of Zaynab,[442] [showing] a dark complexion, very tall, bald, and ambidextrous, walking [head and shoulders above the people] as if he were mounted.

According to Hannād—Sharīk—'Āṣim—Zirr: I saw 'Umar coming to the festival, walking barefoot, ambidextrous, and wearing a striped garment tucked up. He was towering over the people as if he were mounted and was saying, "People, perform [2730] the *hijrah* [with sincerity], and do not pretend to be like those who do!"

According to al-Ḥārith—Ibn Sa'd—Muḥammad b. 'Umar—'Umar b. 'Imrān b. 'Abdallāh b. 'Abd al-Raḥmān b. Abī Bakr[443]—'Āṣim b. 'Ubaydallāh[444]—'Abdallāh b. 'Āmir b. Rabī'ah:[445] I noticed 'Umar was a wan man, pale with an overlay of red. [He was also] very tall and with a bald patch.

According to al-Ḥārith—Ibn Sa'd—Muḥammad b. 'Umar—Shu'ayb b. Ṭalḥah[446]—his father—al-Qāsim b. Muḥammad:[447] I heard ['Abdallāh] b. 'Umar describe 'Umar as follows, "He is wan with an overlay of red. Very tall, white-haired, and with a bald patch."

According to al-Ḥārith—Muḥammad b. Sa'd—Muḥammad b. 'Umar—Khālid b. Abī Bakr:[448] 'Umar used to dye his beard yellow and comb his hair with henna.

His Birth and Age

According to al-Ḥārith—Ibn Sa'd—Muḥammad b. 'Umar—Usāmah b. Zayd b. Aslam[449]—his father—his grandfather: I

---

442. This is probably Zaynab bt. (al-)Jaḥsh, one of the Prophet's wives, who died in 20/641. Cf. Ṭabarī, I, 2595. 'Umar did however have a wife named Zaynab and also a daughter; see pages 100–1, below.

443. An unidentified narrator.

444. 'Āṣim b. 'Ubaydallāh b. 'Āṣim b. 'Umar b. al-Khaṭṭāb died at the beginning of the caliphate of Abū al-'Abbās; that is, ca. 132/750. See Ibn Ḥajar, *Tahdhīb*, V, 46–49.

445. 'Abdallāh b. 'Āmir b. Rabī'ah died after 80/699. See Ibn Ḥajar, *Tahdhīb*, V, 270–71.

446. An unidentified narrator.

447. Al-Qāsim b. Muḥammad is perhaps the grandson of Abū Bakr who died ca. 105/723. See Ibn Ḥajar, *Tahdhīb*, VIII, 333–35.

448. Khālid b. Abī Bakr died in 162/778. See Ibn Ḥajar, *Tahdhīb*, III, 81–82.

449. Usāmah b. Zayd al-Laythī died in the caliphate of Abū Ja'far; that is, 136–158/754–775. See Ibn Ḥajar, *Tahdhīb*, I, 207–8.

heard ʿUmar b. al-Khaṭṭāb say, "I was born four years before the last great Conflict."[450]

Abū Jaʿfar [al-Ṭabarī] reported: The early scholars differed on the subject of ʿUmar's age: some said that on the day he was killed he was fifty-five years old.

Some of the Sources of [the Report that He Was Fifty-Five Years Old]

According to Zayd b. Akhzam al-Ṭāʾī[451]—Abū Qutaybah[452]—
[2731] Jarīr b. Ḥāzim[453]—Ayyūb[454]—Nāfiʿ[455]—[ʿAbdallāh] Ibn ʿUmar: ʿUmar b. al-Khaṭṭāb was killed when he was fifty-five years old.

According to ʿAbd al-Raḥmān b. ʿAbdallāh b. ʿAbd al-Ḥakam[456]—Nuʿaym b. Ḥammād[457]—al-Darāwardī[458]—ʿUbaydallāh b. ʿUmar[459]—Nāfiʿ—Ibn ʿUmar: ʿUmar died when he was fifty-five years old.

According to ʿAbd al-Razzāq[460]—Ibn Jurayj[461]—Ibn Shihāb: ʿUmar died at the age of fifty-five exactly.

Others said he was on the day he died fifty-three years old and some months.

---

450. Reference to the last of the four "conflicts" (*fijār*) in pre-Islamic times, that of al-Barrād b. Qays, who killed ʿUrwah al-Raḥḥāl during one of the sacred months when no fighting was permitted. See Lane, *Lexicon*, 2341; *EI*², s.v. (Fück).

451. He died in 257/870. See Ibn Ḥajar, *Tahdhīb*, III, 393.

452. Abū Qutaybah is probably Salm b. Qutaybah, who died in 201/816. See Ibn Ḥajar, *Tahdhīb*, IV, 133–34.

453. Jarīr b. Ḥāzim died in 175/791. See Ibn Ḥajar, *Tahdhīb*, II, 69–72.

454. Ayyūb al-Sakhtiyānī died ca. 131/748. See Ibn Ḥajar, *Tahdhīb*, I, 397–99.

455. Nāfiʿ, the client of ʿAbdallāh b. ʿUmar, died ca. 120/738. See Ibn Ḥajar, *Tahdhīb*, X, 412–15.

456. Al-Miṣrī, the famous Egyptian historian, who died 257/871. See Ibn Ḥajar, *Tahdhīb*, VI, 208; *EI*², s.v. "Ibn ʿAbd al-Ḥakam" (Rosenthal).

457. Nuʿaym b. Ḥammād died ca. 229/844. See Ibn Ḥajar, *Tahdhīb*, X, 458–63; Sezgin, *GAS*, I, 104ff.

458. ʿAbd al-ʿAzīz b. Muḥammad b. ʿUbayd al-Darāwardī died in 82/701. See Ibn Ḥajar, *Tahdhīb*, VI, 353–55.

459. ʿUbaydallāh b. ʿUmar b. Ḥafṣ b. ʿĀṣim b. ʿUmar b. al-Khaṭṭāb, who died in 147/764. See Sezgin, *GAS*, I, 89.

460. ʿAbd al-Razzāq b. Hammām died 211/827. See Ibn Ḥajar, *Tahdhīb*, VI, 310–15; Sezgin, *GAS*, I, 99.

461. ʿAbd al-Malik b. ʿAbd al-ʿAzīz died in 151/768. See Ibn Ḥajar, *Tahdhīb*, VI, 402–6; Sezgin, *GAS*, I, 91.

The Sources of [the Report that He Was Fifty-Three Years Old]

This was reported to me by Hishām b. Muḥammad b. al-Kalbī.

Yet others said he died when he was sixty-three.

The Sources of [the Report that He Was Sixty-Three Years Old]

Ibn al-Muthannā[462]—Ibn Abī ʿAdī[463]—Dāwūd[464]—ʿĀmir [al-Shaʿbī]: ʿUmar died when he was sixty-three.

Yet others said he died at the age of sixty-one.

The Sources of [the Report that He Was Sixty-One Years Old]

This was reported to me on the authority of Abū Salamah al-Tabūdhakī[465]—Abū Hilāl[466]—Qatādah.[467]

Yet others said he died when he was sixty. [2732]

The Sources of [the Report that He Was Sixty Years Old]

According to al-Ḥārith—Ibn Saʿd—Muḥammad b. ʿUmar—Hishām b. Saʿd[468]—Zayd b. Aslam—his father: ʿUmar died when he was sixty. Muḥammad b. ʿUmar reported that this is the most accurate account in our opinion.

It is reported on the authority of al-Madāʾinī that ʿUmar died when he was fifty-seven.

---

462. Abū Mūsā Muḥammad died ca. 252/866. See Ibn Ḥajar, *Tahdhīb*, IX, 425–27.

463. Muḥammad b. Ibrāhīm b. Abī ʿAdī al-Qasmalī died ca. 194/810. See Ibn Ḥajar, *Tahdhīb*, IX, 12ff.

464. Probably Dāwūd b. Abī Hind, who died ca. 141/759. See Ibn Ḥajar, *Tahdhīb*, III, 204ff.

465. Mūsā b. Ismāʿīl died in 223/838. See Ibn Ḥajar, *Tahdhīb*, X, 333–35; Samʿānī, *Ansāb*, III, 18–19.

466. An unidentified narrator.

467. Qatādah b. Diʿāmah al-Sadūsī died in 117/735. See Ibn Ḥajar, *Tahdhīb*, VIII, 351–56; Sezgin, *GAS*, I, 31ff.

468. Hishām b. Saʿd died ca. 160/776. See Ibn Ḥajar, *Tahdhīb*, XI, 39–41.

The Names of His Children and Wives

According to Abū Zayd 'Umar b. Shabbah—'Alī b. Muḥammad [al-Madā'inī] and al-Ḥārith—Muḥammad b. Sa'd—Muḥammad b. 'Umar, and according to Hishām b. Muḥammad [al-Kalbī], all of whose accounts agree, even if there are differences of expression: In the pre-Islamic era 'Umar married Zaynab bt. Maẓ'ūn b. Ḥabīb b. Wahb b. Ḥudhāfah b. Jumaḥ. She bore him 'Abdallāh, 'Abd al-Raḥmān the elder, and Ḥafṣah.

According to 'Alī b. Muḥammad [al-Madā'inī], ('Umar) also married Mulaykah bt. Jarwal al-Khuzā'ī in the pre-Islamic era. She bore him 'Ubaydallāh b. 'Umar. He became separated from her at the time of the Truce.[469] After 'Umar, Abū al-Jahm b. Ḥudhayfah[470] married her.

According to Muḥammad b. 'Umar [al-Wāqidī], the mother of Zayd the younger and 'Ubaydallāh, who was killed at the battle of Ṣiffīn[471] [fighting] with Mu'āwiyah, was Umm Kulthūm bt. Jarwal b. Mālik b. al-Musayyib b. Rabī'ah b. Aṣram
[2733] b. Ḍabīs b. Ḥarām b. Ḥabashiyyah b. Salūl b. Ka'b b. 'Amr b. Khuzā'ah. However, Islam brought about a separation between her and 'Umar.

'Ali b. Muḥammad [al-Madā'inī] reported that ('Umar) also married Quraybah bt. Abī Umayyah al-Makhzūmī in the pre-Islamic era. He became separated from her also at the time of the Truce. 'Abd al-Raḥmān b. Abī Bakr al-Ṣiddīq[472] married her after ('Umar).

There were also other reports that he married Umm Ḥakīm bt. al-Ḥārith b. Hishām b. al-Mughīrah b. 'Abdallāh b. 'Umar b. Makhzūm after the advent of Islam. She bore him Fāṭimah, but he divorced her. But al-Madā'inī reported that it was said he did not divorce her.

He also married after the advent of Islam Jamīlah, the sister of

469. That is, the truce of al-Ḥudaybiyah in 6/627 between the Prophet and the Meccans. See Ibn Hishām, *Sīrah*, II, 316ff. (Guillaume, *Life*, 499ff.).

470. Abū (al-)Jahm 'Āmir/'Ubayd b. Ḥudhayfah. See Ibn al-Athīr, *Usd*, V, 162–63. No date of death is given in the entry, but he accepted Islam when Mecca was conquered in 8/629. He was renowned as a genealogist.

471. The battle of Ṣiffīn took place between 'Alī and Mu'āwiyah in 37/657.

472. A son of the first caliph.

ʿĀṣim b. Thābit b. Abī al-Aqlaḥ, whose name was Qays b. ʿIṣmah b. Mālik b. Ḍubayʿah b. Zayd b. al-Aws of the Helpers. She bore him ʿĀṣim, but he divorced her.

He also married Umm Kulthūm bt. ʿAlī b. Abī Ṭālib, whose mother was Fāṭimah, the daughter of the Messenger of God. He reportedly gave her 40,000 [dirhams] as a dowry. She bore him Zayd and Ruqayyah.

He also married Luhayyah, a Yemeni woman, who bore him ʿAbd al-Raḥmān. Al-Madāʾinī reported that she bore him ʿAbd al-Raḥmān the youngest. He added that there was a report that (Luhayyah) was a concubine. Al-Wāqidī also said this Luhayyah was a concubine. He added that Luhayyah bore him the middle ʿAbd al-Raḥmān. (Al-Wāqidī) also reported that the mother of the youngest ʿAbd al-Raḥmān was a concubine. He also had Fukayhah as a concubine, and, according to several reports, she bore him Zaynab. (Al-Wāqidī) also reported that she was ʿUmar's youngest child.

He also married ʿĀtikah bt. Zayd b. ʿAmr b. Nufayl. Before him she had been married to ʿAbdallāh b. Abī Bakr.[473] When [2734]
ʿUmar died, al-Zubayr b. al-ʿAwwām married her.

Al-Madāʾinī said:[474] (ʿUmar) asked for the hand of Umm Kulthūm bt. Abī Bakr when she was young, and he sent a message regarding her to ʿĀʾishah. The latter told (Umm Kulthūm) that the [marriage] was up to her. Umm Kulthūm replied that she did not want him. "You are turning down the Commander of the Faithful!" ʿĀʾishah exclaimed. "Yes," (Umm Kulthūm) said, "he leads a rough life and is severe with his womenfolk." So ʿĀʾishah sent a message to ʿAmr b. al-ʿĀṣ, telling him [of Umm Kulthūm's decision]. "Leave it to me," was his reply. (ʿAmr) came to ʿUmar and said, "Commander of the Faithful, I have heard some news from which I invoke God's name to protect you!" "What is it?" he asked. (ʿAmr) continued, "You are seeking the hand of Umm Kulthūm bt. Abī Bakr." (ʿUmar) replied, "Yes, do you think I am not good enough for her or she for me?" (ʿAmr) said, "Neither, but she is young and

473. A son of the first caliph.
474. See the account in Balʿami, *Chronique*, III, 535–36.

grew up with kindness and gentleness under the protection of the Mother of the Believers.[475] You are rough and ready. But we are in awe of you and we cannot turn you away from something that is natural to you. How will it be with (Umm Kulthūm) if she disobeys you on any matter and you punish her physically? You will have taken Abū Bakr's place as his child's [guardian] in a fashion that does not befit you." ('Umar) replied, "But how will all this be with 'Ā'ishah? I have already told her [I am going to marry Umm Kulthūm]." ('Amr) said, "I shall deal with her on your behalf. Also I shall show you someone better than (Umm Kulthūm bt. Abī Bakr), [namely] Umm Kulthūm bt. 'Alī b. Abī Ṭālib through whom you will acquire a relationship with the Messenger of God."

Al-Madā'inī said: ('Umar) was seeking the hand of Umm Abān bt. 'Utbah b. Rabī'ah. However she did not like him and said, "He closes his door, keeping away any goodness he has [from others];[476] he enters wearing a frown and comes out wearing a frown!"

[2735]

When He Became a Muslim

Abū Ja'far [al-Ṭabarī] said: It is reported that ('Umar) embraced Islam after forty-five men and twenty-one women.

The Sources of This Report

According to al-Ḥārith—Ibn Sa'd—Muḥammad b. 'Umar [al-Wāqidī]—Muḥammad b. 'Abdallāh[477]—his father: I mentioned the account about 'Umar to (my son) and he said that 'Abdallāh b. Tha'labah b. Ṣu'ayr[478] had told him that 'Umar embraced Islam after forty-five men and twenty-one women.

---

475. That is, 'Ā'ishah, the wife of the Prophet.

476. An accusation of miserliness.

477. Abū Aḥmad al-Zubayrī, who died in 203/818. See Ibn Ḥajar, *Tahdhīb*, IX, 254–56.

478. 'Abdallāh b. Tha'labah b. Ṣu'ayr al-'Udharī died ca. 93/711. See Ibn Ḥajar, *Tahdhīb*, V, 165.

Some of His Memorable Deeds

According to Abū al-Sā'ib [Salm b. Junādah]—Ibn Fuḍayl[479]—Ḍirār[480]—Ḥuṣayn al-Murrī:[481] 'Umar said, "The Arabs are like a tractable camel that follows its leader. So its leader should watch where he is leading it. By the Lord of the Ka'bah, I shall certainly carry them along the [straight] road.

According to Ya'qūb b. Ibrāhīm—Ismā'īl b. Ibrāhīm[482]—Yūnus[483]—al-Ḥasan [al-Baṣrī]: 'Umar said, "When I find myself in a position when I feel comfortable, but that means my people have no access [to me], then this [can]not [continue] to be my position; I [must once again] be on the same level as my people. [2736]

According to Khallād b. Aslam[484]—al-Naḍr b. Shumayl[485]—Qaṭan[486]—Abū Yazīd al-Madīnī[487]—a client of 'Uthmān b. 'Affān: I was riding behind 'Uthmān b. 'Affān one hot day when there was an extremely hot wind blowing and he came to the alms-animal pen. There was a man wearing a waist wrapper and an upper garment with another wrapped around his head. He was driving camels into the pen; that is, the alms-camel pen. 'Uthmān said, "Who do you think this is?" We finally reached him and he was 'Umar b. al-Khaṭṭāb. ('Uthmān) said, "He is indeed 'the strong, the trustworthy one'!"[488]

According to Ja'far b. Muḥammad al-Kūfī[489] and 'Abbās b.

---

479. Muḥammad b. Fuḍayl b. Ghazwān al-Ḍabbī died ca. 195/811. See Ibn Ḥajar, *Tahdhīb*, IX, 405ff.

480. Ḍirār is perhaps Ibn Murrah al-Kūfī, who died in 132/749. See Ibn Ḥajar, *Tahdhīb*, IV, 457.

481. An unidentified narrator. For the following reports, see Ibn al-Athīr, *Kāmil*, III, 27ff.

482. It is not possible to provide more information on Abū Sa'īd Ismā'īl b. Ibrāhīm al-Asadī. See Translation, I, 255.

483. Possibly Yūnus b. 'Ubayd, who died in 140/757. See Juynboll, *Tradition*, 52.

484. Died ca. 249/863. See Ibn Ḥajar, *Tahdhīb*, III, 171ff.

485. Died ca. 204/820. See Ibn Ḥajar, *Tahdhīb*, X, 437ff.; Sezgin, *GAS*, I, 262.

486. Qaṭan b. Ka'b al-Quṭa'ī appears in Ibn Ḥajar, *Tahdhīb*, VIII, 381–82, but no date of death is given.

487. Abū Yazīd al-Madīnī appears in Ibn Ḥajar, *Tahdhīb*, XII, 280, as al-Madanī, whose date of death is not given.

488. As mentioned in Qur'ān, XVIII:26.

489. An unidentified narrator.

Abī Ṭālib[490]—Abū Zakariyyā' Yaḥyā b. Muṣ'ab al-Kalbī[491]—'Umar b. Nāfi'[492]—Abū Bakr al-'Absī:[493] I entered the alms-animal enclosure with 'Umar b. al-Khaṭṭāb and 'Alī b. Abī Ṭālib. 'Uthmān sat down in the shade to write while 'Alī stood by him, dictating to him what 'Umar was saying. On a very hot day 'Umar was standing in the sun and wearing two black garments, one as a waist wrapper, another wrapped around his
[2737] head, as he counted the alms camels, recording their colors and their ages. 'Alī spoke to 'Uthmān, and I heard him quoting the description of the daughter of Shu'ayb in God's Book, "O father, hire him; the best of those you hire will be the strong, the trustworthy one!" 'Alī pointed at 'Umar and said, "This is 'the strong, the trustworthy one'!"

According to Ya'qūb b. Ibrāhīm—Ismā'īl—Yūnus—al-Ḥasan:
[2738] 'Umar said,[494]

> If I live, I shall certainly travel for a whole year among my subjects, God willing. I know that people have needs that do not reach me. Their governors will not refer them to me, nor will they themselves come to me. I shall travel to Syria and stay there two months. Then I shall travel to the Jazīrah and stay there two months. Then I shall travel to Egypt and stay there two months. Then I shall travel to Bahrain and stay there two months. Then I shall travel to al-Kūfah and stay there for two months. Then I shall travel to al-Baṣrah and stay there for two months. Indeed, what a fine year this will be!

According to Muḥammad b. 'Awf[495]—Abū al-Mughīrah 'Abd al-Quddūs b. al-Ḥajjāj[496]—Ṣafwān b. 'Amr[497]—Abū al-Mukhāriq

---

490. 'Abbās b. Abī Ṭālib died in 258/871. See Ibn Ḥajar, *Tahdhīb*, V, 115–16.

491. An unidentified narrator.

492. 'Umar b. Nāfi' al-Thaqafī has a short notice in Ibn Ḥajar, *Tahdhīb*, VI, 500, which gives, however, no date of death.

493. The text has Abū Bakr al-'Absī, but Ibn Ḥajar, *Tahdhīb*, XII, lists an Abū Bakr al-'Ansī, associating him with 'Umar b. Nāfi' (see preceding note).

494. Cf. Bal'ami, *Chronique*, III, 538.

495. Died ca. 273/886. See Ibn Ḥajar, *Tahdhīb*, IX, 383ff.

496. Abū al-Mughīrah 'Abd al-Quddūs b. al-Ḥajjāj al-Khawlānī died in 212/827. See Ibn Ḥajar, *Tahdhīb*, VI, 369–70.

497. It is not possible to identify this narrator with certainty.

Zuhayr b. Sālim[498]—Ka'b al-Aḥbār: I stayed with a man called Mālik who was under the protection of 'Umar b. al-Khaṭṭāb. I asked him how one could get access to the Commander of the Faithful. He replied that there was no door barring the way to ('Umar) or any obstacle, that he would say his prayers, would then sit down, and anyone who wished could talk to him.

According to Yūnus b. 'Abd al-A'lā—Sufyān [b. 'Uyaynah]—Yaḥyā[499]—Sālim[500]—Aslam: 'Umar sent me off with some alms camels to the designated pasturage and I put my baggage on one of the she-camels. When I was intending to lead them away, he asked me to show him them. I did so and he saw my baggage on a fine she-camel in among them and said, "You wretch! You make use of a she-camel that will provide goodness to a Muslim family! Why not a two-year-old camel constantly discharging urine, or a she with little milk?"[501]

According to 'Umar b. Ismā'īl b. Mujālid al-Hamdānī[502]—Abū Mu'āwiyah[503]—Abū Ḥayyān[504]—Abū al-Zinbā'[505]—Abū al-Dihqānah:[506] 'Umar b. al-Khaṭṭāb was told that there was someone from al-Anbār[507] who had some knowledge of the state register [and was asked] if he would take him on as a secretary. 'Umar replied, "In this case, I would be taking on as a confidant [someone] from outside the [community of the] Believers!" [2739]

According to Yūnus b. 'Abd al-A'lā—Ibn Wahb[508]—'Abd

498. He has a brief notice in Ibn Ḥajar, *Tahdhīb*, III, 344, although no date of death is given.

499. Yaḥyā b. Kathīr died in 129/746. See Ibn Ḥajar, *Tahdhīb*, XI, 268–69.

500. Sālim b. 'Abdallāh b. 'Umar died in 106/724. See Ibn Ḥajar, *Tahdhīb*, III, 438.

501. That is, why do you have to choose a good beast as your baggage camel, when there are inferior ones that could be used?

502. He has a brief notice in Ibn Ḥajar, *Tahdhīb*, VII, 427–28.

503. Abū Mu'āwiyah Muḥammad b. Khāzim al-Ḍarīr died in 195/810. See Ibn Ḥajar, *Tahdhīb*, IX, 137–39.

504. Perhaps Abū Ḥayyān Yaḥyā b. Sa'īd, who died in 145/762. See Ibn Ḥajar, *Tahdhīb*, XI, 214–15.

505. An unidentified narrator.

506. An unidentified narrator.

507. A town on the Euphrates about 45 miles west of Baghdad. See Yāqūt, *Mu'jam*, I, 257–58; Le Strange, *Lands*, 25 and Map II, opposite 25.

508. 'Abdallāh b. Wahb died in 197/813. See Ibn Ḥajar, *Tahdhīb*, VI, 71–74; Sezgin, *GAS*, I, 466.

al-Raḥmān b. Zayd[509]—his father—his grandfather: 'Umar b. al-Khaṭṭāb addressed the people and said, "By Him who sent Muḥammad with the Truth, if one camel were to perish untended on the bank of the Euphrates, I would fear that God would hold the Khaṭṭāb family responsible for it." Abū Zayd[510] added that the Khaṭṭāb family meant himself, no one else.

According to Ibn al-Muthannā—Ibn Abī 'Adī—Shu'bah[511]—Abū 'Imrān al-Jawnī: 'Umar wrote to Abū Mūsā,[512] "There are still prominent men who refer the needs of the people [to me] on their behalf. So honor those prominent men who are in your jurisdiction. It is justice enough for an uninfluential Muslim that he be treated fairly in juridical decisions and in the division [of spoils after being referred to me]."

According to Abū Kurayb[513]—Ibn Idrīs[514]—Muṭarrif[515]—al-Sha'bī: A bedouin came to 'Umar and said, "My stallion camel has both mange and saddle sores; give me a mount." 'Umar replied to him, "Your camel does not have mange and saddle sores!" (The bedouin) turned away, reciting the following:[516]

Abū Ḥafṣ 'Umar has sworn by God's name
That no mange or saddle sores have afflicted [my mount].
Forgive him, God, that he has given a false oath!

('Umar) exclaimed, "O God, forgive me!" He called the bedouin back and gave him a [fresh] mount.

[2740] According to Ya'qūb b. Ibrāhīm—Ismā'īl—Ayyūb—Muḥammad: I was informed that a man who was related to 'Umar asked him [for money]. But he chided him and sent him away. People spoke to ('Umar) about him, and he was asked why he

509. 'Abd al-Raḥmān b. Zayd b. Aslam died in 182/798. See Ibn Ḥajar, *Tahdhīb*, VI, 177–79.

510. Perhaps this is the grandfather, the original source.

511. Shu'bah b. al-Ḥajjāj died in 160/776. See Ibn Ḥajar, *Tahdhīb*, IV, 338–46.

512. His provincial governor in al-Baṣrah.

513. Muḥammad b. al-'Alā' died ca. 248/862. See Ibn Ḥajar, *Tahdhīb*, IX, 385ff.

514. Probably 'Abdallāh b. Idrīs, who died in 192/807 (Ibn Ḥajar, *Tahdhīb*, V, 144–46), rather than 'Abd al-Mun'im b. Idrīs, who died in 228/843 (I, 286 n. 760).

515. It is not possible to identify this narrator with certainty.

516. The meter is *rajaz*.

chided him and sent him away when he begged from him. He replied, "He asked me for some of God's money. What will be my excuse if I meet Him when I am a treacherous ruler? Why did he not ask for some of my money?" (The source) added that ('Umar) sent him 10,000 [dirhams].

According to Muḥammad b. al-Muthannā—'Abd al-Raḥmān b. Mahdī—Shu'bah—Yaḥyā b. Ḥuḍayn[517]—Ṭāriq b. Shihāb:[518] Whenever 'Umar sent governors in charge of provinces, he would say about them, "O God, I have not sent them to take the property (of the people), nor to abuse them physically. Anyone oppressed by his commander has no commander except me."

According to Ibn Bashshār[519]—Ibn Abī 'Adī—Shu'bah—Qatādah—Sālim b. Abī al-Ja'd[520]—Ma'dan b. Abī Ṭalḥah:[521] 'Umar b. al-Khaṭṭāb gave an address to his people and said, "O God, I call You to bear witness to the commanders of the garrison towns that I have sent them only to teach the people their religion and the practice of their Prophet, to distribute among them their spoils and to act with justice. If they have any doubt about any matter, they will refer it to me."

According to Abū Kurayb—Abū Bakr b. 'Ayyāsh[522]—Abū [2741]
Ḥaṣīn:[523] Whenever 'Umar appointed his governors, he would go out with them to bid them farewell, saying, "I have not appointed you governor over Muḥammad's community with limitless authority.[524] I have made you governor over them only to lead them in prayer, to make decisions among them based on what is right, and to distribute [the spoils] among them justly. I have not given you limitless authority over them. Do not flog

517. An unidentified narrator.

518. Ṭāriq b. Shihāb al-Bajalī died in ca. 84/703 or 123/741. See Ibn Ḥajar, *Tahdhīb*, V, 3–4.

519. Muḥammad b. Bashshār died in 252/866. See Ibn Ḥajar, *Tahdhīb*, IX, 70–73.

520. Al-Ashja'ī died ca. 98/716. See Ibn Ḥajar, *Tahdhīb*, III, 432–33.

521. Ma'dan b. Abī Ṭalḥah has a short notice in Ibn Ḥajar, *Tahdhīb*, X, 228, which, however, gives no date of death.

522. He died ca. 194/810. See Ibn Ḥajar, *Tahdhīb*, XI, 34–37.

523. 'Uthmān b. 'Āṣim died ca. 132/750. See Ibn Ḥajar, *Tahdhīb*, VII, 126–28.

524. For the expression *'alā ash'āri-him wa-abshāri-him*, literally "over their hair and their skins," see *Glossarium*, CCCXII.

the Arab [troops] and humiliate them; do not keep them long from their families and bring temptation upon them; do not neglect them and cause them deprivation. Confine yourselves to the [actual text of the] Qur'ān, and do not frequently cite prophetic traditions. I am your partner." He would also allow vengeance to be taken on his governors. If there was a complaint against a governor, he would bring together the governor and the complainant. If there was a genuine case against (the governor) for which punishment was obligatory, he would punish him.

According to Ya'qūb b. Ibrāhīm—Ismā'īl b. Ibrāhīm—Sa'īd al-Jurayrī[525]—Abū Naḍrah[526]—Abū Firās:[527] 'Umar b. al-
[2742] Khaṭṭāb made the Friday address and said, "O people, I do not send governors to you to flog you or to take your possessions. I send them to you to teach you your religion and the way you should follow. If anything other than these is done to anyone, he should refer (the matter) to me. By Him in whose hand is my soul, I shall certainly permit the law of retaliation to be used against (any governor)." Up jumped 'Amr b. al-'Āṣ and said, "Do you really think you will allow the law of retaliation to be used against any commander appointed over your subjects who disciplines one of them?" ('Umar) replied, "Yes indeed, I shall certainly allow that. Why not, as I have seen the Messenger of God allow the law of retaliation against himself? Do not beat Muslims and humiliate them; do not keep them long from their families and bring temptation upon them; do not deny them their rights and turn them into infidels; do not settle them among thickets so that you lose them."[528]

'Umar reportedly would himself patrol at night, seeking out the Muslims' dwellings and personally finding out how they were faring.

---

525. Sa'īd b. Iyās al-Jurayrī died in 144/761. See Ibn Ḥajar, *Tahdhīb*, IV, 5–7.

526. Al-Mundhir b. Mālik al-'Abdī al-'Awqī died ca. 109/728. See Ibn Ḥajar, *Tahdhīb*, X, 302ff.

527. Abū Firās al-Rabī' b. Ziyād al-Nahdī has a brief entry in Ibn Ḥajar, *Tahdhīb*, XII, 201.

528. Perhaps figurative, "do not take them to places they do not know, where they feel ill at ease, and do not lose control of them."

Relevant Information on ['Umar's Night Visits]

According to Ibn Bashshār—Abū 'Āmir[529]—Qurrah b. Khālid[530]—Bakr b. 'Abdallāh al-Muzani:[531] 'Umar b. al-Khaṭṭāb came to the door of 'Abd al-Raḥmān b. 'Awf and knocked on it. His wife came and opened it, saying to him, "Do not enter until [2743] I have entered and sat down." So he did as she had said and entered only after she had told him to do so. He then said, "Is there anything [to eat]?" So she brought him some food and he ate it, while 'Abd al-Raḥmān was standing saying his prayers. ('Umar) asked him to cut them short, so 'Abd al-Raḥmān then recited the blessing [on the Prophet to finish his prayers]. Turning toward him, he asked the Commander of the Faithful what brought him at that time. ('Umar) replied that there was a group of travelers who had stopped in the area of the market and that he was afraid they might be about to be robbed. [He urged 'Abd al-Raḥmān] to go [with him] and that they should both stand guard over them. So off they went and came to the market. They sat down on some elevated ground to talk and, [when it became dark], saw [the light of] a lamp from afar. 'Umar said, "Did I not forbid the [use of] lamps after bedtime?" They went off [toward the light] and came across a group of people drinking. ('Umar) said [to 'Abd al-Raḥmān], however, "You go on your way, for I know who it is." In the morning ('Umar) sent for (the culprit) and said, "So and so, you and your pals were drinking last night!" He replied, "How do you know, Commander of the Faithful?" ('Umar) said, "It was something which I saw with my own eyes." (The man) replied, "Did God not forbid you to spy [on people]?" (The source) continued: So he forgave him.

According to Bakr b. 'Abdallāh al-Muzanī: 'Umar banned [the use of] lamps because the mice would take the wicks [to get at the oil] and drop them on the roofs of houses and they

529. 'Abd al-Malik b. 'Amr al-'Aqadī died ca. 205/821. See Ibn Ḥajar, *Tahdhīb*, VI, 409ff.

530. Qurrah b. Khālid al-Sadūsī died ca. 170/786. See Ibn Ḥajar, *Tahdhīb*, VIII, 371–72.

531. Bakr b. 'Abdallāh al-Muzanī died in 108/726. See Ibn Ḥajar, *Tahdhīb*, I, 484–85.

would catch fire. The roofs of houses at that time were made of palm-branches.

According to Aḥmad b. Ḥarb[532]—Muṣʿab b. ʿAbdallāh al-Zubayrī[533]—his father—Rabīʿah b. ʿUthmān—Zayd b. Aslam—his father: I was going with ʿUmar b. al-Khaṭṭāb to Ḥarrat Wāqim,[534] and when we reached Ṣirār[535] there suddenly appeared a fire which had been lit. He said, "I think, Aslam,[536]
[2744] these people must be riders overtaken by nightfall and cold. Let's go!" So off we went at a good pace and we drew near to them. They were a woman with some young boys, and there was a pot set up over the fire. Her boys were all screaming. ʿUmar said, "Greetings, people of the light," not wishing to call them people of the fire.[537] (The woman) returned the greeting. He asked if he might approach. She replied, "Bring us some good or leave [us] alone." (ʿUmar) asked what was the matter. She told him that nightfall and cold had overtaken them. He asked what was making her children cry. She told him it was hunger. "What is in this pot?" he asked. "Water," she replied, "to keep them quiet until they fall asleep. [I ask] God [to judge] between us and ʿUmar!" ʿUmar said, "God have mercy upon you, how can ʿUmar know anything about you?" She told him, "He is in authority over us, and yet he neglects us." (ʿUmar) turned to me and said, "Let's go." So off we went at a good pace and reached the flour store. He took out a measure [of flour and put] a ball of fat into it. Then he said, "Let me carry [all this]." But I replied, "I will carry it on your behalf." But he insisted twice or three times, "Let me carry all this," while I was saying, "I will carry it on your behalf." He finally said to me, "Will you carry

532. Perhaps Aḥmad b. Ḥarb al-Ṭāʾī, who died in 263/876. See Ibn Ḥajar, *Tahdhīb*, I, 23.

533. Died ca. 235/851. See Rosenthal, *Historiography*, 379.

534. The lava field (*ḥarrah*) east of Medina and still known by this name today. See Bilādī, *Muʿjam*, II, 283ff. For this anecdote, see Ṭanṭāwī, *Akhbār*, 439ff.

535. Three miles from Medina into the area of Ḥarrat Wāqim. See Hamdānī, *Ṣifah*, 124; Bilādī, *Muʿjam*, V, 138ff.

536. That is, the source of the story, Zayd's father.

537. *Aṣḥāb al-nār* would indicate those in Hell, so ʿUmar uses the expression *aṣḥāb al-ḍawʾ* for this family party.

my burden for me on the Day of Resurrection, you wretch?!" So I allowed him to carry (all the food). He made off and I with him, hastening to get back to (the woman). He gave her this [food], taking some of the flour and saying to her, "Sprinkle [it] over (the contents of the pot), while I stir it for you." He also began to blow beneath the pot—now because he had a large beard, I could see the smoke through it—until it was cooked and [the contents [2745]
of] the pot were fit to eat. He put (the pot) down [off the fire] and said, "Get something for me." So she brought a large bowl and he emptied (the contents of the pot) into it. He then said, "Feed them, while I flatten [the bread in the bowl] for you." And he continued to do this until they were satisfied. Then he left what remained of this [food] with her. He got up and I with him. "God give you a good reward," she said, "you have done better in this matter than the Commander of the Faithful!" He replied, "Speak well [of him], for when you come to the Commander of the Faithful, you will find me there, God willing." He stepped away from her a little, then faced her and lay down as a wild beast does. I told him that he had other things to do, but he did not speak to me until I saw that the children were romping around and laughing, and then they fell quiet and went to sleep. He then got up, praising God, then he turned to me and said, "Aslam, hunger kept them awake and made them cry. I did not want to leave until I could see them doing what I see [now]!"

When ʿUmar wanted to order the Muslims to do something that was of benefit to them or to forbid them doing something that was not, he would begin with his own family. He would come to them, exhorting them and threatening [them] not to go against his order. According to Abū Kurayb Muḥammad b. al-ʿAlāʾ—Abū Bakr b. ʿAyyāsh—ʿUbaydallāh b. ʿUmar in Medina—Sālim: When ʿUmar went up into the *minbar* and forbade the people from doing something, he would [first] bring together his own family and say, "I have forbidden the people from doing so and so. They all look at you as birds look—that is, at their [2746]
prey—and I swear in God's name that if I find anyone of you doing (whatever is forbidden) I shall double his punishment!"

Abū Jaʿfar [al-Ṭabarī] said: (ʿUmar) was hard on those of dubious reputations and severe in [seeking out] God's truth until he extracted it, but easygoing in what was owed to him until it was handed over to him and compassionate and full of pity for the weak.

According to 'Ubaydallāh b. Sa'd al-Zuhrī[538]—his paternal uncle—his father—al-Walīd b. Kathīr[539]—Muḥammad b. 'Ijlān[540]—Zayd b. Aslam—his father: Some Muslims had a word with 'Abd al-Raḥmān b. 'Awf and said, "Speak to 'Umar b. al-Khaṭṭāb, for he has inspired so much fear in us that indeed we cannot look him in the face." 'Abd al-Raḥmān b. 'Awf mentioned this to 'Umar and he said, "Did they really say this?! I was indeed lenient with them to such as extent that I was afraid of God. I became severe with them to such an extent that I was afraid of God. I swear an oath in God's name that I am more afraid of them than they are of me!"

According to Abū Kurayb—Abū Bakr—'Āṣim [b. Kulayb]:
[2747] 'Umar appointed someone governor of Egypt. While 'Umar was walking through one of the streets of Medina, he heard someone say, "Good heavens, 'Umar, you appoint someone governor who acts treacherously and you say that you have no responsibility in the matter, when your governor is doing so and so!" So ('Umar) sent for (the governor) and when he arrived gave him a staff, a woolen coat, and sheep, saying to the man whose name was 'Iyāḍ b. Ghanm,[541] "Pasture them, for your father was a shepherd." Then he called him back and mentioned what had been said [about him]. He added, "What if I send you back!" He returned him to his post, saying, "I must have your word that you will not wear any fine cloth, nor ride an expensive horse (*birdhawn*)."[542]

According to Abū Kurayb—Abū Usāmah[543]—'Abdallāh b. al-

538. 'Ubaydallāh b. Sa'd al-Zuhrī died in 260/873. See Ibn Ḥajar, *Tahdhīb*, VII, 15–16.

539. Perhaps al-Walīd b. Kathīr al-Makhzūmī, who died in 151/768. See Ibn Ḥajar, *Tahdhīb*, XI, 148.

540. Muḥammad b. 'Ijlān died in 149/766. See Ibn Ḥajar, *Tahdhīb*, IX, 341–43.

541. There is perhaps a play on words here: *ghanam* is used for sheep—a strange gift anyway—and the governor's father was called Ghanm. For 'Iyāḍ b. Ghanm, see note 224, above.

542. The word cannot mean "nag" or some such inferior horse here. See Morony, *Iraq*, 211.

543. Ḥammād b. Usāmah died in Baghdad in 244/858. See Ibn Ḥajar, *Tahdhīb*, III, 1–4.

Walīd[544]—ʿĀṣim—Ibn Khuzaymah b. Thābit al-Anṣarī:[545] When ʿUmar appointed a governor, he would write him a certificate of investiture that would be witnessed by a group of both Emigrants and Helpers, stipulating that he should not ride an expensive horse, or eat white bread, or wear any fine cloth, or prevent the people's needs [from being satisfied].

According to al-Ḥārith—Ibn Saʿd—Muslim b. Ibrāhīm[546]—Sallām b. Miskīn[547]—ʿImrān:[548] When ʿUmar b. al-Khaṭṭāb was in need, he would go to the treasurer and ask him for a loan. Sometimes he was short of money, and the treasurer would come to (ʿUmar) and demand payment of his debt and would insist on its payment. So ʿUmar would use his wiles against him. At other times his stipend was disbursed [to him], so he paid back (the debt).

According to Abū ʿĀmir al-ʿAqadī —ʿĪsā b. Ḥafṣ[549]—a man of [2748]
Banū Salimah[550]—Ibn al-Barāʾ b. Maʿrūr:[551] ʿUmar went out one day to go to the *minbar*. He complained of being sick and some honey was prescribed for him, there being a skin receptacle [full of it] in the treasury. He said, "If you give me permission [to take] it, I shall do so; otherwise it is forbidden to me."

ʿUmar's Being Called Commander of the Faithful

Abū Jaʿfar [al-Ṭabarī] said: The first person to be called Commander of the Faithful was ʿUmar b. al-Khaṭṭāb. Then this practice continued and the caliphs have used (the title) to this day.

---

544. Perhaps ʿAbdallāh b. al-Walīd b. Maymūn, whose date of death is unrecorded in Ibn Ḥajar, *Tahdhīb*, VI, 70.

545. ʿUmārah b. Khuzaymah b. Thābit al-Anṣārī died in 105/723. See Ibn Ḥajar, *Tahdhīb*, VII, 416.

546. It is not possible to identify this narrator with certainty.

547. Died ca. 167/784. See Ibn Ḥajar, *Tahdhīb*, IV, 286ff.

548. It is not possible to identify this narrator with certainty.

549. ʿĪsā b. Ḥafṣ died in 157/773. See Ibn Ḥajar, *Tahdhīb*, VIII, 208–9.

550. Salimah b. Saʿd, a tribal division (*baṭn*) of the Khazraj, one of the two Arab tribes in Medina in early Islam. See Ibn Ḥazm, *Jamharah*, 358–59; Kaḥḥālah, *Muʿjam*, II, 537.

551. An unidentified narrator.

Information on This Matter

According to Aḥmad b. ʿAbd al-Ṣamad al-Anṣārī[552]—Umm ʿAmr bt. Ḥassān al-Kūfiyyah[553]—her father: When ʿUmar assumed power, he was addressed, "O Caliph of the Caliph of the Messenger of God." ʿUmar said, "This is too long winded. When another caliph comes along, they will say, 'O Caliph of the Caliph of the Caliph of the Messenger of God!' But you are the faithful and I am your commander." So he was called Commander of the Faithful. Aḥmad b. ʿAbd al-Ṣamad said: I asked (Umm ʿAmr) how many years she had lived. She replied, "133 years."

According to Ibn Ḥumayd—Yaḥyā b. Wāḍiḥ[554]—Abū Ḥamzah[555]—Jābir: Some one addressed ʿUmar b. al-Khaṭṭāb, "O
[2749] Caliph of God." He replied, "God turn you away [from such a remark]!"[556] (The man) said, "May God make me your ransom!" (ʿUmar) said, "In that case, God will humiliate you!"[557]

His Institution of the [Islamic] Dating System

Abū Jaʿfar [al-Ṭabarī] said: (ʿUmar) instituted the [Islamic] dating system and recorded it. According to al-Ḥārith—Ibn Saʿd—Muḥammad b. ʿUmar: This was in 16 in Rabīʿ I [April 637]. I have already mentioned the reason for his recording this and the circumstances surrounding it.[558] ʿUmar was also the first to date documents and to stamp them with clay.

He was also the first to assemble the people to one imam to lead them in the special Ramaḍān prayers.[559] He sent out written instructions to the provinces to carry this out. According

---

552. An unidentified narrator.
553. An unidentified narrator.
554. Yaḥyā b. Wāḍiḥ has no date of death provided in Ibn Ḥajar, *Tahdhīb*, XI, 293ff.
555. Abū Ḥamzah Muḥammad b. Maymūn al-Sukkārī died ca. 168/785. See Ibn Ḥajar, *Tahdhīb*, IX, 486ff.
556. Arabic, *khālafa Allāhu bi-ka*. A pun with *khalīfah*, caliph, is intended.
557. The man's reply is meant as an apology, but ʿUmar is not appeased.
558. See in the text, Ṭabarī, I, 2480; Translation, XIII, 59.
559. Arabic, *tarāwīḥ*, the special prayers said after the evening prayer in Ramaḍān. See *SEI*, s.v. (Wensinck).

to al-Ḥārith—Ibn Saʿd—Muḥammad b. ʿUmar: This was in the year 14 [February 25, 635–February 14, 636]. He also appointed two public Qurʾān readers, one to lead the men in prayer, the other the women.

[ʿUmar's] Carrying a Whip and His Instituting the State Registers[560]

He was the first to carry a whip and to use it. He was the first to institute the state registers for the people in Islam. He recorded the [names of] people according to their tribes and assigned them stipends. [2750]

According to al-Ḥārith—Ibn Saʿd—Muḥammad b. ʿUmar—ʿĀʾidh b. Yaḥyā[561]—Abū al-Ḥuwayrith[562]—Jubayr b. al-Ḥuwayrith b. Nuqayd:[563] ʿUmar b. al-Khaṭṭṭāb sought the advice of the Muslims on the matter of establishing state registers. ʿAlī b. Abī Ṭālib advised him to distribute all the wealth that accrued to him every year, without keeping any. ʿUthmān b. ʿAffān remarked on the large amount of wealth that was coming to the people in ample quantities. He said, "If they are not subjected to an official census so that you know who has received [wealth] and those who have not, I am afraid things will get out of hand." Al-Walīd b. Hishām b. al-Mughīrah[564] said to him, "O Commander of the Faithful, I have been to Syria and seen how the rulers there have instituted a state register and conscripted a regular army. So you do the same." (ʿUmar) took his advice and summoned ʿAqīl b. Abī Ṭālib,[565] Makhramah b. Nawfal,[566] and

560. For *dīwān*, see Puin, *Dīwān*, passim; *EI*², s.v. (Duri).
561. An unidentified narrator.
562. Abū al-Ḥuwayrith ʿAbd al-Raḥmān b. Muʿāwiyah died ca. 130/747. See Ibn Ḥajar, *Tahdhīb*, VI, 272–73.
563. Jubayr b. al-Ḥuwayrith b. Nuqayd has a brief notice in Ibn al-Athīr, *Usd*, I, 270.
564. He is unidentified.
565. ʿAqīl b. Abī Ṭālib was the brother of ʿAlī. See Ibn Ḥajar, *Tahdhīb*, VII, 254. For this account, see Yaʿqūbī, *Taʾrīkh*, II, 153.
566. Makhramah b. Nawfal b. Ahīb b. ʿAbd Manāf al-Zuhrī was the father of al-Miswar and the cousin of Saʿd b. Abī Waqqāṣ. He died in 54/674. See Ibn al-Athīr, *Usd*, IV, 337–38.

Jubayr b. Muṭʿim, genealogists of Quraysh, telling them to register people according to their ranks. So they made the registers, beginning with Banū Hāshim,[567] followed by Abū Bakr and his family, then ʿUmar and his family as the first two caliphs. When ʿUmar looked into (the matter), he said, "I would indeed like it to be thus, but begin with the relatives of the Messenger of God, the closest, then the next, until you register ʿUmar in the appropriate place."[568]

According to al-Ḥārith—Ibn Saʿd—Muḥammad b. ʿUmar—Usāmah b. Zayd b. Aslam—his father—his grandfather: I saw
[2751] ʿUmar b. al-Khaṭṭāb, when it was being proposed to him that he should register [the people], with Banū Taym[569] coming after Banū Hāshim and Banū ʿAdī[570] coming after Banū Taym, and I could hear him say, "Put ʿUmar down in the appropriate place. Begin with the closest related to the Messenger of God, then the next." Then Banū ʿAdī came to ʿUmar and said, "You are the caliph of the Messenger of God." He replied, "Or the caliph of Abū Bakr and Abū Bakr was the caliph of the Messenger of God." "This is so," they replied, "What if you placed yourself where these people [who are carrying out the registration] place you!" "Excellent, excellent, Banū ʿAdī," exclaimed (ʿUmar), "You want to take advantage of my position![571] You want me to transfer my good fortune to you. No, indeed, [you must wait] until the call comes to you, even if you come last in the register, even if you are registered after everyone else. I have two

567. That is, the Prophet's clan, a division of Quraysh.

568. ʿUmar is thus refusing to allow his position as caliph to promote his own name in the register and is insisting that relationship to the Prophet alone should be the criterion of order of listing.

569. Banū Taym b. Murrah, the branch of Quraysh to which Abū Bakr al-Ṣiddīq, the first caliph, belonged, hence its position in the register after Banū Hāshim, the Prophet's branch. See Zubayrī, *Nasab Quraysh*, 275ff.; Ibn Ḥazm, *Jamharah*, 135ff.; Kaḥḥālah, *Muʿjam*, I, 138.

570. Banū ʿAdī b. Kaʿb, the branch of Quraysh to which ʿUmar belonged, hence its position in the register after Banū Taym and Banū Hāshim, the branches of Abū Bakr and Muḥammad, respectively. See Zubayrī, *Nasab Quraysh*, 346ff.; Ibn Ḥazm, *Jamharah*, 150ff.; Kaḥḥālah, *Muʿjam*, II, 766.

571. ʿUmar's exclamation (*bakhin bakhin*) to his own tribe, Banū ʿAdī, is sarcastic. The Arabic then reads *aradtum al-akla ʿalā ẓahrī*; literally, "You want to eat off my back!".

colleagues who have gone down a [particular] road already.[572] If I am at variance with them, I myself will be led off in another direction. Indeed, we have achieved excellence only in this world, and we can only hope for God's reward in the hereafter for what we have done through Muḥammad. He is our nobility; his family are the noblest of the Arabs, then the closest related to him, then the next. The Arabs are noble through the Messenger of God. Some of them may share many ancestors with him. We ourselves meet his line of descent after [going back] only a few generations, then do not diverge from it as far back as Adam.[573] Moreover, if non-Arabs carry out [good] deeds and we do not, then they are nearer to Muḥammad than we on the Day of Resurrection. Let no one rely on close relationship, rather let him act for God's reward. For he whose effort falls short cannot get ahead by means of his ancestry."

According to al-Ḥārith—Ibn Sa'd—Muḥammad b. 'Umar—Ḥizām b. Hishām al-Ka'bī[574]—his father: I saw 'Umar b. al-Khaṭṭāb carry the Khuzā'ah[575] register and stop at Qudayd.[576] (Khuzā'ah) would come to him there, where all the women, virgin or otherwise, came to him and he would hand over stipends directly to them, then move on and stop in 'Usfān[577] where he would do the same also. [All this he did] until he died. [2752]

According to al-Ḥārith—Ibn Sa'd—Muḥammad b. 'Umar—'Abdallāh b. Ja'far al-Zuhrī and 'Abd al-Malik b. Sulaymān[578]—

572. That is, the Prophet and Abū Bakr before him, whose policies, he is explaining, he must at all costs follow.

573. Arabic, *wa-la'alla ba'ḍa-hā [al-'Arab] yalqā-hu ilā ābā'in kathīratin wa-mā bayna-nā wa-bayna an nalqā-hu ilā nasabi-hi thumma lā nufāriqu-hu ilā Ādama illā ābā'an yasīratan.*

574. Ḥizām b. Hishām al-Ka'bī is unidentified.

575. A large tribal group of al-Azd inhabiting the general area of Mecca. See Ibn Ḥazm, *Jamharah*, 331; Hamdānī, *Ṣifah*, 120, 179, 211; Kaḥḥālah, *Mu'jam*, I, 338–40.

576. An agricultural area north of Mecca, 23 miles from 'Usfān (see next note). See Hamdānī *Ṣifah*, 120, 185; *al-Manāsik*, 415, 457, etc.; Bilādī, *Mu'jam*, VII, 97.

577. An area of cultivation 36 miles from Mecca. See Hamdānī, *Ṣifah*, 185; Bilādī, *Mu'jam*, VI, 100.

578. An unidentified narrator.

Ismāʿīl b. Muḥammad b. Saʿd—al-Sāʾib b. Yazīd:[579] I heard ʿUmar say three times, "By God, there is no other god but He!" [He added], "Everyone has a right to some of this [community] wealth, whether he has been granted it or not. No one has more right to it than another, except a slave. I am exactly like other people in (this matter of wealth). But we [are eligible] according to our ranks [as derived] from God's book and our allotments from the Messenger of God. [It is] a man's achievement in Islam, his precedence in Islam, his usefulness in Islam, and his need [that count]. If indeed I remain alive, the shepherd where he is on the mountain of Ṣanʿāʾ shall certainly receive his share of this wealth!"[580]

Ismāʿīl b. Muḥammad said that he mentioned this to his father and he knew the account also.

According to al-Ḥārith—Ibn Saʿd—Muḥammad b. ʿUmar—Muḥammad b. ʿAbdallāh—al-Zuhrī—al-Sāʾib b. Yazīd: I discovered that ʿUmar b. al-Khaṭṭāb had some horses that had the following brand on their thighs: To be used only in God's
[2753] cause.

According to al-Ḥārith—Ibn Saʿd—Muḥammad b. ʿUmar—Qays b. al-Rabīʿ[581]—ʿAṭāʾ b. al-Sāʾib[582]—Zādhān[583]—Salmān:[584] ʿUmar said to him, "Am I a king or a caliph?" Salmān replied, "If you collect from Muslim territory 1 dirham—or less or more—then you put it to use other than for what it is by right intended, you are a king, not a caliph." ʿUmar wept.

According to al-Ḥārith—Ibn Saʿd—Muḥammad b. ʿUmar—

---

579. Al-Sāʾib b. Yazīd died in the 80s/ca. 700. See Ibn Ḥajar, *Tahdhīb*, III, 450–51. If this is a correct identification, he must have been very young when he heard ʿUmar's words.

580. Ṣanʿāʾ in the Yemen has in fact two mountains: Nuqum in the east and ʿAybān in the west. See Hamdānī, *Ṣifah*, 125. Here, however, ʿUmar means *anyone anywhere* will receive his fair share of community wealth.

581. Qays b. al-Rabīʿ died in the late 160s/early 780s. Ibn Ḥajar, *Tahdhīb*, VIII, 391–95.

582. ʿAṭāʾ b. al-Sāʾib died in the 130s/747–757. See Ibn Ḥajar, *Tahdhīb*, VII, 203–7.

583. Zādhān is Abū ʿAbdallāh/ʿUmar al-Kindī, who died in 82/701. See Ibn Ḥajar, *Tahdhīb*, III, 302–3.

584. Salmān al-Fārisī died in the 30s/650s. See Ibn Ḥajar, *Tahdhīb*, IV, 137–39.

Usāmah b. Zayd—Nāfiʿ, the client of Āl al-Zubayr:[585] I heard Abū Hurayrah say, "God have mercy on Ibn Ḥantamah.[586] I saw him in the Year of the Distruction[587] carrying on his back two provision bags with a skin of olive oil in his hand. He and Aslam were taking it in turns. When he saw me, he said, 'Where are you coming from, Abū Hurayrah?' I told him from near at hand, and I began to take my turn to carry. So we all eventually came to Ṣirār where there were about twenty isolated tents of Muḥārib.[588] 'Umar said, 'What has brought you here?' They replied it was exhaustion. They brought out for us some broiled carrion skin that they were eating and some powdered old bones that they were scooping into their mouths with their hands. I saw 'Umar throw his upper garment [over his shoulder], then adjust his waist wrapper. He continued cooking for them until they were satisfied. Then he sent Aslam to Medina and he brought some stallion camels on which he mounted them and set them down in al-Jabbānah.[589] He then gave them clothes, visiting them and others [in similar circumstances] frequently until God relieved the people of this drought."

According to al-Ḥārith—Ibn Saʿd—Muḥammad b. 'Umar— [2754]
Mūsā b. Yaʿqūb[590]—his paternal uncle—Hishām b. Khālid:[591] I heard 'Umar b. al-Khaṭṭāb say, "None of you (women) should sprinkle flour [into it] before the water is hot. Then you can sprinkle a little at a time and stir it in with a stirrer. This makes it more abundant and it is less apt to go lumpy."

According to al-Ḥārith—Ibn Saʿd—Muḥammad b. Muṣʿab al-

585. Āl al-Zubayr b. al-'Awāmm is a tribal group (*baṭn*) of Banū Asad b. 'Abd al-'Uzzā of Quraysh. See Zubayrī, *Nasab Quraysh*, 236ff.; Ibn Ḥazm, *Jamharah*, 121–22; Kaḥḥālah, *Mu'jam*, II, 467.

586. Ḥantamah was 'Umar's mother, so Ibn Ḥantamah means 'Umar himself. See page 95, above.

587. 'Ām al-Ramādah (the "Year of Destruction") occurred in the year 17 or 18/638–639, a year in which much destruction took place as a result of drought. See Lane, *Lexicon*, III, 1154–55; Ṭanṭāwī, *Akhbār*, 140.

588. Muḥārib is probably Muḥārib b. Fihr of 'Adnān, but Kaḥḥālah, *Mu'jam*, III, 1042–44, lists several tribes of this name.

589. I take this to be a place name here, as Bilādī (*Mu'jam*, II, 115) indicates that the area near the burial ground of Medina was known by this name. Apart from "burial ground", the word *jabbānah* also means "place of prayer."

590. Mūsā b. Yaʿqūb al-Zamʿī's death date is not recorded. See Ibn Ḥajar, *Tahdhīb*, X, 378ff.

591. An unidentified narrator.

Qarqasānī[592]—Abū Bakr b. ʿAbdallāh b. Abī Maryam[593]—Rāshid b. Saʿd:[594] ʿUmar b. al-Khaṭṭāb was brought some wealth and he began to distribute it among the people who all thronged around him. Saʿd b. Abī Waqqāṣ pushed his way roughly through the people and reached ʿUmar. (The latter) assailed him with his whip, saying, "You come here showing no respect for God's authority on earth! I want to teach you that God's authority will show you no respect!"

According to al-Ḥārith—Ibn Saʿd—Muḥammad b. ʿUmar—ʿUmar b. Sulaymān b. Abī Ḥathmah[595]—his father: al-Shafā bt. ʿAbdallāh[596] said, "I saw some young men walking along at a moderate pace, talking softly." She asked who they were and was told they were ascetics. She said, "When ʿUmar spoke, he made [people] hear; when he walked, he moved quickly; when he beat [someone], he brought pain. He in truth was the ascetic!"

[2755] According to ʿUmar—ʿAlī b. Muḥammad [al-Madāʾinī]—ʿAbdallāh b. ʿĀmir: ʿUmar helped a man carry something, so the man blessed him, saying, "May your sons be of benefit to you, Commander of the Faithful!" (ʿUmar) replied, "Rather may God enable me to do without them!"

According to ʿUmar—ʿAlī b. Muḥammad—ʿUmar b. Mujāshiʿ:[597] ʿUmar b. al-Khaṭṭāb said, "Strength in what one does [comes only] when you do not put off today's deed until tomorrow. Trustworthiness [comes only] when what is kept secret does not run counter to what is made public. Fear God; piety [comes only] through fear; anyone fearing God will be preserved by Him."[598]

---

592. Muḥammad b. Muṣʿab al-Qarqasānī's *nisbah* I vocalize from the Leiden text and from Yāqūt (*Muʿjam*, IV, 327), who briefly mentions a place called Qarqasān. His date of death is given in Ibn Ḥajar's *Tahdhīb*, IX, 458–60, as 280 or 288/893 or 901. Cf. Translation, I, 267 n. 633.

593. According to Ibn Ḥajar's *Tahdhīb*, XII, 28–30, Abū Bakr b. ʿAbdallāh died in 256/870, but this does not find universal support. Cf. Translation, I, 217 n. 350.

594. It is not possible to identify this narrator with certainty.

595. An unidentified narrator.

596. An unidentified narrator.

597. An unidentified narrator.

598. Arabic, *man yattaqi Allāha yaqi-hi*.

According to ʿUmar—ʿAlī—ʿAwānah[599]—al-Shaʿbī and someone other than ʿAwānah, one adding to what the other had to say: ʿUmar used to wander around the markets, reciting the Qurʾān and making judgments among the people wherever litigants caught up with him.

According to ʿUmar—ʿAlī—Muḥammad b. Ṣāliḥ[600]—Mūsā b. ʿUqbah:[601] A group of people came to ʿUmar and said, "Our family is large and the burden is heavy. Increase our stipends." He replied, "You are responsible (for your own problems)! From God's wealth you have married fellow wives and have taken servants. Yes indeed, I would like to be on a ship[602] with you [2756]
out at sea, traveling east and west. It would not then be difficult for those (on board) to appoint one of them as their leader. If he went straight, they would follow him. If he deviated from the right course, they would kill him." Ṭalḥah said, "Why did you not say, 'If he deviated, they would dismiss him.'?" (ʿUmar) replied, "No, killing is a better deterrent to anyone coming after him. Beware of the young man of Quraysh and the son of their nobleman[603] who always sleeps content and who laughs when angry, dealing with those above him and those below him [in the same way]."

According to ʿUmar—ʿAlī—ʿAbdallāh b. Dāwūd al-Wāsiṭī[604]—Zayd b. Aslam: ʿUmar said, "We used to reckon that someone lending [money] was stingy, but it was only showing friendly concern."[605]

---

599. ʿAwānah b. al-Ḥakam al-Kalbī died ca. 150/767. See Rosenthal, *Historiography*, 89ff.

600. Muḥammad b. Ṣāliḥ b. Dīnār died in 168/785. See Ibn Ḥajar, *Tahdhīb*; IX, 225ff.

601. Mūsā b. ʿUqbah, the famous *maghāzī* writer, died in 141/759. See Duri, *Rise*, 32–33; Guillaume, *Life*, xvi, xliii etc.; Rosenthal, *Historiography*, 131ff., 393ff.

602. Although there seems to be no convincing support for the Cairo reading *fī safīnatin* (singular) rather than the Leiden *fī safīnatayn* (dual), I accept the former as it clearly makes more sense and the following verb *tadhhabu* is singular.

603. The reference here eludes me.

604. He has a short notice in Ibn Ḥajar, *Tahdhīb*, V, 200–1, although no date of death is given.

605. Or "[a means of] sharing [wealth]."

According to ʿUmar—ʿAlī—Ibn Daʾb[606]—Abū Maʿbad al-Aslamī[607]—Ibn ʿAbbās:[608] ʿUmar said to a group of Quraysh, "I have heard that you are all sitting apart, no two of you sitting together, until it is asked who so-and-so's friends are, who are the people who usually sit with so-and-so. The result is that meetings are being avoided. I swear by God that this will quickly damage your faith and your honor and will quickly damage also the state of friendship among you. It is indeed as if I can see those who will come after you saying, 'This is so-and-so's opinion; they have divided Islam.' Make your meetings accessible to you all and sit together, for this will make your fellowship last longer and increase your respect for one another. O God, they have had enough of me and I of them. I am fed up with myself and they are fed up with me also. I do not know through which one of us the [real] calamity will come about. But I am aware that they have others on their side, so take me unto Yourself!"

According to ʿUmar—ʿAlī—Ibrāhīm b. Muḥammad[609]—his father: ʿAbdallāh b. Abī Rabīʿah[610] took delivery of some mares
[2757] in Medina, but ʿUmar forbade him [to keep them]. He was urged to allow him, [but] he said, "I shall only allow him [to keep them] if he brings in fodder from outside Medina." So he kept them tethered and brought in fodder from some land he had in the Yemen.[611]

According to ʿUmar—ʿAlī—Abū Ismāʿīl al-Hamdānī[612]—Mujālid: I heard that some people mentioned a certain man to ʿUmar b. al-Khaṭṭāb, saying, "Commander of the Faithful, [he is]

606. An unidentified narrator.

607. Abū Maʿbad Nāfidh al-Aslamī was Ibn ʿAbbās's client; he died in Medina in 104/722. See Ibn Ḥajar, *Tahdhīb*, X, 404.

608. ʿAbdallāh b. ʿAbbās b. ʿAbd al-Muṭṭalib, the cousin of the Prophet and ʿAlī b. Abī Ṭālib, died ca. 70/689. See *EI*[2] s.v. (Veccia Vaglieri).

609. An unidentified narrator.

610. He was governor of the Yemen. See Ibn Ḥajar, *Tahdhīb*, V, 208.

611. It seems unlikely that ʿAbdallāh would go all the way to the Yemen to provide fodder, and it should be noted, the word *yaman* is used all over the Arabian Peninsula to indicate the south, whether near or far, just as *al-shām* indicates the north. This may, therefore, mean "in the south [of Medina]."

612. An unidentified narrator.

excellent; he knows nothing of evil." ('Umar) replied, "In this case there is more likelihood of evil happening to him!"[613]

Some Excerpts from His Addresses

According to 'Umar—'Alī—Abū Ma'shar—Ibn al-Munkadir[614] and others, and Abū Mu'ādh al-Anṣārī[615]—al-Zuhrī, and Yazīd b. 'Iyāḍ[616]—'Abdallāh b. Abī Bakr,[617] and 'Alī b. Mujāhid—Ibn Isḥāq—Yazīd b. 'Iyāḍ[618]—'Abdallāh b. Abī Isḥāq[619]—Yazīd b. Rūmān[620]—'Urwah b. al-Zubayr:[621] 'Umar delivered an address. He praised and extolled God in a worthy manner. Then he reminded the people of God and the last day. He then said,

> O people, I have been appointed over you; were it not for the hope that I shall prove to be the best of you for you, the toughest on you, and best able of you to undertake your constantly changing and preoccupying affairs, I would not have undertaken this [responsibility] from you. Waiting to meet the [day of] reckoning for taking your rights as I do and placing them where I do and for conducting myself among you as I do is enough to preoccupy and sadden 'Umar. My Lord is the One whose help must be sought. For 'Umar no longer trusts in [2758]
> strength and strategem if God does not continue to extend to him His mercy, help and support.

---

613. The text of De Goeje's *Selection* ends at this point. See note 394.

614. Muḥammad b. al-Munkadir died ca. 130/748. See Ibn Ḥajar, *Tahdhīb*, IX, 473–75; Sezgin, *GAS*, I, 65.

615. His date of death is not given in the biographies. He has an entry in Ibn Ḥajar, *Tahdhīb*, IV, 168–69.

616. Yazīd b. 'Iyāḍ b. Ju'dubah died in al-Baṣrah during the caliphate of the Abbasid al-Mahdī (158–169/775–785). See Ibn Ḥajar, *Tahdhīb*, XI, 352–54.

617. 'Abdallāh b. Abī Bakr b Muḥammad b. 'Amr b. Ḥazm al-Anṣārī died ca. 135/752. See Ibn Ḥajar, *Tahdhīb*, V, 164–65.

618. I have retained this name in translation, although there appears to be dittography here.

619. 'Abdallāh b. Abī Isḥāq died in 129/746. See Ibn Ḥajar, *Tahdhīb*, V, 148. This could, however, be dittography, the "'Abdallāh b." from 'Abdallāh b. Abī Bakr and the "Isḥāq" from Ibn Isḥāq.

620. Yazīd b. Rūmān al-Asadī died in 130/747. See Ibn Ḥajar, *Tahdhīb*, XI, 325.

621. 'Urwah b. al-Zubayr, the famous early historian, died ca. 95/714. See Duri, *Rise*, 76–8 and passim; Rosenthal, *Historiography*, 130ff., 395; Sezgin *GAS*, I, 278ff.

Another Address

God has put me in charge of your affairs, because I am aware of what is most advantageous for you in your present situation. I ask God to assist me to carry out (this task) and to preserve me as I do it as He has preserved me in other (tasks) and to inspire me with justice when I make distributions among you in the way He has commanded. I am a Muslim, but am a weak servant, except for as long as God assists me. What I have undertaken in my position as your caliph will never change anything of my nature, God willing. Greatness belongs to God, not to (His) servants. Let none of you say that ʿUmar has changed for the worse since he took office. I shall ascertain what is right by myself and I shall proceed [on this basis]. I shall explain to you what I am doing. So any man who has a need, or who suffers any oppression, or who blames us for our behavior, should inform me. I am only a man from among you. You must show piety toward God in your secret and open dealings, and as far as what is inviolable and your honor are concerned. Proclaim what is right on your own and do not compel one another to seek litigation before me, for I show no particular leniency in my dealings with any person. Your welfare is dear to me; your criticism is of concern to me; you are people the general mass of whom are settled dwellers in God's land and people of a region without crops and livestock except for what God provides. God has promised you much bounty. I am responsible for the trust placed in me and for the position I am in. I shall personally inspect closely what faces me at the present time, God willing. I shall not
[2759] delegate responsibility to anyone else. I can do only what is remote from (what immediately faces me at the present time) with the help of trusty supporters and those who give good advice from among you to the people at large. I shall not place my trust in anyone else's hands, God willing.

Another Address

After praising and extolling God and blessing the Prophet, (ʿUmar) said,

> O people, some greed [breeds a sense of] poverty; some despair [of not getting what one wants breeds a sense of] freedom from want. You bring together what you do not consume and you hope for what you do not attain. You have been placed for a defined period of time in a "deceiving abode."[622] You were dealt with through the revelation in the time of the Messenger of God: those who kept things secret were dealt with according to their secrecy. Those who did things openly were dealt with according to their openness. But [now] show us the best of your character, while God knows your secrets well. For those who show us what is bad,[623] yet claim that what they keep secret is good, will not be believed by us; as for those who show us something good openly, we shall think good of them. You should know that some avarice is a part of hypocrisy. "Spend what is good for yourselves; those who are saved from their own avarice, they are the successful ones."[624]
>
> O people, make good your abode, put your affairs aright, and fear God, your Lord. Do not dress your womenfolk in fine cotton clothes (*qabāṭī*), for [even] if they are not transparent, yet they will allow [the shape of their bodies] to be visualized.
>
> O people, I would indeed like to be delivered on a completely even basis, neither to my advantage nor to my disadvantage. I do also hope that, however long I am permitted to live, I do what is right among you, God willing, and that no Muslim will remain—even if he is in his own home—to whom his right and his share of [2760]
> God's wealth has not come, nor [that] he exerts himself

---

622. That is, the lower world. See Qur'ān, III:185.
623. The texts read *shay'an,* which is emended to *sayyi'an.*
624. Qur'ān, LXIV:16.

for it without his having it allotted to him. Put your wealth that God has provided for you in good order. A little [gained] gently is better than much violently. Being killed is one form of death that afflicts the pious and the impious alike. The [true] martyr is he who sacrifices himself [to seek God's reward]. If one of you wants a stallion camel, he should go for a large, tall one. He should strike it with his stick and if he finds it is spirited, he should buy it.[625]

Another Address

God has imposed upon you gratitude and instituted the pilgrimage for you as part of the bounty of the hereafter and this world that He has provided for you, without your asking Him or wishing it from Him. He created you, after you were nothing, for Himself and for you to worship Him. He had the power to make you subservient to the weakest of His creation, but rather He made subservient to you the general mass of His creation. He did not make you subservient to anything other than He. And He "subjected to you what is in the heavens and on earth and made His favors abound upon you, both open and hidden."[626] "He carried you by land and sea."[627] "And He gave you of good things, perchance you might be grateful."[628] Then He made for you hearing and sight. Of God's favors to you are those that He granted to mankind in general and others that He granted exclusively to the people of your faith. These general and special favors are continued during your turn of fortune, your time, and your generation. None of these favors has come to anyone in particular without, if he were to share out what he received among all the people, their

625. The abrupt change of subject may indicate that the camel here is metaphorical, rather than real. The meaning would therefore be: if you want something in life, go for the best and do all you can to acquire it.

626. Qur'ān, XXXI:20.

627. After Qur'ān, XVII:70.

628. Qur'ān, VIII:26.

gratitude for it being difficult for them and their right to have it overburdening them, except with God's help along with faith in God and His Messenger. You are appointed successors on earth and conquerors of its people. God has given your faith victory. No other community who differs from you in faith is left except two: one rendered submissive to Islam and to those who follow it, they paying you tribute, while (the Muslims) take the best of their livelihood, what they have earned and [produced with] the sweat of their brow; they must work hard, while you have the benefit;[629] and a [second] community waiting for God's battles and attacks every day and night. God has filled their hearts with terror. They have no refuge to which they can flee or an escape by means of which they can guard against attack.[630] God's armies came upon them suddenly and right into their own territory. [All this you have been granted] along with an abundance of food, a pouring out of wealth, the repeated dispatch of [victorious] troops and the [successful] defense of the frontier areas with God's permission, together excellent general security better than which this community had not experienced since Islam came into existence—God be praised!—along with the great conquests in every land. With all this, what might the gratitude of the grateful, the utterances of those who mention [God] and the striving of those who strive, along with these favors that are innumerable, incalculable and the debt that cannot be paid except with God's help, mercy, and kindness, achieve? We ask God—there is no other than He—who has conferred this upon us to grant us that we act in obedience to Him and hasten to do what pleases Him. [2761]

Remember, o servants of God, God's favor among you and seek to have an increase in His favor to you and in

629. That is, the Persians in the east, most of whom have been subjugated by the Muslims.

630. That is, the Byzantines in the west, so far subjugated only in Syria.

your meeting places "in twos and singly."[631] God said to Moses, "Bring out your people from the darkness into the light and remind them of God's days."[632] To Muḥammad he said, "Remember when you were few
[2762] and considered weak in the land."[633] Even if, when you were weak and deprived of the goodness of this lower world, you had been following a part of the truth, believing in it, secure in it with knowledge of God and His faith, and thereby hoping for goodness after death, this would be so. But [in fact] you struggled the most for a livelihood [in this world] and were [at the same time] the most confirmed in your ignorance of God. If (Islam) that He [sent] to save you had come without affluence in this world, but were nonetheless a security for you in the hereafter to which you will return, while you continued to struggle for your livelihood as you had before, you would still do your best to hold fast to your share of Islam and put it above others. [All the more is this true], as He has [in fact] combined for you the excellence of the lower world and the bounty of the hereafter. He [then] among you who wishes to combine it for him, I would remind of God who intervenes between [a man and his] heart, charging you to recognize God's right and act accordingly, to force yourselves to obey Him and to combine your pleasure in His favors with a fear of them and their being removed and a feeling of unease because of them and their being changed. For there is nothing that deprives you more of favor than not being grateful for it. Gratitude is a safeguard against [what] the changing fortunes of time [will bring about], a way of increasing favor and establishing a claim to more. [All] this is for God binding upon me in the orders I give you and in the prohibitions I make.

631. Qur'ān, XXXIV:46.
632. Qur'ān, XIV:5.
633. Qur'ān, VIII:26.

Those Who Have Lamented and Elegized 'Umar—Some of the Elegies Written about Him

According to 'Umar—'Alī—Abū 'Abdallāh al-Burjumī[634]—Hishām b. 'Urwah:[635] A woman weeping for 'Umar said, "Alas, my heart burns for 'Umar; a burning sensation that has spread and filled all mankind!" Another woman said, "Alas, my heart burns for 'Umar; a burning sensation that has spread until it has [2763] become known throughout the whole of mankind!"

According to 'Umar—'Alī—Ibn Da'b and Sa'īd b. Khālid[636]—Ṣāliḥ b. Kaysān—al-Mughīrah b. Shu'bah: When 'Umar died, Ibnat Abī Ḥathmah[637] said, "Alas for 'Umar; he straightened whatever was crooked; he made better anyone suffering pain; he put an end to dissensions; he revived the [true] practices [of religion]; he went out in clean clothes, free from blemish."[638]

According to al-Mughīrah b. Shu'bah: When 'Umar was buried, I came to 'Alī, wanting to hear something about 'Umar from him. He came out shaking his head and his beard, having washed himself and wrapped himself in a garment and not doubting that the caliphate would finally be his. He said, "God have mercy on Ibn al-Khaṭṭāb! Ibnat Abī Ḥathmah was right. [In death,] he has taken away the good of (the lower world)[639] and escaped from its evil. Oh indeed, she did not [herself] speak; but rather she was inspired."

'Ātikah bt. Zayd b. 'Amr recited the following about 'Umar b. al-Khaṭṭāb:[640]

---

634. An unidentified narrator.

635. Hishām b. 'Urwah b. al-Zubayr died in 146/763. See Ibn Ḥajar, *Tahdhīb*, XI, 48–51.

636. It is not possible to identify this narrator with certainty.

637. She is unidentified.

638. The speaker delivers her elegy in rhymed prose: *al-awad* (crooked)/*al-'amad* (suffering pain); *al-fitan* (dissensions)/*al-sunan* (religious practices); *al-thawb* (clothing)/*al-'ayb* (blemish).

639. I take this vague feminine pronoun to refer to *dunyā*.

640. The meter is *ṭawīl*. See Ibn al-Athīr, *Kāmil*, III, 30. The poetess 'Ātikah bt. Zayd b. 'Amr had, according to Iṣfahānī, *Aghānī*, XVI, 133ff., some famous husbands in her time on whose deaths she composed elegies: Zubayr b. al-'Awwām, 'Abdallāh b. Abī Bakr, 'Umar himself, and Ḥusayn b. 'Alī. See page 101, above.

Fayrūz[641]—may his wealth not be abundant!—has caused me distress
by [the death of] one full of honor,[642] who recited the Book and was obedient to God;
Compassionate to those closest [to him], tough against his enemies,
someone to trust in times of bad fortune and answering [the demands of his people].
Whenever he gave his word, his deeds did not belie his word;
[he was] swift to [perform] good deeds, and not with a frown.

[2764] She also recited as follows:[643]

O my eye, shed all your tears copiously
and weary not of [weeping] for the noble imam.
Fate brought me distress with [the death of] the horseman wearing the badge of courage
on the day when there was agitation and [much] to-ing and fro-ing.
[He was] the protection of his people, their helper against Fate,
the succor of the afflicted and the deprived.
Tell those who are happy and those in distress, "Die!
Fate has given ('Umar) Death's cup from which to drink."

Another woman recited the following, weeping over him:[644]

The women of the tribe will weep for you;
grieving, they will weep,
Scratching their faces, [previously] like
[shining] dinars, [all] pure,
And wearing clothes of grief
after their finery (*qaṣabiyyāt*).

641. That is, Abū Lu'lu'ah, the assassin of 'Umar; see note 399.
642. That is, 'Umar himself.
643. The meter is *khafīf*. See Ibn al-Athīr, *Kāmil*, III, 30.
644. The meter is *hazaj*.

Some of ʿUmar's Meritorious Deeds Not Previously Recorded

According to ʿUmar b. Shabbah—ʿAlī b. Muḥammad [al-Madā-ʾinī]—Ibn Juʿdubah[645]—Ismāʿīl b. Abī Ḥakīm[646]—Saʿīd b. al-Musayyab:[647] ʿUmar went on the pilgrimage and when he was at Ḍajnān,[648] he said, "There is no god but God, the Great, the Sublime, the Giver of what He wishes to whomsoever He wishes. I used to pasture the camels of al-Khaṭṭāb in this wadi, wearing a woolen tunic. (My father) was a harsh man and used to wear me out when I was working and beat me when I slacked off. Now I find myself in a situation in which there is no one between me and God." Then he quoted the following verses as an example [of his own situation]:[649]

There is nothing of what you see whose joy lasts; [2765]
God endures, whereas wealth and children perish.
His treasures have never been of any avail to any Persian ruler,
and ʿĀd[650] have tried to achieve eternal life, but they were not eternal.
There is no Solomon, despite the fact that the winds swept for him,[651]
while men and jinn mixed together hastened [to his command].
Where are the rulers to whose gifts
riders came from all directions?
At the inevitable pool of death there
[we] must drink one day, as [others already] have.

---

645. Ibn Juʿdubah is Yazīd b. ʿIyāḍ. See note 616, above.

646. Ismāʿīl b. Abī Ḥakīm al-Qurashī died in 130/747. See Ibn Ḥajar, *Tahdhīb*, I, 289.

647. Saʿīd b. al-Musayyab died ca. 94/713. See Ibn Ḥajar, *Tahdhīb*, IV, 84–88; Sezgin, *GAS*, I, 276.

648. A small mountain 25 miles north of Mecca on the Medina road. See Bilādī, *Muʿjam*, V, 189–91.

649. The meter is *basīṭ*. See Ibn al-Athīr, *Kāmil*, III, 30.

650. One of the pre-Islamic tribes mentioned in the Qurʾān who refused to accept the message to abandon their gods and worship God. See Qurʾān, XXVI:129, where they are accused by their messenger, Hūd, of "taking to yourselves strongholds, perchance you might live forever."

651. In the Qurʾān (XXXIV:12) Solomon is given the wind by God, and (XXXVIII:36) God made the wind subservient to him.

According to ʿUmar b. Shabbah—ʿAlī—Abū al-Walīd al-Makkī:[652] While ʿUmar was sitting down a lame man came up to him leading a limping she-camel. He stopped and recited the following:[653]

You have been made our ruler whereas we are the subjects;
you, ʿUmar, are summoned by virtue of your mark of distinction.
When the evil of an evil day falls on its evil men,
[then, by contrast] Muḍar[654] has today placed upon you [the glory] of their noble deeds.

(ʿUmar) exclaimed, "There is no might and power except in God!"[655] The man complained that his she-camel was lame. So
[2766] ʿUmar took the she-camel, gave him a red camel as a fresh mount and provisioned him, and he went on his way. ʿUmar left later on pilgrimage, and while he was traveling along, he came across a rider who was reciting the following:[656]

No one has ruled over us like you, Ibn al-Khaṭṭāb,
[no one] more beneficent to those distant [from you], nor to his friends,
after the Prophet, him of the Book.

So ʿUmar prodded him with a stick he was carrying and said, "What about Abū Bakr?"

According to ʿUmar—ʿAlī b. Muḥammad—Muḥammad b. Ṣāliḥ—ʿAbd al-Malik b. Nawfal b. Musāḥiq:[657] ʿUmar appointed ʿUtbah b. Abī Sufyān[658] as governor of Kinānah.[659] He

---

652. Abū al-Walīd al-Makkī is Yasār b. ʿAbd al-Raḥmān. See Ibn Ḥajar, *Tahdhīb*, XII, 274.

653. The meter is *ṭawīl*.

654. Muḍar is a huge tribal conferation amounting to a very large proportion of all the northern Arab tribes known collectively as ʿAdnān. See Kaḥḥālah, *Muʿjam*, III, 1107.

655. ʿUmar is apologizing for not having done his duty.

656. The meter is *rajaz*.

657. ʿAbd al-Malik b. Nawfal b. Musāḥiq has a brief notice without date of death in Ibn Ḥajar, *Tahdhīb*, VI, 428.

658. ʿUtbah b. Abī Sufyān b. Ḥarb was the brother of Muʿāwiyah.

659. This is in all probability the large tribal group in the Mecca area, Kinānah b. Khuzaymah. See Ibn Ḥazm, *Jamharah*, 11ff., 180; Zubayrī, *Nasab Quraysh*, 10ff.; Kaḥḥālah, *Muʿjam*, III, 996–98.

arrived back, bringing some wealth with him. ('Umar) asked him what it was. He said it was wealth he had taken with him and with which he had engaged in business. ('Umar) said, "What are you doing taking wealth with you in this way?" ('Umar) put it in the treasury. Now when 'Uthmān became caliph, he said to Abū Sufyān,[660] "If you demand what 'Umar took from 'Utbah, I shall return it to him." Abū Sufyān replied, "If you contradict your predecessor, the people will think badly of you. Beware of going against your predecessor, lest your successor go against you!"

According to al-Sarī—Shu'ayb—Sayf—al-Rabī' b. al-Nu'mān,[661] Abū al-Mujālid Jarād b. 'Amr,[662] Abū 'Uthmān, Abū Ḥārithah,[663] and Abū 'Amr,[664] the client of Ibrāhīm b. Ṭalḥah[665]—Zayd b. Aslam—his father: Hind bt. 'Utbah[666] paid her respects to 'Umar b. al-Khaṭṭāb and asked him for a loan from the treasury of 4,000 [dirhams] with which to engage in business, and at the same time making herself responsible for (the sum). ('Umar) lent her the money and she took it off to the territory of Kalb,[667] where she bought and sold. She heard that Abū Sufyān and 'Amr b. Abī Sufyān[668] had gone to Mu'āwiyah, so she left [2767]
Kalb territory and came to see Mu'āwiyah. (This was when Abū Sufyān had already divorced her.) "What brings you here, mother?" Mu'āwiyah asked. She replied, "To see you, my son. [You know that] 'Umar works only [to please] God. Your father, [I note], has already been to you, and I was afraid that you will give him all sorts of things, as he is worthy of this. But people

660. Abū Sufyān b. Ḥarb was the father of 'Utbah.

661. Al-Rabī' b. al-Nu'mān has a brief entry in Ibn al-Athīr, *Usd*, II, 165.

662. An unidentified narrator.

663. An unidentified narrator.

664. An unidentified narrator.

665. An unidentified narrator.

666. Hind bt. 'Utbah, wife of Abū Sufyān, mother of Mu'āwiyah and 'Amr (see note 668, below).

667. There are several tribes of this name, but one can perhaps assume Kalb b. Wabarah is meant here, a tribal group (*baṭn*) of Quḍā'ah, by origin a southern, Qaḥṭānī tribe. If this is the case, Hind would have been conducting her business in the northern Ḥijāz and the Jawf area in the north of the Peninsula. Ibn Ḥazm, *Jamharah*, 455ff.; Kaḥḥālah, *Mu'jam*, III, 990–92; *EI*[2], s.v. "Kalb" (Fück/Dixon).

668. 'Amr b. Abī Sufyān, brother of Mu'āwiyah and son of Hind.

will not know the source of the wherewithall you had to make the gift, so they will blame you severely, and ʿUmar will too and so will never absolve her of the (money) owed [to the treasury]." So (Muʿāwiyah) sent [only] a hundred dinars [from Hind's money] to his father and brother [ʿAmr], clothed them, and gave them mounts. But ʿAmr considered this too much and Abū Sufyān said, "Do not think [it is too much], for Hind has been involved in this gift and was present at a discussion [about it]." So they all returned and Abū Sufyān said to Hind, "Did you make any profit?" "God knows best!" she replied, "I [still] have some business in Medina." When she reached Medina and sold [her goods], she complained about what had been paid out to them. ʿUmar said to her, "If the money [you owe] were mine, I would leave it to you. But it is the Muslims' money and this is a discussion in which Abū Sufyān has been involved." So (ʿUmar) sent for (Abū Sufyān) and detained him until she paid (the money) in full. (ʿUmar) asked (Abū Sufyān), "How much did Muʿāwiyah give you?" He replied, "A hundred dinars."

According to ʿUmar—ʿAlī—Maslamah b. Muḥārib[669]—Khālid al-Ḥadhdhāʾ[670]—ʿAbdallāh b. Abī Ṣaʿṣaʿah[671]—al-Aḥnaf: ʿAbdallāh b. ʿUmayr[672] came to ʿUmar as he was assigning state stipends to the people. Now (ʿAbdallāh's) father was killed a martyr at the battle of Ḥunayn,[673] so he said, "O Commander of the Faithful, give me a stipend." But (ʿUmar) paid no attention to him. So he gave (ʿUmar) a prod. ʿUmar cried, "Ouch!"
[2768] and then turned to him and said, "Who are you?" He told him he was ʿAbdallāh b. ʿUmayr, so (ʿUmar) said [to his servant], "Yarfaʾ, give him 600." He gave him 500, but (ʿAbdallāh) did not accept it and said, "The Commander of the Faithful has given orders that I receive 600." And he went back and told (ʿUmar). He said, "Give him 600 and a complete garment,

669. An unidentified narrator.

670. An unidentified narrator.

671. ʿAbdallāh b. Abī Ṣaʿṣaʿah has a brief entry in Ibn Ḥajar, *Tahdhīb*, V, 265.

672. It is not possible to identify this man with certainty.

673. This battle took place in 8/629 and the Prophet and his Muslim forces defeated a Meccan army. Ḥunayn is a wadi only about 10 miles from Mecca itself. See Ṭabarī, I, 1654ff.; Ibn Hishām, *Sīrah*, II, pp. 442ff.; Guillaume, *Life*, 566ff. For the lcoation of the wadi, see Bilādī, *Muʿjam*, III, 70–73.

Yarfa'." So the latter did. ('Abdallāh) put the garment on and threw away what he had been wearing. But 'Umar said to him, "My son, take these clothes of yours for serving your family and [keep] this one to make you look smart!"

According to 'Umar—'Alī—Abū al-Walīd al-Makkī—one of the sons of Ṭalḥah—Ibn 'Abbās: I went with 'Umar on one of his journeys. We were traveling one night, and I came near to him as he struck the front of his saddle with his whip and recited the following:[674]

You have lied, by the house of God! Will Ahmad be killed[675]
 when we have not yet come to his defense with spears and arrows?
Shall we surrender him before we are slain around him
 and neglect our sons and spouses?

Then he said, "I ask God for forgiveness [for implying ill of the Prophet's house]!" He went on without speaking for a little while, then he recited as follows:[676]

No she-camel has borne on her saddle
 one more pious and more faithful when he makes a covenant than Muḥammad;
One more generous to give away a red and black striped garment before it is worn out
 and who gives away more thoroughbred horses.

Then he said, "I ask God for forgiveness, Ibn 'Abbās! What prevented 'Alī from coming with us?" I replied, "I do not know." He continued, "Ibn 'Abbās, your father is the paternal uncle of the Messenger of God. You are his cousin. What has kept your people from [putting] you [in authority]?" I replied that I did not know. He continued, "But I do know; they do not [2769]

674. The poem was composed by Abū Ṭālib after the battle of Badr. See Ibn Hishām, *Sīrah*, II, 24. The meter is *ṭawīl*.

675. The poem was uttered by the dying 'Ubaydah b. al-Ḥārith after the battle of Badr, in fact quoting Abū Ṭālib's composition. The *Sīrah* version (Ibn Hishām, II, 24) reads *yubzā Muḥammadun*, that is, "will Muhammad be maltreated," rather than the Ṭabarī text *yuqtalu Aḥmadu*. The "Aḥmad" of the text means "Muḥammad." See also Wāqidī, *Maghāzī*, I, 70.

676. By Anas b. Zunaym al-Dīlī; see Guillaume, *Life*, 559. The meter is *ṭawīl*.

like your being put in charge of them." I said, "Why, when we are good to them?" ('Umar) replied, "O God, [grant] forgiveness. They do not like you to combine the prophethood and the caliphate among yourselves, lest it bring about self-aggrandizement and pride. You will perhaps say, 'Abū Bakr did this.' No indeed, but Abū Bakr did the most resolute thing he could. If he had made (the caliphate) yours, he would not have benefited you despite your close ties of relationship [to the Prophet]. Recite to me what the poet of poets, Zuhayr, composed:[677]

When Qays b. 'Aylān[678] hasten to a glorious goal,
the one who reaches it first is made chief."

So I recited it to him as dawn broke. ('Umar) said, "Recite 'The Event'."[679] So I recited it. Then he dismounted and said his prayers, reciting "The Event" [in them].

According to Ibn Ḥumayd—Salamah—Muḥammad b. Isḥāq—a source—'Ikrimah[680]—Ibn 'Abbās: As 'Umar b. al-Khaṭṭāb and some of his friends were reciting poetry together, one said that so and so was the best poet. Another said that, rather, so and so was the best poet. (Ibn 'Abbās) continued: I arrived and 'Umar remarked, "The most knowledgeable on the subject has just arrived." And he asked, "Who is the best poet, Ibn 'Abbās?" I replied it was Zuhayr b. Abī Sulmā. 'Umar asked me to provide some of his poetry that would prove what I had said. I said, "He eulogized a group of Banū 'Abdallāh b. Ghaṭafān as follows:[681]

---

677. The meter is *ṭawīl*. The poet is Zuhayr b. Abī Sulmā, one of the greatest of the pre-Islamic poets. See Tha'lab, *Sharḥ*, 234; Iṣfahānī, *Aghānī*, IX, 146ff. The poem in question is quoted on 147.

678. A large tribal confederation of 'Adnān. The name Qays is synonymous with the northern tribes, 'Adnān. See Ibn Ḥazm, *Jamharah*, 468ff., 480ff.; Kaḥḥālah, *Mu'jam*, III, 972–93; *EI*², s.v. (Watt).

679. Sūrat al-Wāqi'ah, Qur'ān, LVI, the "Event" being the day of Judgment. This is perhaps a more specific reference to "those coming first" (*al-sābiqūna*) in verse 10.

680. A client of Ibn 'Abbās and famous narrator; he died ca. 107/725. See Ibn Ḥajar, *Tahdhīb*, VII, 263–73.

681. A tribal group (*baṭn*) of Sa'd b. Qays b. 'Aylān of 'Adnān, of whom Zuhayr was a member (Shantamarī, *Dīwān*, 150). Cf. Ibn Ḥazm, *Jamharah*, 248–49; Kaḥḥālah, *Mu'jam*, II, 732–33. For the poem itself, see Ibn al-Athīr, *Kāmil*, III, 31. It does not figure in Zuhayr's *Dīwān*. The meter is *basīṭ*.

If there were sitting above the sun [in a position] of nobility
a people by means of their ancestry or their glory, (Banū 'Abdallāh b. Ghaṭafān) would be they.
[They are] a people whose ancestor is a spearhead; when you examine their pedigree, [2770]
they have an excellent one, as do all their offspring.
[They are] men when they feel safe, jinn when they are afraid,
warriors ready to sacrifice themselves when they come together,
Envied for what good things they have;
may God not remove from them the thing for which they are envied."

"Bravo!" exclaimed 'Umar, "I do not know of anyone more worthy of such poetry than this branch of Banū Hāshim[682] because of the excellence of the Messenger of God and their close relationship to him." I said, "May you be granted lasting success, Commander of the Faithful." ('Umar) said, "Do you know, Ibn 'Abbās, what kept your people from [being put] over (Quraysh) after Muḥammad's death?" I did not want to answer, so I said, "If I do not know, then the Commander of the Faithful will tell me." 'Umar said, "They were unwilling for you to combine the prophethood and the caliphate, lest you magnify yourselves above your own people and be proud. Quraysh made the choice for themselves; they were right and have been granted success." I said, "Commander of the Faithful, if you will permit me and not get angry with me, I shall speak." He allowed me to do so, so I said, "As for your saying, Commander of the Faithful, that Quraysh have made their choice for themselves and that they were right and have been granted success, if Quraysh had made the same choice for themselves as God did for them, then right would be theirs, unrejected and unenvied. As for your saying that (Quraysh) were averse to the prophethood and the caliphate being ours, God has described one people as being averse and said, 'This is because they were averse to what God revealed, so He made their works fruitless.'"[683]

682. That is, Banū al-'Abbās.
683. Qur'ān, XLVII: 9. The Qur'ān is clearly referring to unbelievers.

[2771] 'Umar said, "Far from it indeed,[684] Ibn 'Abbās. I used to hear things about you of which I was reluctant to inquire, lest they bring about your removal from your position with me." I said, "What are they, Commander of the Faithful? If they are right, they should not [be such as to] remove me from my position with you; if they are false, then someone like me will remove the falsehood from himself." 'Umar said, "I have heard that you are saying they have turned (the caliphate) away from you out of envy and injustice." I replied, "When you say out of injustice, Commander of the Faithful, it has already become clear to the ignorant and the thoughtful alike; when you say out of envy, Iblīs was envious of Ādam,[685] and we are his offspring who are envied." 'Umar said, "Far from it! Your hearts, Banū Hāshim, have refused [to show anything] other than unchanging envy and increasing spite and malice." I replied, "Take it easy, Commander of the Faithful; do not describe the hearts of a people from whom God has removed uncleanness, and whom He has purified completely, as being envious and malicious. The heart of the Messenger of God is one of the hearts of Banū Hāshim." 'Umar retorted, "Leave me, Ibn 'Abbās." I said I would comply, but, when I went to get up, he became embarrassed at what he had said to me and said, "Stay where you are, Ibn 'Abbās. I shall tend to your right and approve of what gives you pleasure." I replied, "Commander of the Faithful, I have a right that is incumbent upon you and every Muslim. Anyone who preserves it will achieve good fortune; anyone who does not will lose good fortune." Then he got up and went away.

According to Aḥmad b. 'Umar[686]–Ya'qūb b. Isḥāq al-Ḥaḍramī[687]—'Ikrimah b. 'Ammār[688]—Iyās b. Salamah[689]—his father: 'Umar b. al-Khaṭṭāb passed through the market carrying

684. That is, that Quraysh are in any way attempting to thwart the legitimate rights of the 'Alid family.

685. Iblīs, the Devil, was the angel in Islamic tradition who refused to prostrate himself before Adam. See Qur'ān, VII: 11, 19ff.; XX:115ff.

686. Cairo reads Aḥmad b. 'Amr. It is not possible to identify him with certainty.

687. He died in 205/820. See Ibn Ḥajar, *Tahdhīb*, XI, 382.

688. He died in 159/775. See Ibn Ḥajar, *Tahdhīb*, VII, 261–63.

689. He died in Medina in 119/737. See Ibn Ḥajar, *Tahdhīb*, I, 388–89.

his whip. He dealt me a blow with it and caught the edge of my garment, saying, "Get out of the way." The following year he [2772] met me and said, "Are you intending to go on the pilgrimage, Salamah?" When I told him that I was, he took me by the hand to his house and gave me 600 dirhams, saying, "Use them to make your pilgrimage, and you should know that they are by way of compensation for the lash that I gave you." I replied, "But I had not remembered it, Commander of the Faithful." "But I had not forgotten it!" he exclaimed.

According to ʿAbd al-Ḥamīd b. Bayān[690]—Muḥammad b. Yazīd[691]—Ismāʿīl b. Abī Khālid—Salamah b. Kuhayl:[692] ʿUmar b. al-Khaṭṭāb said, "O subjects, you have an obligation to us to give advice on what is unknown and to cooperate in doing good. There is no forbearance (*ḥilm*) dearer to God and more generally advantageous than that of a gentle leader. O subjects, there is no ignorance more hateful to God and more generally evil than that of a harsh leader. O subjects, he who enjoins well-being for someone in his midst, God will bring him well-being from above."

According to Muḥammad b. Isḥāq—Yaḥyā b. Maʿīn[693]—Yaʿqūb b. Ibrāhīm—ʿĪsā b. Yazīd b. Daʾb—ʿAbd al-Raḥmān b. Abī Zayd[694]—ʿImrān b. Sawādah:[695] I said the morning prayer with ʿUmar, and he recited the Subḥān chapter[696] and one other. Then he left. I went off with him, and he asked if there was anything he could do. I told him there was, so he asked me to join him. I did so and, when he entered [his house], he gave me permission [to enter]. There he was on a bed with nothing on it. I told him I wanted to give him some advice. His reply was, [2773] "The person giving good advice is welcome anytime." I said, "Your community finds fault with you on four counts." (ʿUmar) put the top of his whip in his beard and the lower part on his

690. He died in 244/858. See Ibn Ḥajar, *Tahdhīb*, VI, 111.
691. It is not possible to identify this narrator with certainty.
692. Salamah b. Kuhayl al-Ḥaḍramī died ca. 123/741. See Ibn Ḥajar, *Tahdhīb*, IV, 155–57.
693. He died in 233/848. See Rosenthal, *Historiography*, 341.
694. An unidentified narrator.
695. An unidentified narrator.
696. That is, Qurʾān XVII, usually entitled "The Children of Israel."

thigh. Then he said, "Tell me more." I continued, "It has been mentioned that you declared the lesser pilgrimage[697] forbidden during the months of the [full] pilgrimage. The Messenger of God did not do this, nor Abū Bakr, though it is permitted." He answered, "It is permitted. If they were to perform the lesser pilgrimage during the months of the pilgrimage, they would regard it as being in lieu of the full pilgrimage, and (Mecca) would be a deserted place that year, and the pilgrimage would be celebrated by no one, although it is part of God's greatness. You are right." I continued, "It is also said that you have forbidden temporary marriage,[698] although it was a license (*rukhṣah*) given by God. We enjoy a temporary marriage for a handful [of dates],[699] and we can separate after three nights." He replied, "The Messenger of God permitted it at a time of necessity. Then people regained their life of comfort. I do not know any Muslim who has practiced this or gone back to it. Now anyone who wishes to can marry for a handful [of dates] and separate after three nights. You are right." I continued, "You emancipate a slave girl if she gives birth, without her master's [consenting to] the emancipation."[700] He replied, "I added one thing that is forbidden to another, intending only to do some good. I ask God's forgiveness." I continued, "There have been complaints of your raising your voice against your subjects and your addressing them harshly." He raised his whip, then ran his hand down it right to the end. Then he said, "I am Muḥammad's traveling companion"—he had [in fact] sat behind him at the raid on Qarqarat al-Kudr.[701] "Indeed I pasture [my flocks] well until

697. The pilgrimage that can be undertaken at any time of the year. See *SEI*, s.v. "'umra" (Paret).

698. Temporary marriage, *mut'ah*, is recognized by the Twelver Shī'īs only. See *SEI*, s.v. (Heffening); Schacht, *Origins*, 266–67; *Introduction*, 163; Coulson, *History*, 110–11, 115–16.

699. Where temporary marriage was permitted, it was carried out in return for a robe or a handful of dates. See *SEI*, loc. cit.

700. The *umm walad* would normally have to wait until her master died before gaining her freedom.

701. A plain in the area of Khaybar, about 6 miles away from the town. The raid does not appear to be dated precisely in the *sīrah* and *maghāzī* literature, but must have been only a short time before the death of the Prophet in 10/632. See Wāqidī, *Maghāzī*, I, 182ff. (Qarārat al-Kudr); Ibn Hishām, *Sīrah*, II, 618; *al-Manāsik*, 411; Bilādī, *Mu'jam*, VII, 117.

they are satisfied. I water them and quench their thirst. I push back the she-camel that grumbles when milked. I chide the she-camel that does not stick to the road. I keep them moving. I do not drive them too fast. I gather together camels pasturing alone. [2774]
I bring up camels lagging behind. I chide often and beat seldom. I raise my stick. I push away with my hand. Were it not for all this, I would be much at fault!" (The source) continued: Muʿāwiyah heard this and said, "He was indeed knowledgeable about their subjects."

According to Yaʿqūb b. Ibrāhīm—Ibn ʿUlayyah—Ibn ʿAwn[702] —Muḥammad: ʿUthmān said, " ʿUmar used to deny his family and relatives things, seeking God's face, whereas I give freely to my family and relatives, [also] seeking it. No three like ʿUmar will ever be met with again."[703]

According to ʿAlī b. Sahl[704]—Ḍamrah b. Rabīʿah[705]—ʿAbdallāh b. Abī Sulaymān[706]—his father: I arrived in Medina and entered one of the houses there. There was ʿUmar b. al-Khaṭṭāb wearing [only] a striped waist wrapper and smearing the alms camels with tar.[707]

According to Ibn Bashshār—ʿAbd al-Raḥmān [b. Mahdī]—Sufyān [b. ʿUyaynah]—Ḥabīb[708]—Abū Wā'il [Shaqīq]: ʿUmar b. al-Khaṭṭāb said, "Had I known in the beginning what I know now, I would have taken the excess wealth of the rich and distributed it among the poor Emigrants."

According to Ibn Bashshār—ʿAbd al-Raḥmān b. Mahdī— [2775]
Manṣūr b. Abī al-Aswad[709]—al-Aʿmash—Ibrāhīm[710]—al-Aswad

702. An unidentified narrator.

703. That is, only Abū Bakr and ʿUmar had such piety, but I, ʿUthmān, cannot compete with them. See Ṭanṭāwī, *Akhbār*, 542.

704. ʿAlī b. Sahl al-Ramlī does not figure in the major biographical dictionaries, but see Translation, I, 25, 174 n. 45.

705. Ḍamrah b. Rabīʿah al-Ramlī has a brief entry in Ibn Ḥajar, *Tahdhīb*, IV, 460.

706. An unidentified narrator.

707. To treat mange, sores, and other skin problems.

708. Ḥabīb b. Abī Thābit died in 119/773. See Ibn Ḥajar, *Tahdhīb*, II, 178–80.

709. Manṣūr b. Abī al-Aswad al-Laythī is given no date of death in Ibn Ḥajar, *Tahdhīb*, X, 305–6.

710. Ibrāhīm b. Yazīd al-Nakhaʿī died in 96/714. See Ibn Ḥajar, *Tahdhīb*, I, 177–79.

b. Yazīd:[711] Whenever a delegation came to ʿUmar, he would ask them about their leader. They would give a good account of him, so he would ask, "Does he visit your sick?" They would answer that he did, so he would ask, "Does he visit the sick slave?" They would answer that he did, so he would ask, "How does (your leader) treat the weak? Does he sit at his door?" If they replied in the negative regarding any one of these customs, he would dismiss him.

According to Ibn Ḥumayd—al-Ḥakam b. Bashīr[712]—ʿAmr [b. Muḥammad]: ʿUmar b. al-Khaṭṭāb used to say,

> There are four matters connected with Islam that I shall never neglect or abandon for anything: the strength in God's wealth and collecting it so that, when we do collect it, we place it where God orders us, and remain, family of ʿUmar, with nothing of it in our hands at all. [Second, there are] the Emigrants who are beneath the shadow of swords—they should not be restricted, nor detained away from their families; God's immovable booty should be for them and for their families in abundance, and I shall look after their families until they return. [Third, there are] the Helpers who have already given their share to God and all of them fought the enemy—the good deeds of those who do good among them should be accepted as such, whereas the evil deeds of those who do evil deeds should be passed over without punishment and they should be consulted in the matter. [Fourth, there are] the bedouins who are the original Arabs and the mainstay of Islam—their alms should be taken from them in kind—not a single dinar should be
> [2776] taken from them, nor [even] a dirham—and it should be returned to their poor and wretched.

According to al-Sarī—Shuʿayb—Sayf—Ibn Jurayj—Nāfiʿ—ʿAbdallāh b. ʿUmar: ʿUmar said, "I know that all the people [together] are not equal to these two men between whom and Gabriel the Apostle of God was the confidential messenger,

711. Al-Aswad b. Yazīd died ca. 75/694. See Ibn Ḥajar, *Tahdhīb*, I, 342–43.
712. An unidentified narrator.

receiving the revelations from him and dictating them to them."[713]

The Account of the Electoral Council[714]

According to 'Umar b. Shabbah—'Alī b. Muḥammad [al-Madā'inī]—Wakī' [b. al-Jarrāḥ]—al-A'mash—Ibrāhīm, and Muḥammad b. 'Abdallāh al-Anṣārī[715]—Ibn Abī 'Arūbah[716]—Qatādah—Shahr b. Ḥawshab,[717] and Abū Mikhnaf[718]—Yūsuf b. Yazīd[719]—Abū al-'Abbās Sahl[720] and Mubārak b. Faḍālah—'Ubaydallāh b. 'Umar, and Yūnus b. Abī Isḥāq[721]—'Amr b. Maymūn al-Awdī:[722] When 'Umar b. al-Khaṭṭāb was stabbed, it was suggested to him that he should appoint a successor. "Whom shall I appoint caliph?" was his reply. "If Abū 'Ubaydah b. al-Jarrāḥ[723] were alive, I would appoint him, and if my Lord questioned me, I would say, ' I heard Your prophet say that (Abū 'Ubaydah) was the guardian of this community.' If Sālim, client

---

713. That is, 'Uthmān and 'Alī. Five future caliphs had acted as the Prophet's secretaries: Abū Bakr, 'Umar, 'Uthmān, 'Alī, and Mu'āwiyah. Abū Bakr was by this time dead; 'Umar is not talking of himself here; and Mu'āwiyah also is not in question.

714. Arabic *shūrā*, the council of six appointed by 'Umar to decide on the succession. See Ya'qūbī, *Tārīkh*, II, 160; Ibn al-Athīr, *al-Kāmil*, III, 32ff.; Ibn 'Abd Rabbih, *'Iqd*, IV, 273ff.; Bal'ami, *Chronique*, III, 546ff.; Ṭanṭāwī, *Akhbār*, 531ff. The reader's attention is also drawn to Abbott, *Papyri*, 80ff. Pp. 83–87 in particular include the different versions of the account of the council, with full references.

715. It is not possible to identify this narrator with certainty.

716. He died in 150/767–776. See Ibn Ḥajar, *Tahdhīb*, IV, 636.

717. Shahr b. Ḥawshab al-Ash'arī died ca. 112/730. See Ibn Ḥajar, *Tahdhīb*, IV, 369–72.

718. Abū Mikhnaf Lūṭ b. Yaḥyā died ca. 157/774. See U. Sezgin, *Abū Miḫnaf*, passim; Duri, *Rise*, 44ff., 143ff.; Rosenthal, *Historiography*, 70, 90.

719. An unidentified narrator.

720. I read tentatively from the Leiden *apparatus criticus* Sahl b. Sa'd al-Sā'idī who died ca. 88/707. See Ibn Ḥajar, *Tahdhīb*, IV, 252ff.

721. It is not possible to identify this narrator with certainty.

722. 'Amr b. Maymūn al-Awdī died ca. 75/694. See Ibn Ḥajar, *Tahdhīb*, VIII, 109–10.

723. Abū 'Ubaydah b. al-Jarrāḥ was the famous Companion and military leader on the Syrian front against the Byzantines. He died in Syria in 18/639, shortly after the conquest of Jerusalem by the Muslims. See Shaban, *History*, 31, 43; *EI*², s.v. (Gibb).

[2777] of Abū Ḥudhayfah,[724] were alive, I would appoint him, and if my Lord questioned me, I would say, 'I heard your prophet say that Sālim loves God vehemently.'" Someone said to ('Umar), "I can point to someone, 'Abdallāh b. 'Umar." But ('Umar) replied, "God curse you! You were not saying this for God's sake! You wretch! How can I appoint caliph someone who has been unable to divorce his wife! We have no desire [to get involved] in your affairs. I have not found (the caliphate) so praiseworthy that I should covet it for my own family. If things turn out well, we shall have gained our reward from them; but if they turn out badly, then it is enough for the family of 'Umar that [only] one of them should be called to account and held responsible for what happened to Muḥammad's community. I have striven and have kept my own family out. If I succeed in coming out [of all this] even, and no recompense [being given to me], I shall indeed be happy. I shall look [into the matter]: if I do appoint a caliph, then someone better than I has made the appointment; but if I abandon [the idea], someone better than I has [already] done this. God will never neglect His faith."[725]

So (those with him) left and returned in the evening, suggesting to the Commander of the Faithful that he draw up a succession agreement. He replied, "I had decided after talking to you that I would look [into the matter] and appoint someone over you, the most suitable of you to bear you along the true path." And he indicated 'Alī. [He continued], "But I fell into a swoon and saw a man who had entered a garden that he had planted. He began to pick everything, both the young tender plants and the mature ones, clutching them to him and putting them beneath him. I knew that God was in control and was taking 'Umar into His mercy. I do not want to take on the burden (of the caliphate), dead as well as alive. You should [approach] that group of men who the Messenger of God said are 'among the people of paradise.' Sa'īd b. Zayd b. 'Amr b.

724. Sālim figures quite prominently in the early histories, but this is a strange assertion. See Ibn Hishām, *Sīrah*, I, 479, 679, 708, etc.; Wāqidī, *Maghāzī*, I, 9, 148, 154, etc.

725. In the first instance, if he does appoint a caliph, Abū Bakr has already done this. In the second, if he does not, Muḥammad himself did not appoint a caliph. Either way he has a precedent.

Nufayl[726] is one of them. I am not bringing him into the matter, [2778] but rather the following six: 'Alī and 'Uthmān, sons of 'Abd Manāf,[727] 'Abd al-Raḥmān [b. 'Awf] and Sa'd [b. Abī Waqqāṣ], maternal uncles of the Messenger of God, al-Zubayr b. al-'Awwām, the true friend and cousin of the Messenger of God, and Ṭalḥat al-Khayr b. 'Ubaydallāh.[728] Let them select one of themselves. When they appoint a leader, [you all] should give him good help and support. If he entrusts anyone of you with authority, he should convey to him what is committed to his care."

They left and al-'Abbās[729] said to 'Alī, "Do not get involved with them." He replied, "I do not like dissension [in our family]." (Al-'Abbās) said, "Then you will see something you do not like!" When morning came, 'Umar summoned 'Alī, 'Uthmān, Sa'd, 'Abd al-Raḥmān b. 'Awf, and al-Zubayr b. al-'Awwām and said, "I have looked into the matter and consider you to be the chiefs and leaders of the people. This matter will remain among you alone. When the Messenger of God died, he was well pleased with you. I have no fears for you with the people if you remain on the straight path. However, I do fear for you if there is a difference of opinion among you and the people then differ among themselves. Off you go to 'Ā'ishah's room, with her permission, and deliberate. Choose one of you." Then he added, "Do not go to 'Ā'ishah's room; rather stay near at hand." He put down his head, exhausted by the loss of blood.

So they went in and held secret discussions. But then their voices became raised and 'Abdallāh b. 'Umar exclaimed loud enough for ('Umar) to hear, "God heavens, the Commander of

---

726. Sa'īd b. Zayd b. 'Amr b. Nufayl, the brother-in-law of 'Umar, who with his wife, 'Umar's sister, was instrumental in the future caliph's embracing Islam. He died ca. 51/671. See Ibn Hishām, *Sīrah*, I, 226, 253.

727. A reference to the fact that both belonged to Quraysh—as did the other four—and represented both its lines through 'Abd Manāf, where the pedigree split: 'Alī was descended from 'Abd Manāf through Hāshim, whereas 'Uthmān was descended from 'Abd Manāf through 'Abd Shams.

728. Al-Zubayr was the son of the Prophet's paternal aunt. I detect no great significance in his calling Ṭalḥah Ṭalḥat al-Khayr, which I take to be a way of expressing endearment.

729. Al-'Abbās b. 'Abd al-Muṭṭalib, the uncle of both the Prophet and 'Alī. See *EI*[2], s.v. (Watt).

the Faithful is not yet dead!" ('Umar) came to and said, "All of you, stop this! When I am dead, hold your consultations for three days. Let Ṣuhayb lead the people in prayer. Before the fourth day comes you should have your commander from among you. 'Abdallāh b. 'Umar will be there as adviser, but he shall
[2779] have nothing to do with the matter [of the actual appointment]. Ṭalḥah shall share with you in the decision. If he comes within the three days, include him in your decision. If the three days go by and he does not come, make the decision nevertheless. Who will deal with Ṭalḥah for me?" "I shall," responded Sa'd b. Abī Waqqāṣ, "and he will not give a differing view, God willing." 'Umar said, "I hope he will not give a differing view, God willing. I think one of these two, 'Alī or 'Uthmān, will become leader. If it is 'Uthmān, he is a gentle person; if it is 'Alī, he has a sense of humor. How suitable he is to carry them along the true road! If you appoint Sa'd, he is worthy of the office, but if not, the one appointed should seek his assistance. I have never dismissed him for disloyalty or weakness. How perceptive 'Abd al-Raḥmān b. 'Awf is! He is disposed to what is right. [He is] rightly guided and has a protector in God. Listen to what he has to say."

('Umar) said to Abū Ṭalḥah al-Anṣārī, "For a long time had God strengthened Islam through you Helpers, Abū Ṭalḥah. Select fifty Helpers and urge them to choose one of them." To al-Miqdād b. al-Aswad[730] he said, "When you put me into my grave, assemble these people in one room to choose one of their number." To Ṣuhayb he said, "Lead the people in prayer for three days. Let into [the deliberations] 'Alī, 'Uthmān, al-Zubayr, Sa'd, 'Abd al-Raḥmān b. 'Awf, and Ṭalḥah, if he arrives. Have 'Abdallāh b. 'Umar present, but he shall have nothing to do with the matter [of the actual appointment]. Stay with them and if five agree to approve of one man, but one refuses, smash in his head, or strike it off with a sword. If four agree to approve of one man, but two refuse, cut off the (latters') heads. If three approve
[2780] of one of them, and three approve of another, get 'Abdallāh b.

730. Al-Miqdād b. 'Amr/al-Aswad al-Kindī died in 33/653. See Ibn Ḥajar. *Tahdhīb*, X, 285–87.

'Umar to make a decision. Let whichever party in favor of which he makes his judgment select one of themselves. If they do not accept 'Abdallāh b. 'Umar's judgment, be on the same side as 'Abd al-Rahman b. 'Awf. Kill the rest if they do not go along with the general consensus."

So they left. 'Alī said to some Banū Hāshim who were with him, "If your people are obeyed [only] among themselves, you will never be appointed to positions of leadership." Al-'Abbās came to him, and ('Alī) said, "(The caliphate) has slipped from us!"[731] (Al-'Abbās) asked him how he knew. He continued, "('Umar) paired me with 'Uthmān and told us [all] to fall in with the majority. If two approve of one, and two another, [he said], we should be on the same side as 'Abd al-Raḥmān b. 'Awf. Sa'd will not go against his cousin, 'Abd al-Raḥmān, who is related by marriage to 'Uthmān. They will all (three) agree in their opinion. 'Abd al-Raḥmān will appoint 'Uthmān to the caliphate, or 'Uthmān will appoint 'Abd al-Raḥmān. If the other two were with me, they would be of no benefit to me, to say nothing of the fact that I have hope only of one of them." Al-'Abbās said to him, "I have never urged you to do anything without your later responding to me by holding back in a way I do not like. When the Messenger of God died, I ordered you to ask him [on his death bed] who should have the rule, but you refused. After (Muḥammad's) death I ordered you to bring the matter to a speedy conclusion, but you refused. When 'Umar nominated you a member of the electoral council, I advised you to have nothing to do with them, but you refused. Just learn one thing from me: whenever people make you a proposal, say no, unless they are appointing you [caliph]. Watch out for these people; they will continue to push us out of the matter [of the caliphate] until someone else takes our [rightful] place. I swear in God's name, no such person will get (the caliphate) without [2781]
the help of some evil together with which no good will be of benefit!" 'Alī replied, "If 'Uthmān survives, I shall certainly remind him of what has happened. If he dies, they will certainly take (the caliphate) by turns among themselves. If they do, they

731. That is, Banū Hāshim.

will certainly find me in a position they do not like." Then he quoted the following verses, applying them to his own situation:[732]

I swore by the lord of the mares prancing one evening—
[but] in the morning they came, nimble, hastening to al-Muḥaṣṣab.[733]
"The family of Ibn Ya'mar will certainly stand apart, facing
a bloody place, difficult to drink from, they being the sons of al-Shuddākh.[734]

And he turned and saw Abū Ṭalḥah, but did not like his being there. Abū Ṭalḥah said, "Nothing to be afraid of, Abū al-Ḥasan!"[735]

When 'Umar died and his bier was brought out, both 'Alī and 'Uthmān pretended not to mind which of them would pray over him. But 'Abd al-Raḥman said, "Both of you are candidates for the caliphate. This matter has nothing to do with you. It is for Ṣuhayb whom 'Umar appointed to lead the people in prayer for three (nights) until they can agree on a leader." So Ṣuhayb prayed over ('Umar). When he had been buried, al-Miqdād assembled the members of the electoral council in the house of al-Miswar b. Makhramah—another version is that it was in the treasury and yet another that it was in 'Ā'ishah's room with her permission—five in all, accompanied by Ibn 'Umar and with Ṭalḥah [still] absent. They ordered Abū Ṭalḥah to prevent anyone from disturbing them. 'Amr b. al-'Āṣ and al-Mughīrah b.
[2782] Shu'bah arrived and sat at the door, but Sa'd threw pebbles at

---

732. The meter is *ṭawīl*. See Ibn al-Athīr, *Kāmil*, III, 33.

733. A place between Mecca and Minā, nearer to the latter. See *al-Manāsik*, 602; Bilādī, *Mu'jam*, VIII, 43–44.

734. Ya'mar b. 'Awf, nicknamed al-Shuddākh, was during the pre-Islamic period one of the arbitrators of Kinānah who gave a judgment between the tribes of Khuzā'ah and Quṣayy on the question of the Ka'bah. See Ibn Manẓūr, *Lisān*, III, 28; Zabīdī, *Tāj*, VII, 278–79. The second line is the very tentative rendering of

la-yakhtaliyan rahṭu bni Ya'mara marī'an
najī'an banū l-Shuddākhi wirdan muṣallabā.

'Alī here emphasises his isolation in the face of opposition.

735. Abū al-Ḥasan is 'Alī. This seems to indicate Abū Ṭalḥah's support for the Alid family.

them and made them get up, saying, "You want to say, 'We were there; we were members of the electoral council.'" The electoral council argued about the affair and a great deal of talking went on among them. Abū Ṭalḥah said, "I was more afraid that you would reject (the caliphate) than I was that you would compete for it. No, by Him who has taken away 'Umar's soul, I shall give you no more than the three days that you were ordered. Then I shall sit down in my own house and see what you are up to!"

'Abd al-Raḥmān said, "Which one of you will withdraw from the (race for the caliphate), and undertake to appoint the best of you?" No one answered. So he continued, "I withdraw." 'Uthmān said, "I am the first to accept [this]. I heard the Messenger of God say, '('Abd al-Raḥmān) is trustworthy on earth and will be in heaven.'" All the members, with the exception of 'Alī who remained silent, expressed their approval. So ('Abd al-Raḥmān) said, "What do you say, Abū al-Ḥasan?" ('Alī) replied, "Give me your word you will consider truth paramount, you will not follow your whim, you will not show any preference for a relative, and you will not let the community down." ('Abd al-Raḥmān) said [to the others], "Give me your solemn promises you will stand with me against anyone who reneges [on your final decision] and you will approve of anyone I choose for you. I impose a pact with God upon myself that I shall show no preference for a relative, because he is a relative, nor shall I let down the Muslims." He took a promise from them and similarly gave them his word. ('Abd al-Raḥmān) said to 'Alī, "You say you have most right of those present to the office because of your close relationship [to the Prophet] and your long standing in and the good deeds you have done in the cause of Islam, and you have not, [in saying so], said anything remote [from the truth]. But if you were not involved in the matter and were not here at all, whom would you think of them all has [2783]
most right to (the office)?" He replied, "'Uthmān." ('Abd al-Raḥmān) took 'Uthmān on one side and said, "You say you are a shaykh of Banū 'Abd Manāf and related to the Messenger of God by marriage and his cousin, an excellent man of long standing [in Islam]—and you have not said anything remote from the truth and that (the caliphate) cannot therefore be taken from you. But if you were not here, which of the members do

you think has most right to (the office)?" He replied, "'Alī." Then ('Abd al-Raḥmān) took al-Zubayr on one side and addressed him in the same way as he had 'Alī and 'Uthmān. He replied, "'Uthmān." Then ('Abd al-Raḥmān) took Sa'd on one side and spoke to him. He answered "'Uthmān." 'Alī met Sa'd and quoted, "'Fear God by whom you make demands one of another, and the wombs [which bore you]. God is ever watching you.'[736] I am asking you, in the name of the relationship (*raḥim*) of this son of mine[737] with the Messenger of God and that of my paternal uncle, Ḥamzah,[738] with you, not to stand with 'Abd al-Raḥmān, assisting 'Uthmān against me. I have connections 'Uthman does not." 'Abd al-Raḥmān went round at night meeting the Companions of the Messenger of God and those army commanders and nobles who arrived in Medina and consulting with them. Everyone he took to one side gave him instructions to opt for 'Uthmān. Then on the eve of the morning of the deadline, he came to the house of al-Miswar b. Makhramah well into the night and woke him up, saying, "You're asleep, when I have had very little tonight? Off you go and summon al-Zubayr and Sa'd!"

So (al-Miswar) summoned them and ('Abd al-Raḥmān) began
[2784] with al-Zubayr at the back of the mosque under the covering (*ṣuffah*) that adjoins the house of Marwān,[739] saying, "Let the rule go to the sons of 'Abd Manāf!"[740] (Al-Zubayr) said, "I throw in my lot with 'Alī." ('Abd al-Raḥmān) said to Sa'd, "We are cousins. Throw in your lot with me so that I can choose." He replied, "If you choose yourself, that is fine! But if you choose 'Uthmān, then I prefer to support 'Alī. Have yourself accepted [as caliph], give us some respite and raise up our heads." ('Abd al-Raḥmān) said, "Abū Isḥāq, I have withdrawn from (the ca-

736. Qur'ān, IV:1.

737. The text has a singular, "son," presumably al-Ḥasan, who was born from the womb of Fāṭimah, the Prophet's daughter. The parallel text of the *'Iqd* (IV, 278), however, has a dual, "these two sons of mine"; viz., al-Ḥasan and al-Ḥusayn.

738. Ḥamzah b. 'Abd al-Muṭṭalib, the brother of 'Alī's father, Abū Ṭālib.

739. This is perhaps the young Marwān b. al-Ḥakam, the future fourth Umayyad caliph, who died in 65/685.

740. That is, 'Alī and 'Uthmān. See note 727, above.

liphate) on condition that I make the choice. [Even] had I not done so and the choice had come back on me, I would not have wanted (the caliphate). I saw myself in a dream as if in a green meadow rich in fresh herbage.[741] A stallion camel came in—I have never seen such a noble stallion—and passed through like an arrow without paying attention to anything in the meadow right to the other side without stopping. A stallion followed him in immediately after and left the meadow. Then a fine thoroughbred stallion entered, dragging his halter, turning right and left, going where the other two went and leaving. Then a fourth, a stallion camel entered and pastured in the meadow. No indeed, I shall not be the fourth. No one can take the place of Abū Bakr and ʿUmar after their death and [then] be approved of by the people." Saʿd replied, "I am afraid that weakness has overcome you. Do as you think best. You know what ʿUmar's death bed instructions were."

Al-Zubayr and Saʿd left. (ʿAbd al-Raḥmān) sent al-Miswar b. Makhramah for ʿAlī and talked with him in private for a long time, (the latter) not doubting that he was to be selected for the office [of caliph]. Then (ʿAlī) left, and (ʿAbd al-Raḥmān) sent al-Miswar for ʿUthmān, but the call to morning prayer interrupted their private conversation.

According to ʿAmr b. Maymūn: ʿAbdallāh b. ʿUmar told me, [2785] "ʿAmr, anyone who tells you that he knows what ʿAbd al-Raḥmān discussed with ʿAlī and ʿUthmān, does not know what he is talking about! Your Lord's decision fell on ʿUthmān."

When they had said the morning prayers, (ʿAbd al-Raḥmān) convened the members [of the electoral council] and sent for all the Emigrants and the Helpers of long standing [in Islam] and of excellence and the military commanders who were [in Medina]. They all assembled and there was confusion among the people in the mosque. (ʿAbd al-Raḥmān) said, "People, everyone wants those of the garrison towns to return to them, having learned

---

741. The text reads *"Innī urītu ka-rawḍatin khaḍrāʾa"* etc. Much neater is Ibn ʿAbd Rabbih, *ʿIqd*, IV, 278, who has *Innī raʾaytu ka-annī fī rawḍatin khaḍrāʾa*. I have translated the latter. In the anecdote that follows the first noble stallion camel represents the Prophet, the stallion camel Abū Bakr, and the fine thoroughbred ʿUmar. The fourth represents ʿUmar's successor.

who their supreme commander is." Sa'īd b. Zayd said, "We think you are worthy of (the caliphate)." He replied, "Give me some different advice!" 'Ammār [b. Yāsir] said, "If you want the Muslims to be in full agreement, give 'Alī the oath of allegiance." Al-Miqdād b. al-Aswad said, "'Ammār is right; if you give 'Alī the oath of allegiance, we shall say that we are in full agreement with what you are doing." Ibn Abī Sarḥ[742] said, "If you want Quraysh to be in full agreement, give 'Uthmān the oath of allegiance." 'Abdallāh b. Abī Rabī'ah said, "He is right; if you give 'Uthmān the oath of allegiance, we shall say that we are in full agreement with what you are doing." 'Ammār upbraided Ibn Abī Sarḥ, saying, "When did you ever give the Muslims any good advice?!"

Banū Hāshim and Banū Umayyah[743] held talks. 'Ammār said, "O people, God has ennobled us through His Prophet and strengthened us through His religion. How can you take this appointment away from those of the house of your Prophet?" A member of Banū Makhzūm[744] said, "You have gone too far, Ibn Sumayyah! Why should you have anything to do with Quraysh taking the leadership for themselves?"[745] Sa'd b. Abī Waqqāṣ said, "Get it over with, 'Abd al-Raḥmān, before our people fall into civil war." 'Abd al-Raḥmān said, " I have looked into [the matter] and consulted. Do not, members of the electoral council,
[2786] lay yourselves open to criticism." He summoned 'Alī and said, "God's agreement and covenant is binding on you. Will you indeed act in accordance with God's Book, the practice of His Messenger and the example of the two caliphs after him?" ('Alī) replied, "I hope to do this and act thus to the best of my knowledge and ability." ('Abd al-Raḥmān) summoned 'Uthmān and said to him the same as what he had said to 'Alī. ('Uthmān) replied, "Yes." So ('Abd al-Raḥmān) gave him the oath of

---

742. Ibn Abī Sarḥ was 'Iyāḍ b. 'Abdallāh b. Sa'd who died ca. 100/718. See Ibn Ḥajar, *Tahdhīb*, VIII, 200–1.

743. That is, the families of 'Alī and 'Uthmān, respectively.

744. Makhzūm b. Yaqaẓah, a tribal group (*baṭn*) of Lu'ayy b. Ghālib and Banū Umayyah's chief rival among Quraysh. See Zubayrī, *Nasab Quraysh*, 299–346; Ibn Ḥazm, *Jamharah*, 141ff., 464; Kaḥḥālah, *Mu'jam*, III, 1058.

745. Sumayyah was a concubine, and this is therefore an insult. 'Ammār was not of Quraysh. See note 8, above. See also *EI*², s.v. "'Ammār" (Reckendorf).

allegiance. ʿAlī said, "You have always been partial in his favor![746] This is not the first time you have banded together against us. But '[my course is] comely patience and God's help is to be asked against what you describe.'[747] You have appointed ʿUthmān only so that the rule will come back to you. 'Every day God exercises power.'"[748] ʿAbd al-Raḥmān retorted, "Do not lay yourself open to criticism, ʿAlī. I have looked into the matter and consulted the people. They regard no one as the equal of ʿUthmān." ʿAlī left, saying, "[God's] decree will come in its time!" Al-Miqdād said, "You have indeed, ʿAbd al-Raḥmān, passed up the one who makes decisions based 'on the truth and thereby acts justly.'"[749] (ʿAbd al-Raḥmān) replied, "I have indeed exerted all my efforts for the Muslims, Miqdād." (The former) said, "If you sincerely did what you did for God's sake, may He reward you as He does those who do good." [But] al-Miqdād said, "I have never seen such things as have been visited upon the people of this house after the death of their Prophet. I am amazed at Quraysh that they have abandoned someone who cannot be matched in my opinion in knowledge and the ability to act justly. What indeed if I were to find supporters against ʿUthmān!" ʿAbd al-Raḥmān replied, "Fear God, Miqdād, I am afraid you will cause dissension." Someone questioned al-Miqdād, "God have mercy upon you, who are the people of this house and who is this man?" He replied, "The people of the [2787] house are Banū al-Muṭṭalib and the man is ʿAlī b. Abī Ṭālib." ʿAlī said, "The people are looking to Quraysh, while Quraysh are [also] looking to their own house. (Quraysh) say that, if Banū Hāshim are put in authority over you, (the caliphate) will never leave them; but so long as it is in the hands of [clans] other than (Banū Hāshim) of Quraysh, you will pass it around among yourselves."

Ṭalḥah arrived on the day on which the oath of allegiance

---

746. This appears to be what is meant by the Arabic *ḥabawta-hu ḥabwa dahrin*; see *Glossarium*, CCXLV. Ibn ʿAbd Rabbih, *ʿIqd*, IV, 279, has *ḥabawta-hu muḥābātan*.

747. Qur'ān, XII:18.

748. Qur'ān, LV:29.

749. See Qur'ān, VII:159, 181.

was given to ʿUthmān. He was asked to give his own oath to ʿUthmān, but asked, "Do all Quraysh approve of him?" and was told they did. He came to ʿUthman and the latter said, "You still have your options open; if you refuse [to give me the oath of allegiance], I shall reject (the caliphate)." Ṭalḥah said, "Will you really reject it?" ʿUthmān replied that he would. Ṭalḥah asked, "Have all the people given you the oath of allegiance?" ʿUthmān replied that they had. (Ṭalḥah) said, "Then I approve; I shall not go against the general consensus." He gave (ʿUthmān) the oath of allegiance.

Al-Mughīrah b. Shuʿbah said to ʿAbd al-Raḥmān, "You were right to give ʿUthmān the oath of allegiance, Abū Muḥammad." He also said to ʿUthmān, "If ʿAbd al-Raḥmān had given the oath of allegiance to anyone other than you, we would not have agreed." But ʿAbd al-Raḥmān retorted, "You one-eyed liar! If I had given anyone else the oath of allegiance, you would have done so also and would have said what you say now."

Al-Farazdaq said:[750]

Ṣuhayb led the prayer for three nights; then (ʿAbd al-Raḥmān) handed over (the caliphate)
to Ibn ʿAffān, unlimited authority,
A caliphate [which passed on] from Abū Bakr to his colleague,
[Abū Bakr] rightly guided and [ʿUmar] under his command—
they were [all] sincere friends."

[2788] Al-Miswar b. Makhramah used to say, "I have never seen a man get the better of a group of people in the matter in which they were engaged more effectively than ʿAbd al-Raḥmān b. ʿAwf did of (the electoral council) in this case."

Abū Jaʿfar [al-Ṭabarī] said: We [also] have the account of al-Miswar b. Makhramah. According to Salm b. Junādah Abū al-Sāʾib—Sulaymān b. ʿAbd al-ʿAzīz b. Abī Thābit b. ʿAbd al-

750. The meter is *basīṭ*. Al-Farazdaq is the famous poet, Hammām b. Ghālib b. Ṣaʿṣaʿah, always associated with al-Akhṭal and Jarīr. Al-Farazdaq died ca. 111/729. Cf. *EI*², s.v. (Blachère); for a more recent assessment of al-Farazdaq and his work, see Jayyusi, "Umayyad Poetry," 401ff. The poet here is eulogizing the Umayyad caliph Yazīd b. ʿAbd al-Malik and satirizing Yazīd b. al-Muhallab. Cf. al-Farazdaq, *Dīwān*, I, 265.

ʿAzīz b. ʿUmar b. ʿAbd al-Raḥmān b. ʿAwf—his father—ʿAbd-allāh b. Jaʿfar—his father—al-Miswar b. Makhramah, whose mother was ʿĀtikah bt. ʿAwf, in the account the first part of which I have already given concerning the murder of ʿUmar b. al-Khaṭṭāb: The five, the members of the electoral council, went down into the grave of ʿUmar,[751] then left for their homes. But ʿAbd al-Raḥmān called them back, so they followed him, and he eventually came to the house of Fāṭimah bt. Qays al-Fihriyyah, sister of al-Ḍaḥḥāk b. Qays al-Fihrī.[752] Some scholars say she was [not his sister but] his wife, a fine woman, one of perception. ʿAbd al-Raḥmān began by saying, "I have perception; you have insight. Listen and you will learn; respond and you will have knowledge. An arrow that, though lacking power, hits the target is better than one, shot too hard, that goes beyond it. A mouthful of cold, brackish water is more beneficial than sweet that brings infection [after drinking]. You are leaders through whom guidance is brought about; [you are] scholars to whom reference [2789]
is made. Do not blunt your knives by differing among yourselves, nor put your swords in their scabbards away from your enemies and so make them attain their blood revenge and diminish your deeds. Every term has a prescribed end. Every house has a leader at whose command they rise up and at whose forbidding they desist. Put one of you in charge of your affair, and you will walk slowly [forward] and reach your aim. Were it not for blind dissension and complete error, the perpetrators of which say what they think and upon whom calamity alights, your intentions would not go beyond your knowledge or your deeds beyond your intentions. Beware of the advice given at a whim and the tongue that divides. A stratagem introduced into speech is more effective than swords in a wound. Associate your affairs with someone who has ample strength against whatever befalls, is trustworthy with things unknown whatever descends, is pleased with you and all of you are pleased with him, chosen from among you and

---

751. See page 93.

752. Al-Ḍaḥḥāk b. Qays al-Fihrī belonged to the Qurashī clan of Fihr. He was later in charge of Damascus, leader of Qays, the northern tribes, and fought against the Umayyad caliph, Marwān b. al-Ḥakam in 64/684 at the famous battle of Marj Rāhiṭ, where he was defeated and killed. See Ṭabarī, II, 474ff.; Iṣfahānī, *Aghānī*, XVII, 111; *EI*[2], s.v. (Dietrich).

[about whom] all of you have the same opinion. Do not obey an evil doer who gives good advice or go against someone rightly guided who gives his assistance. I am making this speech and I ask God for forgiveness for you and for myself."

'Uthmān b. 'Affān spoke next, saying, "Praise be to God who took Muḥammad as a prophet and sent him as a messenger. He told him truthfully of His promise and granted him His help
[2790] against all those distantly or closely related. God has made us his followers, guided by His command. He is our light. We act at His command when personal opinions diverge and our enemies dispute [with us]. Through His bounty God has made us leaders and through our obedience to Him commanders. Our concern does not extend beyond ourselves; no one else will approach us except those who are oblivious to the truth and shrink from the established aim. How preferable it would be if [dissension] were left alone, Ibn 'Awf! How apt that it should be,[753] if your decision is opposed and your call abandoned. I am the first to agree with you and to call to you, answerable and responsible for what I say. I ask God for forgiveness for you and for myself."

Al-Zubayr b. al-'Awwām spoke after him, saying, "To continue. He who calls upon God is not ignorant and he who answers Him is not rejected when personal opinions diverge and necks turn. Only one deviating from the truth will not comply with what you say. Only a wretch will abandon that for which you call. Were it not for God's ordinances that were made obligatory and God's regulations that were ordained and are restored to those who keep them and remain alive and do not die, death would be an escape from command and flight would be security from authority. But we must answer God's call and make the established practice prevail, lest we die a death of error and lest we suffer from the blindness of a time of ignorance. I agree with you in that to which you summon [us] and will support you in what you have commanded. There is no power and no strength except in God. I ask God for forgiveness for you and for myself."

Sa'd b. Abī Waqqāṣ then spoke, saying, "Praise be to God who

753. Reading *wa-ajdir*. Cairo reads *wa-aḥdhir*, "how wary we should be of its occurring."

was first and will be last. I praise Him because He has saved me from going astray and opened my eyes to error. Through God's [2791] guidance those who are saved are the winners; through His mercy those who are pure are successful. Through Muḥammad b. ʿAbdallāh roads are lit up, paths are straight, and all truth prevails, as all falsehood is no more. Beware, members of the electoral council, of lies and the desire of those who are false. Their desires have already dispossessed a people before you. They inherited what you did and they acquired what you did, so God made them enemies and heaped curses upon them. God said, 'Those of the Israelites who did not believe are cursed by David's tongue and that of Jesus, the son of Mary; this is because they disobeyed and transgressed. They did not restrain one another from evil that they committed. How wretched was what they did!'[754] I have scattered [the arrows in] my quiver and taken my winning arrow. For Ṭalḥah b. ʿUbaydallāh I have adopted [the opinion] of which I approved for myself.[755] I am answerable for him and responsible for what [opinion] I gave on his behalf. The matter is in your hands, Ibn ʿAwf, for you to put your effort into it and the good advice you intended. Upon God depends the ultimate destination and to Him shall be the return. I ask for forgiveness for you and for myself and take refuge in God from your opposition."

ʿAlī b. Abī Ṭālib then spoke, saying, "Praise be to God who sent forth Muḥammad as Prophet from among us and as a messenger to us. We are the house of the prophethood, the mine of wisdom, the security of the people of the world, and a salvation for those who ask for it. We have a right; if we are given it, we take it; if we are refused it, we ride the rumps of our camels, though the night journey be long.[756] If the Messenger of God had given us a commission, we would have carried out his agreement; if he had said [something] to us [as a designation], we would have disputed [with others] over it until we die.[757] No

754. Qur'ān, V:78–79.

755. It will be recalled that Ṭalḥah was absent until the final day of the deliberations, and Saʿd now speaks on his behalf.

756. That is, we take it by force.

757. ʿAlī is here claiming the succession, but making it clear that there is no explicit delegation from the Prophet.

[2792] one will be faster than I to call for truth and [claim] close kinship. There is no power and strength except in God. Listen to and remember what I have to say. Perhaps you will see swords drawn and agreements broken in this matter after this council, until you become one united group, and some of you become leaders over those in error and over partisans (*shī'ah*) of the ignorant." Then he recited the following:[758]

If Jāsim has perished, I,
    because of what Banū 'Abd b. Ḍakhm have done,[759]
Shall [nevertheless] obey anyone [even if he is] unable to find the
    right way in the desert heat,
    knowing well my destination, [guided by] every star.[760]

'Abd al-Raḥmān said, "Which one of you is willing to withdraw from this appointment and appoint someone else?" But they did not respond to his suggestion. He continued, "I withdraw myself and my cousin."[761] So the members gave him the task of settling the matter. At the *minbar* he got them to swear to give the oath of allgiance to whomsoever he gave it, even if he were to give with one hand the oath of allegiance to the other. He remained for three [nights] in his house, which was near the mosque and called today Raḥabat al-Qaḍā' (Courtyard where the Decision was made)—for this reason it was given this name. Ṣuhayb remained also for three [nights] leading the people in prayer.

'Abd al-Raḥmān sent for 'Alī and said to him, "If I do not give you the oath of allegiance, tell me to whom I should." ('Alī) replied, "'Uthmān." Then ('Abd al-Raḥmān) sent for 'Uthmān and asked the same thing of him. ('Uthmān) replied, "'Alī." ('Abd al-Raḥmān) then dismissed them both and summoned al-

---

758. The meter is *wāfir*. See Ibn al-Athīr, *Kāmil*, III, 37.

759. Jāsim is a section of the Amalekite tribe, Banū 'Abd b. Ḍakhm, from the area of al-Ṭā'if. See Ibn Manẓūr, *Lisān*, XII, 354; Fīrūzābādī, *Qāmūs*, IV, 143; Kaḥḥālah, *Mu'jam*, I, 157; II, 725. Ṭabarī, I, 230, however, places Jāsim in Oman.

760. 'Alī's message through this obscure poem is that, despite having been let down badly by his own people and despite having no one on which to depend, he can nevertheless proceed as he thinks fit, because he knows his goal is a righteous and attainable one.

761. That is, Sa'd b. Abī Waqqāṣ.

Zubayr. He asked (al-Zubayr) the same thing and he replied "'Uthmān." Then ('Abd al-Raḥmān) summoned Sa'd and said, "Whom do you advise me [to support], as we two are not candidates for (the caliphate)?" He replied, "'Uthman." On the third night, ('Abd al-Raḥmān) called, "Miswar!" I replied, "At your service!" ('Abd al-Raḥmān) exclaimed, "You are asleep, [2793]
when I have not slept for three [nights]! Go and call 'Alī and 'Uthmān for me. Miswar continued his account: I said, "Which shall I call first, uncle?" He replied, "Whichever one you wish." So I left and came to 'Alī—and he was the one I favored [for the caliphate]—and said, "Will you come to speak with my uncle?" ('Alī) said, "Did he send you to anyone else?" I replied that he had also sent me to 'Uthmān. ('Alī) said, "Which one of us did he order you to come to first?" I replied, "I asked him and he told me whichever one I wished. So I came to you first—you were the one I favored." So he came with me and we reached the place where people sit (*al-maqā'id*), and 'Alī took his seat there. I went in to see 'Uthmān and found him performing the *witr* prayer as dawn came up.[762] I asked him if he would come to speak with my uncle. ('Uthmān) in turn asked me, "Did he send you to anyone else?" I replied that he had also sent me to 'Alī. ('Uthmān) said, "Which one of us did he order you to come to first?" I replied, "I asked him and he told me whichever one I wished. 'Alī is where the people sit." So he came with me and we all went in to see my uncle who was standing in the *qiblah*, praying. He left [his prayers] when he saw us, then he turned to 'Alī and 'Uthmān and said, "I have asked about you and about others. I find that the people regard no one as equal to you two. Will you, 'Alī, give me your oath of office based on God's Book, the practice of His Prophet, and the deeds of Abū Bakr and 'Umar?" ('Alī) replied, "Indeed no, but [only] based on my own effort in all this and in accordance with my own ability." ('Abd al-Raḥmān) turned to 'Uthmān and said, "Will you give me your oath of office based on God's Book, the practice of His Prophet, and the deeds of Abū Bakr and 'Umar?" ('Uthmān) said, "Indeed yes." Then ('Abd al-Raḥmān) made a sign with his

762. The odd number of prostrations performed in prayer at night. See *SEI*, s.v. (Wensinck).

hand to his shoulders[763] and said, "If you will come this way!" So we got up and went to the mosque where someone gave out
[2794] the cry, "Everyone in for prayer!"[764] 'Uthmān [later] said, "I held back, embarrassed by his haste to join 'Alī. I was at the back of the mosque." 'Abd al-Raḥmān appeared wearing the very turban that the Messenger of God had put on him and carrying his sword. He went up into the *minbar* where he stood for a long time. Then he said a prayer that the people did not hear.

('Abd al-Raḥmān) then spoke, "O people, I have questioned you in secret and openly on the question of [who will be] your leader. I have found that none of you regard [anyone else] as equal to one of these two, 'Alī or 'Uthmān. Come forward to me, 'Alī." He did so and stood beneath the *minbar*. 'Abd al-Raḥmān took his hand and said, "Will you give me your oath of office based on God's Book, the practice of His Prophet, and the deeds of Abū Bakr and 'Umar?" He replied, "No, but based on my own effort in all this and in accordance with my own ability." ('Abd al-Raḥmān) let go of ('Alī's) hand and called out, "Come forward to me, 'Uthmān." He took him by his hand, as ('Uthmān) stood where 'Alī had stood, and said, "Will you give me your oath of office based on God's Book, the practice of His Prophet, and the deeds of Abū Bakr and 'Umar?" ('Uthmān) replied, "Indeed yes!" So ('Abd al-Raḥmān) stretched right up to the ceiling of the mosque, his hand still in 'Uthmān's hand. Then he said, "O God, hear and bear witness! O God, I have placed what was my own responsibility in all this upon 'Uthmān." The people crowded round to give 'Uthmān the oath of allegiance, until they reached him at the *minbar*. 'Abd al-Raḥmān sat down where the Prophet sat in the *minbar*, and he sat 'Uthmān down on the second step. The people began to
[2795] give him the oath of allegiance, but 'Alī excused himself. 'Abd al-Raḥmān quoted, "He who breaks his word, does so to his own detriment; he who keeps the agreement he has made with God, He will bring him a great reward."[765] Then 'Alī came back,

---

763. Thus signifying that they should walk on either side of him.
764. Arabic, *al-ṣalātu jāmi'ah*. See Dozy, *Supplément*, I, 216–17.
765. Qur'ān, XLVIII:10.

pushing his way through the people, and gave the oath of allegiance, saying, "Deceit! What deceit!"

'Abd al-'Azīz[766] said, "The reason for 'Alī's mentioning deceit was simply that 'Amr b. al-'Āṣ had met 'Alī during the period the electoral council was meeting and said, "Abd al-Raḥmān is striving hard. The more you show (your) firm resolution, the less keen he is (that you be appointed). But [the more you say you will act according to] (your) effort and ability, the keener he is (that you be appointed). Then ('Amr b. al-'Āṣ) met 'Uthmān and said, "Abd al-Raḥmān is striving hard. He will indeed give you his oath of allegiance only because of firm resolution. So accept (the offer).' It was for this reason that 'Alī mentioned deceit."[767]

Then ('Abd al-Raḥman) went off with 'Uthmān to the house of Fāṭimah bt. Qays, where he sat down with the people. Al-Mughīrah b. Shu'bah got up to make a speech, with 'Alī sitting there, "Praise be to God, Abū Muḥammad, who has granted you success! There was indeed no one other than 'Uthmān for (the caliphate)." 'Abd al-Raḥmān said, "This is none of your business, Ibn al-Dabbāgh! I could give my own oath of allegiance to no one without your saying what you have just said about him!"

Then 'Uthmān sat at the side of the mosque and called for 'Ubaydallāh b. 'Umar, who was confined in the house of Sa'd b. Abī Waqqāṣ. He is the one from whose hand the sword had been snatched after he had killed Jufaynah,[768] al-Hurmuzān, and the daughter of Abū Lu'lu'ah, saying that he was going to kill some of those who were involved in shedding his father's blood, alluding to both the Emigrants and the Helpers. Sa'd had jumped up against him, snatched the sword from his hand and tugged at his hair until he had him on the ground. He held him prisoner in his own house until 'Uthmān brought him out. [2796]
'Uthmān said to a group of Emigrants and Helpers, "Give me your advice on [what to do with] this man who has brought

766. The father of Sulaymān, see the chain of authorities, p. 154, above.

767. 'Amr later appeared as Mu'āwiyah's arbitrator against Abū Mūsā al-Ash'arī, 'Alī's arbitrator, after Ṣiffīn in 38/659. It appears from this text that he had long been against 'Alī.

768. Jufaynah was a Christian slave from al-Ḥīrah; see p. 163, below.

schism into Islam." ʿAlī replied, "I think you should kill him." One of the Emigrants said, "ʿUmar was killed yesterday; will his son be killed today?" But ʿAmr b. al-ʿĀṣ said, "Commander of the Faithful, God has exempted you from this having happened while you were in authority over the Muslims; rather this took place when you had none." ʿUthmān said, "I am now their master. I have decided that blood money should be paid in this case, and I shall bear the cost from my own money."

A Helper called Ziyād b. Labīd al-Bayāḍī recited the following when he saw ʿUbaydallāh b. ʿUmar:[769]

Ah, you have no way of escape, ʿUbaydallāh,
    no place of refuge from Ibn Arwā[770] and no means of protecting yourself.
You spilled blood indeed, completely unlawfully—
    and killing al-Hurmuzān is a dangerous matter—
For no other reason than that someone said,
    "Do you suspect al-Hurmuzān of [killing] ʿUmar?"
When so many things were happening, a fool replied,
    "Yes, do suspect him, since he suggested [it] and gave the command.
The slave's weapon[771] was inside the (Hurmuzān's) house,
    he turning it over [in his hand]. One thing [must] be reckoned in relation to another."

ʿUbaydallāh. b. ʿUmar complained to ʿUthmān of Ziyād b. Labīd and his poem, so ʿUthmān called in Ziyād b. Labīd and forbade him [from reciting it]. Ziyād recited the following, speaking of ʿUthmān:[772]

Abū ʿAmr, ʿUbaydallāh is a hostage—
    have no doubt—for the killing of al-Hurmuzān.
For if you forgive him the offense, [this will be wrong],

---

769. The meter is *ṭawīl*. Ziyād b. Labīd al-Bayāḍī is unidentified. For the poem, see Ibn al-Athīr, *Kāmil*, III, 37.

770. That is, ʿUthmān b. ʿAffān, whose mother was Arwā bt. Kurayz.

771. That is, the double-bladed dagger used by Abū Luʾluʾah to kill ʿUmar.

772. The meter is *wāfir*. See Ibn al-Athīr, *Kāmil*, III, 37.

when the circumstances of the crime are [at least] equally balanced.[773]

Will you forgive ['Ubaydallāh], when you have no right to do so?[774]

[As yet] you have no authority to do what you say.[775]

So 'Uthman summoned Ziyād b. Labīd, forbade him [to recite this], and sent him away. [2797]

According to al-Sarī—Shu'ayb—Sayf—Yaḥyā b. Sa'īd[776]—Sa'īd b. al-Musayyab: On the morning when 'Umar was stabbed 'Abd al-Raḥmān b. Abī Bakr said, "Last evening I passed by Abū Lu'lu'ah, as he was meeting in secret with Jufaynah and al-Hurmuzān. When I came upon them, they sprang up and a dagger with two baldes and its handle in the middle fell out into their midst. Consider (the instrument) with which ('Umar) was killed!" (Abū Lu'lu'ah) had already slipped through the crowd attending the mosque. A Tamīmī[777] went off in search of him and returned to them, having kept after Abū Lu'lu'ah as he left 'Umar, taken him, and killed him. (The Tamīmī) brought the dagger that 'Abd al-Raḥmān b. Abī Bakr had described. 'Ubaydallāh b. 'Umar heard about this, but held back until 'Umar died. Then he wrapped his garments round his sword, came to al-Hurmuzān, and killed him. When the sword was wounding him, he called out, "There is no god but God." Then ('Ubaydallāh b. 'Umar) passed on to Jufaynah, a Christian from al-Ḥīrah, foster son of Sa'd b. Mālik[778] and whom he had brought to Medina as a result of the peace between himself and (the inhabitants) and to teach him writing. As he held the sword over him, ('Ubaydallah) [struck Jufaynah with it], making the

773. The second hemistich reads "*wa-asbābu al-khaṭā farasā rihāni*"; literally, "two horses racing [neck and neck]". That is, it is a question of timing: was 'Uthman in authority when the crime was perpetrated or not?

774. The first hemistich reads *a-ta'fū idh 'afawta bi-ghayri ḥaqqin.*

775. With some hesitation I follow the *Glossarium*, CXCIX. The Arabic reads *fa-mā la-ka bi-lladhī taḥkī yadāni.*

776. Yaḥyā b. Sa'īd b. Mikhnaf, father of Abū Mikhnaf.

777. Tamīm b. Murr, a huge confederation of northern tribal groups inhabiting the general area of Najd, al-Yamāmah and Bahrain. See Ibn Ḥazm, *Jamharah*, 207, 466–67; Kaḥḥālah, *Mu'jam*, I, 126–33.

778. That is, Sa'd b. Abī Waqqāṣ.

sign of the cross between his eyes. Ṣuhayb heard of this and sent ʿAmr b. al-ʿĀṣ to (ʿUbaydallāh). He kept at him, saying "[Give me] the sword, by my mother and father!" until he handed it over to him. Saʿd sprang upon him, took him by the hair and they all came to Ṣuhayb.

[2798]

ʿUmar's Governors in the Garrison Towns

ʿUmar b. al-Khaṭṭāb's governor of Mecca in the year in which he was killed, that is, 23 [November 19, 643–November 7, 644], was Nāfiʿ b. ʿAbd al-Ḥārith al-Khuzāʿī;[779] of al-Ṭā'if, Sufyān b. ʿAbdallāh al-Thaqafī;[780] of Ṣanʿā', Yaʿlā b. Munyah, confederate of Banū Nawfal b. ʿAbd Manāf;[781] of al-Janad,[782] ʿAbdallāh b. Abī Rabīʿah; of al-Kūfah, al-Mughīrah b. Shuʿbah; of al-Baṣrah, Abū Mūsā al-Ashʿarī; of Egypt, ʿAmr b. al-ʿĀṣ; of Ḥimṣ, ʿUmayr b. Saʿd; of Damascus, Muʿāwiyah b. Abī Sufyān; and of Bahrain and its neighboring area, ʿUthmān b. Abī al-ʿĀṣ al-Thaqafī.

According to al-Wāqidī, Qatādah b. al-Nuʿman al-Ẓafārī[783] died in 23 and ʿUmar prayed over him.

In (this year) Muʿāwiyah launched a summer offensive and reached Amorium,[784] accompanied by some of the Companions of the Messenger of God; viz., ʿUbādah b. al-Ṣāmit,[785] Abū

779. I have no further information on Nāfiʿ b. ʿAbd al-Ḥārith al-Khuzāʿī. For the following list, see Yaʿqūbī, *Tārīkh*, II, 161.

780. Sufyān b. ʿAbdallāh al-Thaqafī has a brief entry in Ibn Ḥajar, *Tahdhīb*, IV, 115–16, although no date of death is given.

781. Yaʿlā was more commonly known as Yaʿlā b. Umayyah; see note 205. Nawfal b. ʿAbd Manāf was a tribal group (*baṭn*) of Quraysh. See Zubayrī, *Nasab Quraysh*, 197–205; Ibn Ḥazm, *Jamharah*, 115–17; Kaḥḥālah, *Muʿjam*, III, 1202–3.

782. Al-Janad is very close to, and at the present time a suburb of, the important town of Taʿizz in the southern highlands of the Yemen. It was of great importance in early and medieval times and the seat of one of the three governors in the Yemen, along with Ṣanʿā' and Ḥaḍramawt (not here mentioned). See Hamdānī, *Ṣifah*, 44, 54–55 and passim; Kay, *Yaman*, end map.

783. Qatādah b. al-Nuʿmān al-Ẓafarī fought at Badr, a fact mentioned in the biographies; e.g., Ibn Ḥajar, *Tahdhīb*, VIII, 357–58.

784. Byzantine Amorion, Arabic ʿAmmūriyyah, in the heart of Asia Minor, only approximately 170 miles southeast of Constantinople. See Yāqūt, *Muʿjam*, IV, 158; Runciman, *Crusades*, I, Map 176.

785. ʿUbādah b. al-Ṣāmit died in 34/654 or later. He had been present at the battle of Badr. See Ibn Ḥajar, *Tahdhīb*, V, 111ff.

Ayyūb Khālid b. Zayd,[786] Abū Dharr,[787] and Shaddād b. Aws.[788]

In (this year) Mu'āwiyah conquered Ascalon[789] by making peace [with its inhabitants.]

It was reported that Shurayḥ was judge of al-Kūfah in the year in which 'Umar b. al-Khaṭṭāb died; judge of al-Baṣrah was Ka'b b. Sūr.[790] According to Muṣ'ab b. 'Abdallāh—Mālik b. Anas[791] —Ibn Shihāb: Abū Bakr and 'Umar had no judge.

---

786. Abū Ayyūb Khālid b. Zayd died in 50/670 or 55/675. See Ibn Ḥajar, *Tahdhīb*, III, 90–91.

787. Abū Dharr al-Ghifārī died ca. 32/653. See Ibn Ḥajar, *Tahdhīb*, XII, 90ff.; *EI*[2], s.v. (Robson); Cameron, *Abū Dharr*, passim.

788. Shaddād b. Aws died ca. 64/683. See Ibn Ḥajar, *Tahdhīb*, IV, 315.

789. 'Asqalān on the Mediterranean coast north of Gaza. See Yāqūt, *Mu'jam*, IV, 122; Le Strange, *Palestine*, 400–3 and map opposite 14.

790. For Ka'b b. Sūr al-Azdī, see Wakī', *Akhbār*, I, 274ff.

791. Mālik b. Anas was the author of the famous *Muwaṭṭa'* and died in 179/796. See Ibn Ḥajar, *Tahdhīb*, X, 5–9; Sezgin, *GAS*, I, 457–64.

Bibliography

Abbott, Nabia. *Studies in Arabic Literary Papyri*. I. *Historical Texts*. The University of Chicago Oriental Institute Publcations. Volume LXXV. Chicago, 1957.

ʿAbd al-Bāqī, Muḥammad Fu'ād. *Al-Muʿjam al-mufahras li-alfāẓ al-Qur'ān al-karīm*. [Cairo], 1378 A.H.

Abun-Nasr, Jamil M. *A History of the Maghrib*. Cambridge, 1975.

Arberry, A. J. *The Koran Interpreted*. London, 1965.

al-Balādhurī, Aḥmad b. Yaḥyā. *Futūḥ al-buldān. Liber Expugnationis Regionum*, ed. M. J. de Geoje. Leiden, 1866.

Balʿami; see al-Ṭabarī.

Barthold, W. *An Historical Geography of Iran*, trans. Svat Soucek. Princeton, N.J., 1984.

———. *Turkestan down to the Mongol invasion*. London, 1977.

al-Bayḍāwī, ʿAbdallāh b. ʿUmar. *Beidhawii commentarius in Coranum . . .*, ed. H. O. Fleischer, 3 vols. Leipzig, 1846–78.

Belʿami, Abou-ʿAli Moʿhammed; see al-Ṭabarī.

Ben Shemesh, A. *Taxation in Islam. Abū Yūsuf's Kitāb al-Kharāj*, III. Leiden and London, 1969.

al-Bilādī, ʿĀtiq b. Ghayth. *Muʿjam maʿālim al-Ḥijāz*, 10 vols. Mecca, 1978–84.

Bosworth, Clifford Edmund. *The Islamic Dynasties*. Islamic Surveys 5. Edinburgh, 1967.

———. *The Mediaeval Islamic Underworld. The Banū Sasān in Arabic Society and Literature*, 2 vols. Leiden, 1976.

———. *Sīstān under the Arabs*. Rome, 1968.

Brice, W. C. *An Historical Atlas of Islam*. Leiden, 1981.

Butler, A. J. *The Arab Conquest of Egypt and the Last Years of Roman Domination*, 2nd ed. Oxford, 1978.

Cahen, C. "Coran IX-29: *ḥattā yu'tū l-ǧizyata 'an yadin wa-hum ṣāǧirūna.*" *Arabica* 9 (1962): 76–79.

Cambridge History of Iran, ed. R. N. Frye. IV. *The Period from the Arab Invasion to the Saljuqs*. Cambridge, 1975 [*CHIr*].

Cambridge History of Islam, ed. P. M. Holt, Ann K. S. Lambton, and Bernard Lewis, 2 vols. Cambridge, 1970 [*CHIs*].

Cameron, A. J. *Abū Dharr al-Ghifārī*. London, 1973.

Caskel, Werner. *Ǧamharat an-nasab. Das genealogische Werk des Hišām ibn Muḥammad al-Kalbī*. I. Introd. by Werner Caskel, tables by Gert Strenziok. II. Commentary on the tables by Werner Caskel, index begun by Gert Strenziok, completed by Werner Caskel. Leiden, 1966.

Christensen, A. *L'Iran sous les Sassanides*. Copenhagen, 1936.

Coulson, N. J. *A History of Islamic Law*. Edinburgh, 1964.

Dennett, D. C. *Conversion and the Poll Tax in Early Islam*. Cambridge, Mass., 1950.

Donner, Fred McGraw. *The Early Islamic Conquests*. Princeton, N.J., 1981.

Dozy, R. *Supplément aux dictionnaires arabes*, 2 vols., 3rd ed. Leiden and Paris, 1967.

Duri, A. A. "The Iraq School of History to the Ninth Century—A Sketch." *Historians of the Middle East*, ed. Bernard Lewis and P. M. Holt, London, 1962. pp. 46–53.

———. *The Rise of Historical Writing Among the Arabs*. Princeton, N.J., 1983.

Encyclopaedia Iranica. London, 1982– [*EIr*].

Encyclopaedia of Islam, 1st ed. Leiden, 1913–38; 2nd ed. Leiden, 1960– [*EI*[1] and *EI*[2]].

al-Farazdaq, Hammām b. Ghālib. *Dīwān al-Farazdaq*, ed. 'Abdallāh Ismā'īl al-Ṣāwī, 2 vols. Cairo, 1354/1936.

Fatḥnamah-i-Sind, ed. N. A. Baloch. Islamabad, 1403/1983.

al-Fīrūzābādī, Muḥammad b. Ya'qūb. *Al-Qāmūs al-muḥīṭ*, 4 vols. Cairo, 1952.

Freeman-Grenville, G. S. P. *The Muslim and Christian Calendars*. Oxford, 1963.

Freytag, G. W. F. *Arabum Proverbia*, 3 vols. Bonn, 1838–43.

Goldziher, I. "Ueber Dualtitel." *Wiener Zeitschrift für die Kunde des Morgenlandes* 13 (1899): 321–29.

Guillaume, A. *The Life of Muhammad*. Lahore, Karachi, and Decca, 1967.

al-Hamdānī, al-Ḥasan b. Aḥmad. *Ṣifat Jazīrat al-'Arab*, ed. David Heinrich Müller. Leiden, 1968.

Hill, D. R. *The Termination of Hostilities in the Early Arab Conquests. A.D. 634–656*. London, 1971.

Hinds, Martin. "The First Arab Conquests in Fars." *Iran* 23 (1984): 39–55.

———. *Sayf b. 'Umar's Sources on Arabia*. University of Riyad, Sources for the History of Arabia I/2. Riyadh, 1979.

Hinz, Walther. *Islamische Masse und Gewichte: Umgerechnet ins metrische System*. Leiden, 1970.

Ibn 'Abd Al-Ḥakam. *Futūḥ Miṣr: History of the Conquest of Egypt, North Africa and Spain*, ed. C. C. Torrey. New Haven, Conn., 1922.

Ibn 'Abd Rabbih, Aḥmad b. Muḥammad al-Andalusī. *Kitāb al-'Iqd al-farīd*, ed. Aḥmad Amīn, Aḥmad al-Zayn, and Ibrāhīm al-Abyārī, 7 vols. Cairo, 1367–72/1948–53.

Ibn al-Athīr, 'Alī b. Muḥammad. *Tārīkh al-Kāmil*, III, Cairo, 1301 [1883–4].

———. *Usd al-ghābah fī ma'rifat al-ṣaḥābah*, 5 vols. Cairo, 1280–86/1863–69.

Ibn Ḥajar, Aḥmad b. 'Alī al-'Asqalānī. *Al-Iṣābah fī tamyīz al-ṣaḥābah*, ed. Ṭāhā M. al-Zaynī, 13 vols. Cairo, 1389–96/1969–76.

———. *Tahdhīb al-tahdhīb*, 12 vols. Cairo, 1325–27.

Ibn Ḥazm, 'Alī b. Aḥmad al-Andalusī. *Jamharat ansāb al-'Arab*, ed. 'Abd al-Salām Muḥammad Hārūn. Cairo, 1962.

Ibn Hishām, 'Abd al-Malik. *Al-Sīrah al-nabawiyyah*, ed. Muṣṭafā al-Saqqā et al., 2 vols. Cairo, 1955.

Ibn Manẓūr, Muḥammad b. Mukarram. *Lisān al-'Arab*, 15 vols. Beirut, 1955–56.

Ibn Qutaybah, 'Abdallāh b. Muslim. *Al-Ma'ārif*, ed. Tharwat 'Ukāshah. Cairo, 1969.

Ibn Rasūl, al-Malik al-Ashraf 'Umar b. Yūsuf. *Ṭurfat al-aṣḥāb fī ma'rifat al-ansāb*, ed. K. W. Zetterstéen. Damascus, 1949.

Ibn Sa'd, Muḥammad. *al-Ṭabaqāt al-kubrā*, 9 vols. Beirut, 1380–88/1960–68.

al-Iṣfahānī, Abū al-Faraj 'Alī b. al-Ḥusayn. *Kitāb al-Aghanī*, 20 vols. and indexes. Bulaq, 1285–86/1868–70.

Jayyusi, Salma K. "Umayyad Poetry." A. F. L. Beeston et al., eds., *Cambridge History of Arabic Literature. Arabic Literature to the End of the Umayyad Period*. Cambridge, 1983. pp. 387–433.

Justi, Ferdinand. *Iranisches Namenbuch*. Marburg, 1895.

Juynboll, G. H. A. *Muslim Tradition: Studies in Chronology, Provenence and Authorship of Early Ḥadīth*. Cambridge, 1983.

Kaḥḥālah, 'Umar Riḍā. *Mu'jam qabā'il al-'Arab*, 3 vols. and 2 supplementary vols. Beirut, 1982.

Kay, Henry Cassels. *Yaman, Its Early Mediaeval History*. London, 1892.
Kazimirski, A. De Biberstein. *Dictionnaire arabe-français*, 2 vols. Paris, 1860.
Kennedy, H. *The Prophet and the Age of the Caliphates*. London, 1986.
al-Khaṭīb al-Baghdādī. *Tārīkh Baghdād*. Cairo, 1349/1931.
Kister, M. J. "*ʿAn yadin* (Qur'ān, IX/29), an Attempt at Interpretation." *Arabica* 11 (1964): 272–78.
Lambrick, H. T. *Sind, a General Introduction*. Hyderabad (Sind), 1964.
Lane, Edward William. *An Arabic-English Lexicon*, 8 parts. London and Edinburgh, 1863–93.
Le Strange, G. *The Lands of the Eastern Caliphate*. London, 1966.
———. *Palestine under the Moslems*. London, 1890.
Løkkegard, F. *Islamic Taxation in the Classic Period*. Copenhagen, 1950.
al-Madʿaj, ʿAbd al-Muḥsin Madʿaj M. *The Yemen in Early Islam. 9–233/630–847. A Political History*. London, 1988.
al-Manāsik wa-amākin ṭuruq al-ḥajj wa-maʿālim al-Jazīrah, ed. Ḥamad al-Jāsir. Riyadh, 1969.
al-Masʿūdī, ʿAlī b. al-Ḥusayn. *Les Prairies d'or. Kitāb Murūj al-dhahab wa-maʿādin al-jawāhir*, ed. and trans. C. Barbier de Meynard, IV. Paris, 1914.
Minorsky, V. *Studies in Caucasian History*. Cambridge, 1953.
Morony, Michael. *Iraq after the Muslim Conquest*. Princeton, N.J., 1984.
Nöldeke, T. *Geschichte der Perser und Araber zur Zeit der Sasaniden*, Photographic reproduction. Graz, 1973.
Penrice, John. *A Dictionary and Glossary of the Kor-an*. London, 1873.
Pickthall, Marmaduke. *The Glorious Koran*. London, 1976.
Puin, G. R. *Der Diwan von ʿUmar Ibn al-Ḫaṭṭāb. Ein Beitrag sur frühislamischen Verwaltungsgeschichte*. Bonn, 1969.
al-Qalqashandī, Abū al-ʿAbbās Aḥmad. *Ṣubḥ al-aʿshā fī ṣināʿat al-inshā*. Cairo, 1920.
al-Rāzī, Aḥmad b. ʿAbdallāh. *Tārīkh Madīnat Ṣanʿā'*, ed. Ḥusayn ʿAbdallāh al-ʿAmrī and ʿAbd al-Jabbār Zakkār. Ṣanʿā', 1981.
Rosenthal, Franz. *A History of Muslim Historiography*. Leiden, 1968.
Runciman, Steven. *A History of the Crusades*, 3 vols. Harmondsworth, Eng. 1965.
al-Samʿānī, ʿAbd al-Karīm b. Muḥammad. *Al-Ansāb*, ed. ʿAbd al-Raḥmān b. Yaḥyā al-Muʿallimī et al., 13 vols. Hyderabad, 1382–1402/1962–82.
Sauvaire, M. A. "Matériaux pour servir à l'histoire de la numismatique

et de la métrologie musulmanes." *Journal asiatique* (1879): 455–533.

Schacht, Joseph. *An Introduction to Islamic Law*. Oxford, 1964.

———. *The Origins of Muhammadan Jurisprudence*. Oxford, 1950.

Sezgin, Fuat. *Geschichte des Arabischen Schrifttums*, I. Leiden, 1967 [*GAS*].

Sezgin, U. *Abū Miḫnaf. Ein Beitrag zur Historiographie der umaiyadischen Zeit*. Leiden, 1971.

Shaban, M. A. *Islamic History. A New Interpretation*. I. A.D. 600–750. Cambridge, 1971.

al-Shantamarī, al-A'lam. *Dīwān Zuhayr b. Abī Sulmā wa-sharḥuh*. Leiden 1307 A.H.

Shorter Encyclopaedia of Islam, ed. H. A. R. Gibb and J. H. Kramers. Leiden and London, 1961 [*SEI*].

Spuler, Bertold. *Iran in früh-islamischer Zeit*. Wiesbaden, 1952.

Steingass, F. *A Comprehensive Persian-English Dictionary*. London, 1947.

al-Ṭabarī, Abū Ja'far Muḥammad b. Jarīr. *Ta'rīkh al-rusul wa-al-mulūk*, ed. M. J. De Goeje et al. *Annales quos scripsit Abu Djafar . . . at-Tabari*, 13 vols. and 2 vols. *Indices* and *Introductio, glossarium, addenda et emendanda* [Ṭabarī and *Glossarium*].

———. Ed. Muḥammad Abū al-Faḍl Ibrāhīm, 10 vols. Cairo, 1960–69 [Cairo].

———. *The History of al-Ṭabarī*. Albany, N.Y., 1985–, [Translation].

———. *Chronique de Abou-Djafar-Mo'hammed-ben-Djarir-ben-Yezid Tabari. Traduite sur la version persane d'Abou-'Ali Mo'hammed Bel'ami . . . par M. Hermann Zotenberg*, III. Paris, 1958.

———. *Selection from the Annals of Tabari*, ed. M. J. De Goeje. Semitic Study Series 1. Leiden, 1951 [*Selection*].

al-Ṭanṭāwī, 'Alī, and al-Ṭanṭāwī, Nājī, *Akhbār 'Umar b. al-Khaṭṭāb*. Damascus, 1379/1959.

Tha'lab, Aḥmad b. Yaḥyā al-Shaybānī. *Sharḥ Dīwān Zuhayr b. Abī Sulmā*. Cairo, 1363/1944.

Wakī', Muḥammad b. Khalaf. *Akhbār al-quḍāh*. I. ed. 'Abd al-'Azīz Muṣṭafā al-Murāghī. Cairo, 1366/1947.

al-Wāqidī, Muḥammad b. 'Umar. *Kitāb Futūḥ Miṣr wa-al-Iskandariyyah*, ed. H. A. Hamaker. Leiden, 1825.

———. *Kitāb al-Maghāzī*, ed. Marsden Jones, 3 vols. London, 1966.

Watt, W. Montgomery. *Muhammad at Mecca*. Oxford, 1965.

———. *Muhammad at Medina*. Oxford, 1962.

Wright, W. *A Grammar of the Arabic Language*, 3rd ed., rev. W. Robertson Smith and M. J. De Goeje, 2 vols. Cambridge, 1951.

al-Yaʿqūbī, Aḥmad b. Abī Yaʿqūb. *Tārīkh al-Yaʿqūbī*, 2 vols. Beirut, 1960.

Yāqūt b. ʿAbdallāh al-Ḥamawī. *Muʿjam al-Buldān*, 5 vols. Beirut, 1979.

al-Zabīdī, Muḥammad Murtaḍā. *Tāj al-ʿarūs min jawāhir al-qāmūs*, ed. ʿAbd al-Sattār Aḥmad Faraj et al. Kuwait, 1965–.

Zarrīnkūb, ʿAbd al-Ḥusayn. "The Arab Conquest of Iran and Its Aftermath." R. N. Frye, ed., *The Cambridge History of Iran*, IV. Cambridge, 1975. pp. 1–57.

al-Zubayrī, al-Muṣʿab b. ʿAbdallāh. *Kitāb Nasab Quraysh*, ed. E. Lévi-Provençal. Cairo, 1953.

Index

The index contains all proper names of persons, places, and tribal and other groups, as well as topographical data, occurring in the foreword, the text, and the footnotes, together with some technical terms. As far as the footnotes are concerned, however, only those names that belong to the medieval or earlier periods are listed.

The definite article, the abbreviations b. *(for* ibn, *son) and* bt. *(for* bint, *daughter), and everything in parentheses have been disregarded for the purposes of alphabetization. Where a name occurs in both the text and the footnotes on the same page, only the page number is given.*

A

Abān b. Abī ʿAmr b. Umayyah b. ʿAbd Shams 91 n. 404
Ābān Jādhawayh, governor of al-Rayy 52
ʿAbbād b. Ziyād 76 n. 339
al-ʿAbbās b. ʿAbd al-Muṭṭalib 145, 147
ʿAbbās b. Abī Ṭālib, *rāwī* 103, 104
ʿAbd al-ʿAzīz, *rāwī* 161
ʿAbd al-Ḥamīd b. Bayān, *rāwī* 139
ʿAbd al-Malik b. Marwān 42
ʿAbd al-Malik b. Nawfal b. Musāḥiq, *rāwī* 132
ʿAbd al-Malik b. Sulaymān, *rāwī* 117
ʿAbd al-Munʿim b. Idrīs, *rāwī* 106 n. 514
ʿAbd al-Qays 53 n. 251
ʿAbd al-Raḥmān, the eldest son of ʿUmar b. al-Khaṭṭāb 100, 101
ʿAbd al-Raḥmān, the middle son of ʿUmar b. al-Khaṭṭāb 101
ʿAbd al-Raḥmān, the youngest son of ʿUmar b. al-Khaṭṭāb 101
ʿAbd al-Raḥmān b. ʿAbdallāh b. ʿAbd al-Ḥakam al-Miṣrī, *rāwī* 98
ʿAbd al-Raḥmān b. Abī Bakr al-Ṣiddīq 100, 163
ʿAbd al-Raḥmān b. Abī Zayd, *rāwī* 139
ʿAbd al-Raḥmān b. ʿAmr 13
ʿAbd al-Raḥmān b. ʿAwf 90–93, 109, 112, 145–58, 160, 161
ʿAbd al-Raḥmān b. Jazʾ al-Sulamī, religious scholar 45, 46
ʿAbd al-Raḥmān b. Khālid b. al-Walīd al-Makhzūmī 46
ʿAbd al-Raḥmān b. Mahdī, *rāwī* 10, 107, 141
ʿAbd al-Raḥmān b. Rabīʿah, Dhū al-Nūr 5, 34, 35, 37–42

'Abd al-Raḥmān b. Zayd, *rāwī* 105
'Abd al-Razzāq b. Hammām, *rāwī* 98
'Abd Shams 91 n. 404, 145 n. 727
'Abdallāh b. 'Abdallāh b. 'Itbān 3–9, 44, 73, 74, 77
'Abdallāh b. Abī Bakr 101, 123, 129 n. 640
'Abdallāh b. Abī Isḥāq *rāwī* 123
'Abdallāh b. Abī Rabī'ah, governor of the Yemen 122, 152, 164
'Abdallāh b. Abī Ṣa'ṣa'ah, *rāwī* 134
'Abdallāh b. Abī Sulaymān, *rāwī* 141
'Abdallāh b. Abī 'Uqayl al-Thaqafī 54
'Abdallāh b. Aḥmad b. Shabbawayh al-Marwazī, *rāwī* 68
'Abdallāh b. 'Āmir al-Qurashī 58 n. 276
'Abdallāh b. 'Āmir b. Rabī'ah, *rāwī* 97, 120
'Abdallāh b. 'Amr 13
'Abdallāh b. Budayl b. Warqā' al-Khuzā'ī 4, 5 n. 22, 74
'Abdallāh b. Dāwūd al-Wāsiṭī, *rāwī* 121
'Abdallāh b. al-Ḥārith b. Warqā' al-Asadī 4, 83
'Abdallāh b. Ja'far b. Abī Ṭālib, *rāwī* 85, 155
'Abdallāh b. Ja'far al-Zuhrī 89, 117
'Abdallāh b. Kathīr al-'Abdī, *rāwī* 83, 87–89
'Abdallāh b. Mas'ūd 5, 6, 14, 16
'Abdallāh b. Qays al-Ash'athī 9
'Abdallāh b. Tha'labah b. Ṣu'ayr, *rāwī* 102
'Abdallāh b. 'Umar, son of 'Umar b. al-Khaṭṭāb 12, 92, 98, 100, 142, 144–48, 151
'Abdallāh b. 'Umayr 75, 134, 135
'Abdallāh b. al-Walīd, *rāwī* 112, 113
'Abdallāh b. Warqā' al-Riyāḥī 4, 6, 7, 9, 83
'Abdallāh b. al-Zubayr 12
Abū al-'Abbās, Abbasid caliph 97 n. 444
Abū al-'Abbās Sahl b. Sa'd al-Sā'idī, *rāwī* 143
Abū 'Abd al-Raḥmān al-Fazārī, *rāwī* 55
Abū 'Abdallāh al-Burjumī, *rāwī* 129
Abū 'Āmir 'Abd al-Malik b. 'Amr al-'Aqadī, *rāwī* 109, 113
Abū 'Amr. *See* 'Uthmān b. 'Affān
Abū 'Amr, client of Ibrāhīm b. Ṭalhah, *rāwī* 85, 133
Abū 'Amr b. al-'Alā', *rāwī* 71
Abū 'Amr Dhakwān, *rāwī* 96
Abū Ayyūb Khālid b. Zayd, Companion 164, 165
Abū Bakr b. 'Abdallāh b. Abī Maryam, *rāwī* 120
Abū Bakr al-'Absī, *rāwī* 104
Abū Bakr b. 'Ayyāsh, *rāwī* 107, 111, 112
Abū Bakr b. Ismā'īl b. Muḥammad b. Sa'd, *rāwī* 93
Abū Bakr al-Ṣiddīq, xiii, xiv, 92–94, 97 n. 447, 102, 116, 132, 136, 140, 141 n. 703, 143 n. 713, 144 n. 725, 151, 154, 159, 160, 165
Abū Dharr al-Ghifārī, Companion 165
Abū al-Dihqānah, *rāwī* 105
Abū Dujānah 32
Abū Firās al-Rabī'ah b. Ziyād al-Nahdī, *rāwī* 108
Abū Ḥafṣ, *kunyah* of 'Umar b. al-Khaṭṭāb 57, 95, 106
Abū Ḥamzah Muḥammad b. Maymūn al-Sukkārī, *rāwī* 114
Abū Ḥārithah, *rāwī* 133
Abū al-Ḥasan. *See* 'Alī b. Abī Ṭālib
Abū Hāshim b. 'Utbah b. Rabī'ah b. 'Abd Shams 15
Abū Ḥaṣīn 'Uthmān b. 'Āṣim, *rāwī* 107
Abū Ḥayyān Yaḥyā b. Sa'īd, *rāwī* 105
Abū Ḥazrah Ya'qūb b. Mujāhid, *rāwī* 96
Abū Hilāl, *rāwī* 99
Abū Ḥudhayfah 2 n. 8, 144
Abū Hurayrah al-Dawsī 40, 119
Abū al-Ḥuwayrith 'Abd al-Raḥmān b. Mu'āwiyah, *rāwī* 115
Abū 'Imrān al-Jawnī, *rāwī* 10, 106

Abū Isḥāq. *See* Sa'd b. Abī Waqqāṣ
Abū Ismā'īl al-Hamdānī, *rāwī* 122
Abū Ja'far. *See* al-Ṭabarī
Abū Ja'far, Abbasid caliph 97 n. 449
Abū al-Jahm b. Ḥudhayfah 100
Abū Janāb, *rāwī* 83, 87
Abū al-Janūb 'Uqbah b. 'Alqamah al-Yashkurī, *rāwī* 55
Abū Kurayb Muḥammad b. al-'Alā', *rāwī* 106, 107, 111, 112
Abū Lu'lu'ah Fayrūz al-Nihāwandī xvii, 89, 90, 92, 103, 161, 163
Abū Ma'bad Nāfidh al-Aslamī, *rāwī* 122
Abū Ma'shar, *rāwī* 17, 64, 68, 94, 123
Abū Mikhnaf Lūṭ b. Yaḥyā, *rāwī* 143, 163 n. 776
Abū Mu'ādh al-Anṣārī, *rāwī* 123
Abū Mu'āwiyah Muḥammad b. Khāzim al-Ḍarīr, *rāwī* 105
Abū Mufazzir al-Aswad b. Quṭbah 26
Abū al-Mughīrah 'Abd al-Quddūs b. al-Ḥajjāj al-Khawlānī, *rāwī* 104
Abū al-Muḥajjal al-Rudaynī, *rāwī* 83
Abū Muḥammad. *See* 'Abd al-Raḥmān b. 'Awf
Abū al-Mujālid Jarād b. 'Amr, *rāwī* 133
Abū al-Mukhāriq Zuhayr b. Sālim, *rāwī* 104, 105
Abū Mūsā al-Ash'arī 3, 4, 8, 9, 21 n. 111, 34, 43, 44, 47, 49, 50, 63, 70, 79, 80–83, 106, 161 n. 767, 164
Abū Naḍrah al-Mundhir b. Mālik al-'Abdi al-'Awqī, *rāwī* 108
Abū Qutaybah, *rāwī* 98
Abū al-Sā'ib. *See* Salm b. Junādah
Abū Salamah al-Tabūdhakī, Mūsā, *rāwī* 99
Abū Sirwa'ah 13
Abū Ṣufrah, father of al-Muhallab 69
Abū Sufyān, father of Mu'āwiyah and 'Utbah 133, 134
Abū Sufyān, *rāwī* 67
Abū Ṭalhah al-Anṣārī 91, 146, 148, 149
Abū Ṭālib, father of 'Alī 135 nn. 674–75, 150 n. 738
Abū al-Ṭufayl 'Āmir b. Wāthilah, *rāwī* 48
Abū 'Ubaydah b. al-Jarrāḥ 143
Abū 'Umar Dithār b. Abī Shabīb, *rāwī* 71
Abū Usāmah Ḥammād b. Usāmah, *rāwī* 112
Abū 'Uthmān al-Nahdī, *rāwī* 71, 133
Abū Wā'il. *See* Shaqīq b. Salamah
Abū al-Walīd Yasār b. 'Abd al-Raḥmān al-Makkī, *rāwī* 132, 135
Abū al-Yaqẓān. *See* 'Ammār b. Yāsir
Abū Yazīd al-Madīnī, *rāwī* 103
Abū Yūsuf 5, 6 n. 31
Abū Zakariyyā' Yaḥyā b. Muṣ'ab al-Kalbī, *rāwī* 104
Abū Zayd, grandfather of 'Abd al-Raḥmān b. Zayd, *rāwī* 106
Abū Zayd, *rāwī*. *See* 'Umar b. Shabbah
Abū al-Zinbā', *rāwī* 105
al-Abwāb 32 n. 169, 36
'Ād 131
Adam 117, 138
adhān, call to prayer 95 n. 427
Ādharbiyān, ruler of Sābūr 70
'Adnān 55 n. 268, 119 n. 588, 132 n. 654, 136 n. 678
Afghanistan 53 n. 250
aḥdāth, police 16
ahl al-siyar, historians 51
Aḥmad. *See* Muḥammad b. 'Abdallāh, the Prophet
Aḥmad b. 'Abd al-Ṣamad al-Anṣārī, *rāwī* 114
Aḥmad b. Ḥarb al-Ṭā'ī, *rāwī* 110
Aḥmad b. Thābit al-Rāzī, *rāwī* 17, 64, 68, 94
Aḥmad b. 'Umar, *rāwī* 138
al-Aḥnaf b. Qays 9, 51, 53–60, 62, 83, 134
al-Ahwāz 8, 43 n. 207, 78
'Ā'idh b. Yaḥyā, *rāwī* 115
'Ā'ishah, wife of the Prophet 86 n. 380, 92, 93, 96, 101, 102, 145, 148
al-Akhṭal, poet 154 n. 750

Āl al-Zubayr b. al-ʿAwāmm 119 n. 585
al-ʿAlāʾ, governor of Bahrain 65
Alexandria xv
ʿAlī b. Abī Ṭālib 2 n. 8, 5 n. 22, 44, 45, 55, 72, 85 n. 379, 86, 91, 93, 100 n. 471, 104, 115, 121 n. 608, 129, 135, 143 n. 713, 144–53, 157–61
ʿAlī b. Muḥammad, *rāwī*. *See* al-Madāʾinī
ʿAlī b. Mujāhid, *rāwī* 74, 123
ʿAlī b. Sahl al-Ramlī, *rāwī* 141
Allān 37
ʿAlqamah b. ʿAbdallāh al-Muzanī, *rāwī* 10
ʿAlqamah b. Marthad, *rāwī* 83
ʿAlqamah b. al-Naḍr al-Naḍrī 54
ʿĀm al-Ramādah. *See* Destruction
al-Aʿmash, Sulaymān b. Mihrān, *rāwī* 141, 143
ʿĀmir b. Abī Muḥammad, *rāwī* 94
ʿĀmir al-Shaʿbī 15, 48, 73, 95, 99, 106, 120
ʿAmmār b. Yāsir 2, 3, 5, 6, 14, 16, 43, 47–49, 152
ʿAmmūriyyah. *See* Amorium
Amorion. *See* Amorium
Amorium 164
ʿAmr, proper name in poetry 39
ʿAmr b. Abī Sufyān 133, 134
ʿAmr b. ʿAlī, *rāwī* 10
ʿAmr b. al-ʿĀṣ 13, 14, 101, 102, 108, 148, 161, 162, 164
ʿAmr b. Bilāl b. al-Ḥārith 19
ʿAmr b. Maʿdī Karib al-Zubayrī 12, 40
ʿAmr b. Maymūn al-Awdī, *rāwī* 143, 151
ʿAmr b. Muḥammad, *rāwī* 2, 18, 43, 51, 64, 70, 73, 80, 95, 142
Āmul 76
Anas b. Zunaym al-Dīlī 135 n. 676
ʿAnazah 80
al-Anbār 105
Anṭābulus 13
Antioch 15
Anūshīrvān 38 n. 189
Apostasy, wars of. *See* Riddah wars
ʿAqīl b. Abī Ṭālib, genealogist 115
ʿAqīlah, slave girl 80 n. 358, 81, 82
aqṭaʿa, grant as a land concession 74 n. 329
Arabian Peninsula xiii, 122 n. 611, 133 n. 667
Aras, river 37 n. 182, 38 n. 188
arbāʿ, quarters (of Khurāsān) 60 n. 278
Ardashīr Khurrah 64, 66 n. 296
Armenia 36, 37, 45
Armenians 35, 36
Arwā bt. Kurayz, mother of ʿUthmān b. ʿAffān 162 n. 770
Asad b. Mūsā, *rāwī* 88
Ascalon 165
al-Ashʿath b. Qays 13
Asia Minor 32, 164 n. 784
Asīd b. al-Mutashammis, *rāwī* 9, 83
ʿĀṣim, son of ʿUmar b. al-Khaṭṭāb 101
ʿĀṣim b. Abī al-Najjūd, *rāwī* 96, 97
ʿĀṣim b. ʿAmr al-Tamīmī 75
ʿĀṣim b. Kulayb, *rāwī* 66, 112, 113
ʿAṣim b. Thābit b. Abī al-Aqlah 101
ʿĀṣim b. ʿUbaydallāh, *rāwī* 97
Aslam, father of Zayd b. Aslam, *rāwī* 105, 110, 111, 119
ʿAsqalān. *See* Ascalon
al-Aswad b. Yazīd, *rāwī* 141, 142
ʿAṭāʾ b. al-Sāʾib, *rāwī* 118
athqāl, treasures 59
ʿĀtikah bt. ʿAwf, mother of al-Miswar b. Makhramah 89, 155
ʿĀtikah bt. Zayd b. ʿAmr b. Nufayl, wife of ʿUmar b. al-Khaṭṭāb 101, 129
al-ʿAtīqah, ancient Rayy 25
ʿAttāb b. Asīd, governor of Mecca 42
ʿAwānah b. al-Ḥakam al-Kalbī, *rāwī* 121
ʿAwf b. Mālik al-Ashjaʿī, *rāwī* 94
ʿAybān, mountain 118 n. 580
Ayyūb al-Shakhtiyānī, *rāwī* 98, 106
al-Azd 117 n. 575
al-Azdahāq. *See* Shahrak
Azerbaijan xv, 1, 3, 10, 17, 21, 22, 26, 31–34, 36, 44, 45
Azhd Dahāk 70 n. 312

B

al-Bāb 32, 34, 36, 37 n. 184, 38, 40, 41, 44, 45
Bābil. *See* Babylon
Babylon xiv, 48
Badr 91 n. 405, 135 nn. 674–75, 164 nn. 783–85
Baghdad xv, 3 n. 15, 4 n. 20, 51 n. 246
Bahrain 15, 65 n. 290, 66 n. 295, 69, 104, 163 n. 777, 164
Bahrām 25
Bahrām b. al-Farrukhzādh 32, 33
Bakr b. 'Abdallāh al-Muzanī, *rāwī* 109
Bakr b. Wā'il 18 n. 93, 55
al-Balādhurī, Aḥmad b. Yaḥyā xix, 4 n. 22, 6 n. 33, 13 n. 67, 14 n. 72, 16 n. 86, 17 n. 90, 21 n. 111, 24 nn. 131 and 133, 27 n. 150, 28 n. 155, 30 n. 165, 31 n. 167, 45 n. 217, 51 n. 246, 53, 64 n. 285, 68 n. 304, 71 n. 314, 73 n. 320, 75 n. 330, 76 n. 338, 77 nn. 340 and 344
Bal'amī, Abū 'Alī Muḥammad xix, 2 nn. 5 and 7, 6 n. 33, 10 nn. 53 and 55, 14 n. 69, 20 n. 101, 21 n. 114, 22 n. 119, 24 n. 133, 31 n. 167, 64 n. 285, 73 n. 320, 75 n. 330, 76 n. 337, 77 n. 340, 79 n. 352, 89 n. 394, 95 n. 429, 101 n. 474, 104 n. 494, 143 n. 714
Balanjar 38, 39
Balkh and river 54, 56, 58, 60, 75
al-Balqā' 15
Banū al-'Abbās 137 n. 682
Banū 'Abd b. Ḍakhm 158
Banū 'Abd Manāf 145, 149, 150
Banū 'Abd b. Quṣayy 3Banū 'Abdallāh b. Ghaṭafān 136, 137
Banū Abī Mu'ayṭ 91
Banū 'Adī b. Ka'b 116
Banū 'Anazah 80 n. 357
Banū Asad b. 'Abd al-'Uzzā 4, 118 n. 585
Banū Bāsil b. Ḍabbah 23
Banū al-Ḥārith b. Ka'b 93
Banū Hāshim 91, 116, 137, 138, 145 n. 727, 147, 152, 153
Banū al-Ḥublā 4
Banū Kinānah 39
Banū Makhzūm 152
Banū Māzin 71
Banū Mu'āwiyah 19
Banū al-Muṭṭalib 153
Banū Nawfal b. 'Abd Manāf 164
Banū Salimah b. Sa'd 113
Banū Taym b. Murrah 116
Banū Umayyah 152
Barce. *See* Barqah
Barqah 13, 14
al-Barrād b. Qays 98 n. 450
bashīr, bearer of good news 22
al-Baṣrah xv, 1, 3, 4, 6, 9 n. 45, 15, 18 n. 93, 34, 43, 44, 45, 49, 50, 53, 62, 63, 70, 72, 73, 76, 79, 80, 82, 85, 104, 123 n. 616, 164, 165
al-Bathaniyyah 15
baṭn, tribal division 4 n. 19, 18 n. 93, 91 n. 403, 113 n. 550, 118 n. 585, 133 n. 667, 136 n. 681, 152 n. 744, 164 n. 781
al-Bayḍā' 39
Bayrūdh 78, 79, 80
Bayrūt. *See* Bayrūdh
Bilād al-Sūdān 14 n. 72
birdhawn, expensive horse 112
Birūdh. *See* Bayrūdh
Bīshāpūr. *See* Shāpūr
Bisṭām 28
booty xviii, 22, 26, 27, 33, 34, 60, 66, 67, 72, 77, 82, 84, 107
Bukayr b. 'Abdallāh al-Laythī 3, 22, 26, 31–34, 37
Bukhārā 54 n. 258, 76 n. 338
Būshahr (Bushire) 68 n. 302
Byzantines xiv, 127 n. 630, 143 n. 723

C

Caspian Sea 30 n. 166, 37 n. 182
Caucasus 32, 38
Children of Israel. *See* Subḥān
China 54, 59, 60, 61

Cilicia 15
Constantinople 164 n. 784
Ctesiphon 4 n. 20, 48

D

Ḍabbah b. Miḥṣan 80–82
Ḍabbah b. Shihāb b. Mu'āwiyah 19 n. 95
Ḍabbah b. Udd 19 n. 95
al-Ḍaḥḥāk b. Qays al-Fihrī 155
Dajnān 131
Damascus 15, 155 n. 752, 164
Damāvand 25 n. 136
Dāmghān 28 n. 156
Ḍamrah b. Rabī'ah al-Ramlī, *rāwī* 141
daqal, poor quality dates 77
Darābjird 70, 71
al-Darāwardī, 'Abd al-'Azīz b. Muḥammad, *rāwī* 98
Dastabā 20, 21, 22, 24
David 157
Dāwūd b. Abī Hind, *rāwī* 99
Daylam 20, 21, 23 n. 121, 27 n. 149
Destruction, Year of the 119
dhimmah, protection 23 n. 124
Dhū al-Ḥājibayn 10, 12
Dhū al-Qarnayn 42 n. 201
Dihistān 29
dihqān, village headman 80 n. 359
al-Dīnawar 18, 19, 43 n. 206, 44 n. 212
Ḍirār b. Murrah al-Kūfī, *rāwī* 103
dīwān, state register 115
Dujayl 8 n. 41
Dunbāwand 25–27

E

Egypt xv, 15, 104, 112, 164
electoral council, *shūrā* xvii, 93, 95, 143, 147–49, 152, 154, 155
Emigrants 92, 113, 141, 142, 151, 161, 162
Euphrates 5, 6, 106
Event, The, Sūrat al-Wāqi'ah 136

F

al-Fādhūsafān 7–9
al-Farazdaq, Hammām b. Ghālib b. Ṣa'ṣa'ah, poet 154
Farghānah 56, 59, 62
farj, frontier region 29 n. 158
(al-)Farrukhān 25, 30
Fārs xiv, xv, 1, 10, 52, 64 nn. 283–84, 65, 67–69, 71, 73
al-Fārūq, epithet of 'Umar b. al-Khaṭṭāb 95, 96
Fasā 70, 71
Fāṭimah, daughter of the Prophet Muḥammad 101
Fāṭimah, daughter of 'Umar b. al-Khaṭṭāb 100, 150 n. 737
Fāṭimah bt. Qays al-Fihriyyah, sister of al-Ḍaḥḥāk b. Qays al-Fihrī 155, 161
fay', immovable booty 18 n. 94
Fayrūz. *See* Abū Lu'lu'ah
al-Fayrūzān 19, 53
fifth (of booty) 22, 77, 80
Fihr 155 n. 752
fijār, conflicts 98 n. 450
Fīrūzābād 66 n. 296
al-Fīrūzābādī, Muḥammad b. Ya'qūb 58 n. 276, 158 n. 759
Fukayhah, concubine of 'Umar b. al-Khaṭṭāb 101
furūj. *See farj*

G

Gabriel 142
Gaza 165 n. 789
Georgia 37 n. 183
ghanam, sheep 112 n. 541
Ghūrak 56
al-Ghuṣn b. al-Qāsim, *rāwī* 39
Ghūzak. *See* Ghūrak
Gog 42 n. 201

H

Ḥabīb b. Abī Thābit, *rāwī* 141

Ḥabīb b. Maslamah al-Fihrī 34, 35, 45, 46
Ḥaḍramawt 164 n. 782
Ḥafṣah, daughter of ʿUmar b. al-Khaṭṭāb 100
al-Ḥajjāj, witness 46
al-Ḥajjāj b. Dīnār al-Ashjaʿī, *rāwī* 88
al-Ḥakam b. Abī al-ʿĀṣ b. Bishr b. Duhmān al-Thaqafī 68–70
al-Ḥakam b. ʿAmr al-Taghlibī 77, 78
al-Ḥakam b. Bashīr, *rāwī* 142
Hamadhān xv, 2 n. 6, 3, 17–24, 31, 64
Ḥamalah b. Juwayyah 38
Hamdān 22 n. 117
al-Hamdānī, al-Ḥasan b. Aḥmad 110 n. 535, 117 nn. 575–77, 118 n. 580, 164 n. 782
Ḥammād b. Salamah, *rāwī* 10
Ḥamzah, paternal uncle of ʿAlī b. Abī Ṭālib 150
Ḥanbal b. Abī Ḥarīdah, *rāwī* and judge of Qūhistān 74
Ḥanīfah 18
Hannād b. al-Sarī, *rāwī* 96, 97
Ḥantamah bt. Hāshim, mother of ʿUmar b. al-Khaṭṭāb 95
al-Ḥārith b. Ḥassān al-Dhuhlī 53
al-Ḥārith b. Muḥammad, *rāwī* 89, 93, 95–97, 99, 100, 102, 113–20
ḥarrah, lava field 110 n. 534
Ḥarrat Wāqim 110
al-Ḥasan, *rāwī* 67, 83
al-Ḥasan b. ʿAlī b. Abī Ṭālib 150 n. 737
al-Ḥasan al-Baṣrī 8, 15, 103, 104
Ḥātim b. al-Nuʿmān al-Bāhilī 54, 58
Ḥawrān 15
Helpers 92, 101, 113, 142, 146, 151, 161, 162
Heraclius xiv
Herat 52 n. 248, 53, 60 n. 278
Ḥijāz 133 n. 667
Hijrah 17, 94
ḥilm, forbearance 139
Ḥimṣ 5, 13, 15, 44, 164
Hind b. ʿAmr al-Jamalī/al-Murādī 27, 30, 31
Hind bt. ʿUtbah 133, 134
al-Ḥīrah 48, 89, 161 n. 768, 163
hirbadh, religious leader 67
Hishām b. ʿAbd al-Raḥmān al-Thaqafī, *rāwī* 48
Hishām b. Khālid, *rāwī* 119
Hishām b. Muḥammad al-Kalbī, *rāwī* 95, 99, 100
Hishām b. Saʿd, *rāwī* 99
Hishām b. ʿUrwah b. al-Zubayr, *rāwī* 129
Ḥizām b. Hishām al-Kaʿbī, *rāwī* 117
Hūd 131 n. 650
al-Ḥudaybiyah 100
Ḥudhayfah b. Asīd al-Ghifārī 5, 34, 37
Ḥudhayfah b. al-Yamān 5, 6, 13, 18, 19
Ḥulwān 4, 18, 51 n. 246
Ḥunayn 134
al-Hurmuz 45, 46
al-Hurmuzān 10, 53, 161, 162, 163
(al-)Ḥusayn b. ʿAlī b. Abī Ṭālib 129 n. 640, 150 n. 737
Ḥusayn al-Murrī, *rāwī* 103
ḥushira, be recruited for military service/suffer distress 33 n. 172
al-Ḥutayʾah, Abū Mulaykah Jarwal b. Aws 81, 82

I

Iblīs 138
Ibn ʿAbbās, *rāwī* 122, 135–38
Ibn ʿAbd al-Ḥakam 13 n. 67
Ibn ʿAbd Rabbih, Aḥmad b. Muḥammad al-Andalusī xix, 26 n. 142, 89 n. 394, 143 n. 714, 151 n. 741, 153 n. 746
Ibn Abī ʿAdī, Muḥammad al-Qasmalī *rāwī* 99, 106, 107
Ibn Abī ʿArūbah, *rāwī* 143
Ibn Abī Sarḥ, ʿIyāḍ b. ʿAbdallāh b. Saʿd 152
Ibn ʿAffān. *See* ʿUthmān b. ʿAffān
Ibn Arwā. *See* ʿUthmān b. ʿAffān
Ibn al-Athīr, ʿIzz al-Dīn xix, 3 nn. 10 and 12, 6 n. 33, 8 n. 43, 12 n. 58,

14 n. 70, 17 n. 90, 20 nn. 105–6, 21 nn. 110–11, 24 n. 133, 25 n. 137, 26 n. 141, 30 n. 162, 34 nn. 174 and 176, 46 n. 244, 49 n. 243, 53 n. 255, 65 nn. 286–87, 66 n. 295, 67 n. 300, 68 nn. 301 and 304, 79 nn. 355–56, 83 n. 368, 89 nn. 391 and 394, 92 n. 412, 94 n. 423, 95 n. 429, 100 n. 470, 103 n. 481, 115 nn. 563 and 566, 129 n. 640, 130 n. 643, 131 n. 649, 133 n. 661, 136 n. 681, 143 n. 714, 148 n. 732, 158 n. 758, 162 nn. 769 and 772
Ibn ʿAwf. *See* ʿAbd al-Raḥmān b. ʿAwf
Ibn ʿAwn, *rāwī* 141
Ibn al-Barāʾ b. Maʿrūr, *rāwī* 113
Ibn Bashshār, Muḥammad, *rāwī* 107, 109, 141
Ibn Budayl. *See* ʿAbdallāh b. Budayl
Ibn Daʾb, *rāwī* 122, 129
Ibn al-Dabbāgh. *See* al-Mughīrah b. Shuʿbah
Ibn Fudayl, Muḥammad al-Ḍabbī, *rāwī* 103
Ibn Ḥajar, Aḥmad b. ʿAlī al-ʿAsqalānī 2 n. 4, 3 nn. 9–10, 12, and 14, 5 nn. 24, 26, and 28, 6 n. 34, 8 nn. 42–44, 9 n. 46, 10 nn. 47–49, 13 n. 66, 14 n. 69, 15 nn. 74–75 and 77, 19 n. 99, 20 nn. 104–5, 21 nn. 109–10, 26 nn. 141 and 143, 34 nn. 175–76, 37 n. 181, 40 n. 196, 42 n. 205, 48 nn. 233–35, 49 n. 243, 53 nn. 251, 253, and 255, 55 nn. 266–67, 65 nn. 286–87, 66 nn. 293 and 295, 68 nn. 304 and 306, 69 n. 310, 71 nn. 316–17, 74 n. 326, 83 nn. 370 and 374–75, 88 nn. 386–90, 89 nn. 393, 395, and 397–98, 90 n. 401, 91 nn. 405–7, 94 nn. 418, 420–21, and 426, 96 nn. 432–41, 97 nn. 444–45 and 447–49, 98 nn. 451–58 and 460–61, 99 nn. 462–65 and 467–68, 103 nn. 479–80 and 484–87, 104 nn. 490, 492–93, and 495–96, 105 nn. 498–500, 502–4, and 508–9, 106 nn. 511 and 513–14, 107 nn. 518–23, 108 nn. 525–27, 109 nn. 529–31, 110 n. 532, 112 nn. 538–40 and 543, 113 nn. 554–45, 547, and 549, 114 nn. 554–55, 115 nn. 562 and 565, 118 nn. 581–84, 121 nn. 600, 604, and 607, 122 n. 610, 123 nn. 614–17 and 619–20, 129 n. 635, 131 nn. 646–47, 132 nn. 652 and 657, 134 n. 671, 136 n. 680, 138 nn. 687–89, 139 nn. 690 and 692, 141 nn. 705 and 708–10, 142 n. 711, 143 nn. 716–17, 720, and 722, 146 n. 730, 152 n. 742, 164 nn. 780, 783, and 785, 165 nn. 786–88 and 791
Ibn Ḥantamah. *See* ʿUmar b. al-Khaṭṭāb
Ibn Ḥazm, ʿAlī b. Aḥmad al-Andalusī 3 n. 10, 4 n. 19, 10 nn. 50 and 52, 18 n. 93, 23 n. 122, 53 n. 253, 55 n. 268, 80 n. 357, 91 n. 404, 113 n. 550, 116 nn. 569–70, 117 n. 575, 118 n. 585, 119 nn. 590 and 592–93, 132 n. 659, 133 n. 667, 136 nn. 678 and 681, 152 n. 744, 163 n. 777, 164 n. 781
Ibn Hishām, ʿAbd al-Malik 42 n. 204, 43 n. 290, 65 n. 290, 100 n. 469, 134 n. 673, 135 nn. 674–75, 140 n. 701, 144 n. 724, 145 n. 726
Ibn Ḥumayd, Muḥammad al-Rāzī, *rāwī* 15, 95, 114, 136, 142
Ibn Idrīs, ʿAbdallāh, *rāwī* 106
Ibn Isḥāq, Muḥammad, *rāwī* 15, 95, 123
Ibn Jaʿfar. *See* ʿAbdallāh b. Jaʿfar b. Abī Ṭālib
Ibn Juʿdubah, *rāwī*. *See* Yazīd b. ʿIyāḍ
Ibn Jurayj, ʿAbd al-Malik b. ʿAbd al-ʿAzīz, *rāwī* 98, 142
Ibn al-Khaṭṭāb. *See* ʿUmar b. al-Khaṭṭāb
Ibn Khuzaymah b. Thābit al-Anṣārī, ʿUmārah, *rāwī* 113
Ibn Manẓūr, Muḥammad b. Mukarram 58 n. 276, 148 n. 734, 158 n. 759
Ibn Masʿūd. *See* ʿAbdallāh b. Masʿūd
Ibn al-Munkadir, Muḥammad, *rāwī* 123

Ibn al-Muthannā, Abū Mūsā, *rawi* 99, 106
Ibn Rasūl, al-Malik al-Ashraf ʿUmar b. Yūsuf 93 n. 414
Ibn Saʿd, Muḥammad, *rāwī* and biographer 2 n. 8, 5 nn. 24 and 29, 14 n. 69, 15 n. 83, 46 n. 224, 89, 93, 95–97, 99, 100, 102, 113–20
Ibn Shihāb al-Zuhrī, *rāwī* 94, 96, 118, 123, 165
Ibn Sumayyah. *See* ʿAmmār b. Yāsir
Ibn Ṭarīf. *See* ʿIṣmah
Ibn ʿUlayyah, *rāwī* 141
Ibn ʿUmar. *See* ʿAbdallāh b. ʿUmar
Ibn Umm Ghazal al-Hamdānī 54
Ibn Wahb, ʿAbdallāh, *rāwī* 105
Ibn Yaʿmar 148
Ibn Ziyād. *See* Salm b. Ziyād
Ibn al-Zubayr. *See* ʿAbdallāh b. al-Zubayr
Ibnat Abī Ḥathmah 129
Ibrāhīm b. Muḥammad, *rāwī* 122
Ibrāhīm b. Ṭalhah, *rāwī* 88 n. 366
Ibrāhīm b. Yazīd al-Nakhaʿī, *rāwī* 141, 143
Īdhaj 43, 44
Ifrīqiyah 14 n. 72
ʿIjl 18
ikhshīd, ruler 56 n. 271
ʿIkrimah, *rāwī* 136
ʿIkrimah b. ʿAmmār, *rāwī* 138
ʿImrān, *rāwī* 113
ʿImrān b. Sawādah, *rāwī* 139
Indus xv, 77 n. 343
iqāmah, second call to prayer 95 n. 427
Iran xiii, 1, 2 n. 6
Iraq xiv, 1, 44
ʿĪsā b. Ḥafṣ, *rāwī* 113
ʿĪsā b. al-Mughīrah, *rāwī* 55
ʿĪsā b. Yazīd b. Daʾb, *rāwī* 139
isbahbadh, ruler 17
Iṣfahān xv, 1, 44, 52, 53, 80, 83
al-Iṣfahānī, Abū al-Faraj 13 n. 66, 24 n. 131, 26 n. 142, 38 n. 185, 55, 81 n. 364, 129 n. 640, 136 n. 677, 155 n. 752
Isfandiyādh, brother of Rustam 21, 31–33
Isḥāq b. ʿĪsā, *rāwī* 17, 64, 68, 94
ʿIṣmah b. ʿAbdallāh b. ʿUbaydah b. Sayf b. ʿAbd b. al-Ḥārith al-Ḍabbī 6, 9, 20, 21 n. 116
Ismāʿīl b. Abī Ḥakīm al-Qurashī, *rāwī* 131
Ismāʿīl b. Abī Khālid, *rāwī* 48, 139
Ismāʿīl b. Ibrāhīm al-Asadī, *rāwī* 103, 104, 106, 108
Ismāʿīl b. Muḥammad b. Saʿd, *rāwī* 118
Israelites 35, 157
Iṣṭakhr 64, 66–68, 70
ʿIyāḍ b. Ghanm al-Fihrī 46, 112
Iyās b. Salamah, *rāwī* 138

J

al-Jabal 20 n. 102
al-Jabbānah 119
Jābir b. ʿAmr al-Muzanī 5
Jābir b. Yazīd al-Juʿfī, *rāwī* 94, 114
Jaʿfar b. ʿAwn, *rāwī* 83, 87, 89
Jaʿfar b. Muḥammad al-Kūfī, *rāwī* 103
Jalūlāʾ 51
Jamīlah, wife of ʿUmar b. al-Khaṭṭāb 100
Jamshad 70 n. 312
al-Janad 164
Jarīr, poet 154 n. 750
Jarīr b. ʿAbdallāh al-Bajalī 47, 48
Jarīr b. Ḥāzim, *rāwī* 98
Jarmīdhāh b. al-Farrukhzādh 31
Jarmīdhān 20
al-Jārūd b. ʿAmr al-ʿAbdī, Abū al-Mundhir 69
Jāsim 158
al-Jawf 133 n. 667
Jaxartes, river 54 n. 258, 56 n. 272
Jayy 7, 44, 53, 80
al-Jazīrah 15, 34, 44, 45, 46 n. 224, 50, 104
Jerusalem 143 n. 723
Jesus 157

al-Jibāl 3 n. 15, 4 n. 18, 43, 44 n. 214
jīl, ruler of Jīlān 30
Jīlān 20 n. 108, 30, 40
Jīraft 73 n. 322, 74
jizyah. *See* tribute
Jordan 15
Jubayr b. al-Ḥuwayrith b. Nuqayd, *rāwī* 115
Jubayr b. Muṭ'im 14, 116
Jufaynah 161, 163
Jundub 33
Jūr 66, 67, 69
Jurjān xv, 17, 27, 28–30, 46
Jurjistān. *See* Georgia
Jurzān 45

K

Ka'b al-Aḥbār 90, 92, 105
Ka'b b. Sūr al-Azdī, *qāḍī* 165
Ka'bah 148 n. 734
Kābul 76 n. 338
Kalb 133
Kandahar 75
Kangavar. *See* Kinkiwar
Khālid b. Abī Bakr, *rāwī* 97
Khālid b. al-Ḥadhdha', *rawi* 134
Khālid b. al-Walīd 6 n. 34, 13, 42, 46 n. 222
khalīfah, caliph 114 n. 556
Khallād b. Aslam, *rāwī* 103
khāqān, ruler of the Turks 54
kharāj 3 n. 16, 6 n. 30, 29 n. 158, 43, 75, 84, 86
al-Khaṭṭāb, father of 'Umar 131
Khaybar 140 n. 701
Khazars 37 n. 184, 39 n. 188
al-Khazraj 4 n. 19, 113 n. 550
Khulayd b. Dhafarah al-Namarī, *rāwī* 49, 95
khulla', sing. *khālin*, herdsmen 57 n. 275
Khurāsān xv, 3, 30, 51–56, 59, 60, 74, 75
Khusrawshunūm 19
al-Khuwār 27
Khuzā'ah 117, 148 n. 734
Khūzistān 8 n. 41, 10 n. 53, 43 nn. 207–8, 78 n. 352
Kilāb b. Murrah 3 n. 10
Kinānah 132, 148 n. 734
Kindah 13 n. 62
Kinkiwar 20
Kirmān xv, 1, 5 n. 22, 8, 9, 52, 60, 73, 74, 77
al-Kūfah xiv, xv, 1–6, 10, 11 n. 57, 13, 14, 16, 19, 21 n. 109, 24 n. 131, 31, 43–45, 47–51, 53, 62, 63, 70, 83, 104, 164, 165
Kulayb b. Abī al-Bukayr al-Laythī 90
Kur, river 37 n. 183
Kurdistān 43 n. 206, 44 n. 214
Kurds 71, 78, 83
kuwar, regions 60 n. 278

L

land tax. *See kharāj*
al-Lāriz 27
Libya 13 n. 67
Lu'ayy b. Ghālib 152 n. 744
Luhayyah, wife of 'Umar b. al-Khaṭṭāb 101

M

Ma'arrat Maṣrīn 15
al-Madā'in xiv, 4, 8 n. 43, 25, 48, 69
al-Madā'inī, 'Alī b. Muḥammad, *rāwī* 30, 74, 94, 95, 99–102, 120–23, 129, 131, 132, 134, 135, 143
Ma'dan b. Abī Ṭalhah, *rāwī* 107
Madhḥij 93 n. 414
Maghrib 14 nn. 71–72
Magians 62
Magog 42 n. 201
Māh 18, 44
māh, region 1, 18
Māh al-Baṣrah 18 n. 91, 44 n. 211
Māh Dīnār 44

Māh al-Kūfah 18 n. 91
al-Mahdī, Abbasid caliph 123 n. 616
Makhlad al-Bakrī, *rāwī* 83
Makhramah b. Nawfal, genealogist 115
Makrān xv, 53 n. 251, 77, 78
Malādh, river 28
Mālik 105
Mālik b. Anas 165
Malwiyyah, rock 19
Manādhir 79
Manṣūr b. Abī al-Aswad al-Laythī, *rāwī* 141
Manṣūr b. al-Muʿtamir al-Sulamī, *rāwī* 88
Maʿqil b. Yasār al-Muzanī, *rāwī* 9, 10, 12
Mardānshāh, ruler of Dunbāwand 27
Marḍī b. Muqarrin 37
marj, field 18
Marj al-Qalʿah 18
Marj Rāhiṭ 155 n. 752
Marw 52, 53 n. 256, 58–61, 76 n. 338
Marw al-Rūdh 53, 54, 56, 58, 60
Marw al-Shāhijān 52 n. 248, 53, 54, 58
Marwān b. al-Ḥakam 150, 155 n. 752
Mary 157
marzaba, to appoint governor 25
marzbān, governor 67 n. 229, 73
Māsabadhān 43
masāliḥ, frontier regions 20 n. 107
Masjid Simāk, in al-Kūfah 24 n. 131
Maslamah b. Muḥārib, *rāwī* 134
masmughān, religious leader 26
al-Masʿūdī, ʿAlī b. al-Ḥusayn 10 n. 53, 89 n. 394, 95 n. 429
Maṭar b. Thalj al-Tamīmī, *rāwī* 40–42
Mecca 15, 42, 91 n. 403, 100 n. 470, 117 nn. 575–77, 131 n. 648, 132 n. 659, 134 n. 673, 140, 148 n. 733, 164
Medina xiii, xvi–xviii, 12 n. 59, 15, 73, 82, 110 nn. 534–35, 111, 112, 113 n. 550, 119, 122, 131 n. 648, 134, 138 n. 689, 141, 150, 151, 163
Messenger of God. *See* Muḥammad b. ʿAbdallāh, the Prophet
Mihrajānqadhaq 44, 49, 53
Minā 148 n. 733
minbar 111, 113, 158, 160
al-Miqdād b. ʿAmr/al-Aswad al-Kindī 146, 148, 152, 153
al-Miswar b. Makhramah 89, 148, 150, 151, 154, 155, 159
Moses 128
Mosul 3 n. 16, 4, 44, 45
Muʿāwiyah b. Abī Sufyān 15, 20 n. 104, 21 n. 109, 34 n. 176, 42, 44, 45, 46 n. 222, 76, 100, 132 n. 658, 133, 134, 141, 143 n. 713, 161 n. 767, 164, 165
(al-)Mubārak b. Faḍālah, *rāwī* 8, 143
Muḍar 132
al-Muḍārib al-ʿIjlī 26, 27
Mūghān. *See* Mūqān
al-Mughīrah b. Shuʿbah 10–12, 14, 17, 21, 50, 51, 63, 89, 92, 129, 148, 154, 161, 164
Mūghkān. *See* Mūqān
al-Muhājir b. Ziyād 79
Muhalhil b. Zayd al-Tamīmī 19, 20, 21 n. 116
al-Muhallab b. Abī Ṣufrah 69
al-Muhallab b. ʿUqbah al-Asadī, *rāwī* 2, 9, 18, 43, 51, 64, 70, 73, 80
Muḥammad b. ʿAbdallāh, the Prophet, the Messenger of God xiii, xiv, 11, 19, 25 n. 137, 39, 42 n. 204, 52, 66, 84, 89, 91–93, 96, 106–8, 116–18, 121 n. 608, 125, 127, 128, 132, 134 n. 673, 135, 137, 138, 140, 143 n. 713, 144, 145, 147, 149, 150, 151 n. 741, 152, 153, 156, 157, 159, 160, 164
Muḥammad b. ʿAbdallāh al-Anṣārī, *rāwī* 143
Muḥammad b. ʿAbdallāh b. Sawād, *rāwī* 2, 9, 18, 43, 51, 64, 70, 73, 80, 106, 118
Muḥammad b. ʿAbdallāh al-Zubayrī, *rāwī* 50, 102
Muḥammad b. ʿAwf, *rāwī* 104
Muḥammad b. Ibrāhīm, *rāwī* 96
Muḥammad b. ʿIjlān, *rāwī* 112

Muḥammad b. Isḥāq, *rāwī* 136, 139, 141
Muḥammad b. Muṣʿab al-Qarqasānī, *rāwī* 119–20
Muḥammad b. Muslim b. Shihāb al-Zuhrī. *See* Ibn Shihāb
Muḥammad b. al-Muthannā, *rāwī* 107
Muḥammad b. Saʿd. *See* Ibn Saʿd
Muḥammad b. Ṣāliḥ b. Dīnār, *rāwī* 121, 132
Muḥammad b. Sūqah, *rāwī* 66
Muḥammad b. ʿUmar. *See* al-Wāqidī
Muḥammad b. Yazīd, *rāwī* 139
Muḥārib b. Fihr 119
al-Muḥaṣṣab 148
Mujālid b. Saʿīd b. ʿUmayr, *rāwī* 48, 73, 95, 122
Mujāshiʿ b. Masʿūd al-Sulamī 65, 66
al-Mukaʿbir, Āzādh Furūz b. Jushnas 69
al-Mukhtār b. Abī ʿUbayd b. Masʿūd al-Thaqafī 47
Mukkurān. *See* Makrān
Mukrān. *See* Makrān
Mulaykah bt. Jarwal, wife of ʿUmar b. al-Khaṭṭāb 100
mūmisah, prostitute 5 n. 27
al-Mundhir b. ʿAmr 25
Mūqān 37, 38
Murghāb, river 52 n. 248
Mūsā b. ʿUqbah, *rāwī* 121
Mūsā b. Yaʿqūb al-Zamʿī, *rāwī* 119
Muṣʿab b. ʿAbdallāh al-Zubayrī, *rāwī* 110, 165
Muslim b. Ibrāhīm, *rāwī* 113
Mūtā, leader of the Daylam 21, 23, 24
mutʿah, temporary marriage 140
Muṭarrif, *rāwī* 106
Muṭarrif b. ʿAbdallāh b. al-Shikhkhīr al-Ḥarashī 53
Mūthā. *See* Mūtā
al-Muwaṭṭaʾ 165 n. 791

N

al-Naḍr b. Shumayl, *rāwī* 103
Nāfiʿ, client of ʿAbdallāh b. ʿUmar, *rāwī* 98, 142
Nāfiʿ, client of Āl al-Zubayr, *rāwī* 119
Nāfiʿ b. ʿAbd al-Ḥārith al-Khuzāʿī, governor of Mecca 164
Nahr Tīrā 79, 80
al-Najāshī, Qays b. ʿAmr 55
Najd 163 n. 777
Najrān 93 n. 414
nār, fire 52
Naysābūr 53, 54, 60
Nihāwand, xv, 2–4, 6, 8 n. 43, 11 n. 57, 12 n. 59, 18, 19, 22, 23 n. 126, 43 n. 206, 44 nn. 211–13
Nuʿaym b. Ḥammād, *rāwī* 98
Nuʿaym b. Muqarrin 3, 19, 21–27, 31
Nubia 14 n. 72
al-Nuʿmān b. Muqarrin 3 n. 14, 5, 6, 9, 10, 12, 13, 18, 20, 37 n. 181, 44
Nuqum, mountain 118 n. 580
al-Nusayr b. ʿAmr al-ʿIjlī 73
al-Nusayr b. Daysam b. Thawr al-ʿIjlī. *See* al-Nusayr b. Thawr
al-Nusayr b. Thawr 18

O

Oman 66 n. 295, 158 n. 759
Oxus, river 54 n. 258, 56 n. 270, 75 n. 336, 76 n. 338

P

Palestine 15
Peninsula. *See* Arabian Peninsula
Persepolis 64 n. 283
Persia 1, 51, 62
Persians xv, 18, 22, 23, 37, 52, 59, 60, 91, 127 n. 629
Prophet. *See* Muḥammad b. ʿAbdallāh, the Prophet
Pulvar, river 64 n. 283

Q

qabāṭī, fine cotton clothes 125
al-Qabj 32
al-Qādisiyyah xiv, xv, 2 n. 7, 19 n. 96,

20 n. 106, 21 n. 115, 23 n. 126, 26 n. 143, 44, 60, 61 n. 405
qal'ah, castle 18
qalāsim, trees (?) 23
al-Qalqashandī, Abū al-'Abbās Aḥmad 93 n. 414
al-Qandahār. *See* Kandahar
al-Qa'qā' b. 'Amr 19, 75
Qaraẓah b. 'Amr b. Ka'b al-Khuzā'ī 21
Qarmīsīn 20 n. 101
Qarqarat al-Kudr 140
qaṣabah, provincial center 18 n. 91
qaṣabiyyāt, finery 130
al-Qāsim b. Muḥammad, *rāwī* 97
Qaṣr al-Luṣūṣ 20
Qatādah b. Di'amah al-Sadūsī, *rāwī* 99, 107, 143
Qatādah b. al-Nu'mān al-Ẓafārī 164
Qaṭan b. Ka'b al-Quṭa'ī, *rāwī* 103
al-Qayrawān 14 n. 71
Qays 155 n. 752
Qays b. 'Aylān 136
Qays b. 'Iṣmah b. Mālik b. Ḍubay'ah b. Zayd b. al-Aws 101
Qays b. al-Rabī', *rāwī* 118
Qazwīn 21 n. 113, 24 n. 134
qiblah 159
Qihā 24
Qinnasrīn 15, 44
Quḍā'ah 133 n. 667
Qudayd 117
Qufs 73
Qūhistān 53 n. 249, 74
Qūmis xv, 25, 27, 28
qurā, settlements 74 n. 323
Qur'ān 28 nn. 153–54, 30 n. 160, 42 n. 201, 46 n. 221, 48, 49 n. 241, 57 n. 273, 62 nn. 279–81, 82, 92 n. 408, 103 n. 488, 108, 115, 121, 125 nn. 622 and 624, 126 nn. 626–28, 128 nn. 631–33, 131 nn. 650–51, 137 n. 683, 138 n. 685, 139 n. 696, 150, 153 nn. 747–49, 157 n. 754, 160 n. 765
Quraybah bt. Abī Umayyah, wife of 'Umar b. al-Khaṭṭāb 100
Quraysh 14 n. 69, 91 n. 403, 115, 116 nn. 567 and 569–70, 118 n. 585, 121, 137, 138 n. 684, 145 n. 727, 152–54, 164 n. 781
Qurrah b. Khālid al-Sadūsī, *rāwī* 109
Quṣayy 148 n. 734

R

Rabāḥ, witness 46
al-Rabī' b. al-Nu'mān, *rāwī* 133
al-Rabī' b. Sulaymān, *rāwī* 88
al-Rabī' b. Ziyād 79, 80, 82
Rabī'ah b. 'Uthmān 21, 110
radm, wall, rampart 42 n. 201
rāfiḍah, those refusing to serve 'Alī 44 n. 215
Raḥabat al-Qaḍā' 158
raḥim, relationship 150
Rāmahurmuz 43, 44
Rāshid b. Sa'd, *rāwī* 120
Rāsil, ruler of Makrān 70
al-Rayy xv, 1, 3 n. 15, 17, 20 n. 103, 21–27, 31, 51, 52
al-Rāzī, Aḥmad b. 'Abdallāh 42 n. 205
Rib'ī b. 'Āmir al-Ṭā'ī/al-Tamīmī 19, 54
Rib'ī b. Ka's 55
Riddah wars xiv
rikāb, riding camels 18
Rīshahr 68
Rukhkhaj 75 n. 333
rukhṣah, license 140
al-Rūm 32
Ruqayyah, daughter of 'Umar b. al-Khaṭṭāb 101
al-Rusāris b. Junādib 38
Rustam xiv, 21
rustāq, district 7
Rustāq al-Shaykh 7
Rutbīl 76 n. 337
Ruzbān Ṣūl b. Ruzbān 28, 29

S

Sābūr 65, 70

Sa'd b. Abī Waqqāṣ xiv, xv, 2, 5, 51, 52, 91, 93, 120, 145–48, 150–52, 156, 157 n. 755, 158 n. 761, 159, 161, 163 n. 778, 164
Sa'd b. Mālik 163
Sa'd b. Mas'ūd al-Thaqafī 47–49
Sa'd b. Qays b. 'Aylān 136 n. 681
sadd, wall, rampart 42 n. 201
Safwān b. 'Amr, *rāwī* 104
al-Sā'ib b. al-Aqra' 8, 9
al-Sā'ib b. Yazīd, *rāwī* 118
Sa'īd b. 'Amr b. Sa'īd al-'Āṣ, *rāwī* 50
Sa'īd al-Jurayrī, *rāwī* 108
Sa'īd b. Khālid, *rāwī* 129
Sa'īd b. al-Marzbān, Abū Sa'd al-Baqqāl, *rāwī* 2, 9, 18, 43
Sa'īd b. al-Musayyab, *rāwī* 131, 163
Sa'īd b. Zayd b. 'Amr b. Nufayl 144, 145, 152
Ṣakhr. *See* al-Aḥnaf
Salamah, father of Iyās 139
Salamah b. Faḍl al-Azraq, *rāwī* 15, 95
Salamah b. Kuhayl al-Ḥaḍramī, *rāwī* 139
Salamah b. Qays al-Ashja'ī 83, 84, 86–89
Ṣāliḥ b. Kaysān, *rāwī* 96, 129
Sālim, client of Abū Ḥudhayfah 143, 144
Sālim b. 'Abdallāh b. 'Umar, *rāwī* 105
Sālim b. Abī al-Ja'd al-Ashja'ī, *rāwī* 107, 111
Sālim b. Ghanm b. 'Awf b. al-Khazraj 4 n. 19
Sallām b. Miskīn, *rāwī* 113
Salm b. Junādah, Abū al-Sā'ib, *rāwī* 89, 103, 154
Salm b. Ziyād, governor of Sijistān 76
Salmān al-Fārisī, *rāwī* 118
Salmān b. Rabī'ah 5, 34, 37, 39, 40
al-Sam'ānī, 'Abd al-Karīm b. Muḥammad 99 n. 465
Samarqand 54 n. 258
Sāmarrā 51 n. 246
Ṣan'ā' 118, 164
Sarakhs 53
al-Sarī b. Yaḥyā, *rāwī* 2, 8, 9, 17, 39, 43, 47–51, 55, 64, 66, 67, 70, 71, 73, 80, 82, 87, 133, 142, 163
Sāriyah b. Zunaym al-Du'alī al-Kinānī 65, 70–73, 95
al-Sawād 6, 48
Sawād b. Quṭbah al-Tamīmī 30, 31
al-Sawāḥil 15
ṣawāmi', religious buildings 46
Sayf b. 'Umar, *rāwī* xiii, 1, 2, 8, 9, 17, 18, 19 n. 96, 21, 34, 39, 43, 47–51, 55, 64, 66, 67, 70, 71, 73, 80, 82, 87, 95, 133, 142, 163
Seleucia 4 n. 20
al-Sha'bī. *See* 'Āmir al-Sha'bī
Shaddād b. Aws, Companion 165
al-Shafā bt. 'Abdallāh, *rāwī* 120
shāh, ruler of Sijistān 76
Shahr b. Ḥawshab al-Ash'arī, *rāwī* 143
Shahrak, governor of Fārs 67–70
Shahrām 25
Shahrbarāz, ruler of al-Bāb 35, 36, 38–42
Shahrbarāz Jādhawayh 7
al-Shām 35
al-Shammākh b. Ḍirār 38
al-Shammūs, horse 58
Shāpūr, river 64 n. 284, 65 n. 288
Shaqīq b. Salamah al-Asadī, *rāwī* 88, 141
Sharīk b. 'Abdallāh al-Nakha'ī, *rāwī* 94, 97
shaykh, leader 7
shī'ah, partisans 158
Shibl b. Ma'bad al-Bajalī/al-Muzanī 67, 68
Shihāb b. Khirāsh al-Ḥawshabī, *rāwī* 88
Shihāb b. al-Mukhāriq b. Shihāb 77
Shī'īs 44 n. 215
Shīr 74
Shīrāz 65 n. 289
al-Shirriz 27
Shu'ayb 104
Shu'ayb b. Ibrāhīm al-Tamīmī, *rāwī* 2, 8, 9, 17, 39, 43, 47–51, 55, 64, 66, 67, 70, 71, 73, 80, 82, 87, 95
Shu'ayb b. Ṭalhah, *rāwī* 97

Shu'bah b. al-Ḥajjāj, *rāwī* 106, 107
al-Shuddākh, Ya'mar b. 'Awf 148
shūrā. *See* electoral council
Shurayḥ b. al-Ḥārith al-Kindī, *qāḍī* 16, 165
Ṣiffīn 2 n. 8, 4, 5 n. 22, 42 n. 205, 100, 161 n. 767
Sijistān xv, 75, 76
Simāk, mosque 24
Simāk b. Kharashah al-Anṣārī 20, 21 n. 116, 22, 26, 31–33
Simāk b. Makhramah al-Asadī 20, 21 n. 116, 22, 24, 27, 30, 31
Simāk b. 'Ubayd al-'Absī/al-'Ansī 20, 21 n. 116, 22, 31
Sind 75, 77, 78
Ṣirār 110, 119
Siyāwakhsh b. Mihrān b. Bahrām Shūbīn 24, 25
Soghdia 54, 56
Solomon 131
spoils. *See* booty
Subḥān, Sūrat 139
ṣuffah, covering 150
Sufyān b. 'Abdallāh al-Thaqafī, governor of al-Ṭā'if 164
Sufyān b. Sa'īd al-Thawrī, *rāwī* 96
Sufyān b. 'Uyaynah, *rāwī* 105, 141
Ṣuḥār b. Fulān/Ṣakhr al-'Abdī 53, 77, 78 n. 345
Suhayb b. Sinān 91, 93, 95, 146, 148, 154, 164
Suhayl b. 'Adī 8, 9, 73, 77, 78
Sulaymān b. 'Abd al-'Azīz b. Abī Thābit b. 'Abd al-'Azīz b. 'Umar b. 'Abd al-Raḥmān b. 'Awf, *rāwī* 89, 154, 155
Sulaymān b. Buraydah, *rāwī* 83, 87
Sulaymān b. Ṣāliḥ al-Laythī, *rāwī* 68
Sumayrah al-Ḍabbiyyah 19
Sunnīs 44 n. 215
Surāqah b. 'Amr, Dhū al-Nūr 34–38
Suwayd b. Muqarrin 3 n. 14, 5, 19, 27–30, 37 n. 181
Syria xiv, 15, 44, 45, 46 n. 224, 104, 115, 127, 143 n. 723

T

Ṭāb, river 68 n. 302
al-Ṭabarī, Abū Ja'far Muḥammad b. Jarīr xiii–xvi, xix, 1, 2 nn. 4 and 6, 3 n. 17, 4 n. 22, 5 n. 26, 8 n. 44, 11 n. 57, 12 n. 59, 13 n. 64, 15 nn. 73 and 85, 17 n. 96, 21 n. 111, 34 nn. 175–76, 38 n. 187, 39 n. 193, 43 n. 209, 45 nn. 216–17, 46 nn. 222 and 224, 51 n. 246, 53 nn. 251 and 255, 54 nn. 259–60, 63, 65 nn. 286 and 290, 66 n. 295, 75 n. 331, 76 n. 339, 89, 93–95, 97 n. 442, 98, 102, 111, 113, 114, 134 n. 673, 135 n. 675, 154, 155 n. 752
Ṭabaristān xv, 17, 25, 28, 30, 76 n. 338
Ṭabas al-Tamr 53 n. 249
Ṭabas al-'Unnāb 53 n. 249
al-Ṭabasayn 53, 74
Taflī, envoy of Tiflīs in Jurzan 45
al-Ṭā'if 15, 66 n. 295, 158 n. 759, 164
Ta'izz 164 n. 782
Ṭalḥah 135, 148
Ṭalḥah b. al-A'lam al-Ḥanafī, *rāwī* 2, 9, 18, 43, 51, 64, 70, 73, 80
Ṭalḥah b. 'Ubaydallāh 86, 91, 121, 145, 146, 153, 154, 157
Ṭalḥat al-Khayr b. 'Ubaydallāh. *See* Ṭalḥah b. 'Ubaydallāh
Tamīm b. Murr xiii, 9 n. 45, 163 n. 777
tarāwīḥ, Ramaḍān prayers 114 n. 559
Ṭāriq b. Shihāb al-Bajalī, *rāwī* 107
Ṭāwūs 65
Tawwaj 64–66, 69
thaniyyah, mountain road 18
Thaniyyat al-'Asal 19
Thaniyyat al-Rikāb 18
Thaqīf 8 n. 43
thughūr, frontier districts 20 n. 107
Tiflīs 37, 45, 46
Tigris 4 n. 20, 5, 6
Tikrīt xiv
Torah 90
tribute xvi, 9, 13, 28, 29, 33, 46, 66
Truce. *See* al-Ḥudaybiyah
Ṭukhāristān 54
Turks 29, 38, 40, 56–60, 62, 75

U

'Ubādah b. al-Ṣāmit, Companion 164
'Ubayd, *rāwī*. *See* 'Ubaydallāh b. Sulaymān
'Ubaydah b. al-Ḥārith 135 n. 675
'Ubaydallāh, *rāwī* 68
'Ubaydallāh b. Ma'mar al-Taymī 67, 70
'Ubaydallāh b. Sa'd al-Zuhrī, *rāwī* 112
'Ubaydallāh b. Sulaymān, *rāwī* 69; *see also* 'Ubaydallāh
'Ubaydallāh b. 'Umar b. al-Khaṭṭāb, *rāwī* 98, 100, 111, 143, 161–64
'Umar b. 'Imrān b. 'Abdallāh b. 'Abd al-Raḥmān b. Abī Bakr, *rāwī* 97
'Umar b. Ismā'īl b. Mujālid al-Hamdānī, *rāwī* 105
'Umar b. al-Khaṭṭāb xiii–xviii, 1–10, 11 n. 57, 12–15, 19, 21, 22, 25–27, 31–39, 42–44, 47–51, 53, 56, 59, 60, 62, 63, 65 n. 290, 66, 67, 70–72, 74, 77–100, 102–25, 129–39, 141–48, 151, 154, 155, 159, 160, 163–65
'Umar b. Mujāshi', *rāwī* 120
'Umar b. Nāfi', *rāwī* 104
'Umar b. Shabbah, *rāwī* 30, 94, 95, 100, 120–23, 129, 131, 134, 135, 143
'Umar b. Sulaymān b. Abī Ḥathmah, *rāwī* 120–22
'Umar b. Surāqah al-Makhzūmī, governor of al-Baṣrah 3, 4, 43, 50, 83
'Umayr b. Sa'd al-Anṣārī 15, 164
Umayyah 91 n. 404
Umm Abān bt. 'Utbah b. Rabī'ah 102
Umm 'Amr bt. Ḥassān al-Kūfiyyah, *rāwī* 114
Umm Ḥakīm bt. al-Ḥārith, wife of 'Umar b. al-Khaṭṭāb 100
Umm Kulthūm, daughter of 'Alī b. Abī Ṭālib and wife of 'Umar b. al-Khaṭṭāb 72, 85, 86, 88, 101, 102
Umm Kulthūm bt. Abī Bakr 101, 102
Umm Kulthūm bt. Jarwal, wife of 'Umar b. al-Khaṭṭāb 100
umm walad, concubine 13 n. 63, 140 n. 700
'umrah, lesser pilgrimage 140 n. 697
'Uqbah b. Nāfi' al-Fihrī 14
'Urwah, envoy of Nu'aym b. Muqarrin 22
'Urwah al-Raḥḥāl 98
'Urwah b. al-Zubayr, *rāwī* 123
Usāmah b. Zayd b. Aslam al-Laythī, *rāwī* 97, 116, 119
'Usfān 117
'Uṭārid b. Ḥājib b. Zurārah b. 'Udas/'Udus al-Tamīmī 43, 47
'Utaybah b. al-Nahhās al-Bakrī 26, 27, 30, 31
'Utbah b. Abī Sufyān, governor of Kinānah 132, 133
'Utbah b. Farqad al-Sulamī 3, 31–34
'Uthman b. 'Abd al-Raḥmān, *rāwī* 94
'Uthmān b. Abī al-'Āṣ al-Thaqafī 66–70, 164
'Uthmān b. 'Affān 21 n. 111, 30, 34 n. 176, 39, 40, 45 n. 217, 59, 60, 63, 67, 70, 91, 93–95, 103, 104, 115, 132, 141, 143 n. 713, 145–54, 156, 158–162, 163 n. 773
'Uthmān al-Akhnasī 94
'Uthmān b. Ḥunayf 6, 14, 16

W

Wāj (al-)Rūdh 21–24, 31
Wakī', Muḥammad b. Khalaf 165 n. 790
Wakī' b. al-Jarrāḥ b. Malīḥ, *rāwī* 96, 143
al-Walīd b. 'Abd Shams 49
al-Walīd b. Hishām b. al-Mughīrah 115
al-Walīd b. Jumay', *rāwī* 47
al-Walīd b. Kathīr, *rāwī* 112
al-Wāqidī, Muḥammad b. 'Umar 4 n. 19, 13–15, 17, 20, 21, 42, 43 n. 209, 47, 64, 65 n. 290, 89, 93, 95–97, 99–102, 114–20, 135 n. 675, 140 n. 701, 144 n. 724, 164
washal, little water 77

al-Wāzi' b. Zayd b. Khulaydah, *rāwī* 55
wazīr, administrative assistant 6 n. 32
witr, prayer 159

Y

Yaḥyā b. Ḥuḍayn, *rāwī* 107
Yaḥyā b. Kathīr, *rāwī* 105
Yaḥyā b. Ma'īn, *rāwī* 139
Yaḥyā b. Sa'īd b. Mikhnaf, father of Abū Mikhnaf, *rāwī* 163
Yaḥyā b. Wāḍiḥ, *rāwī* 114
Ya'lā b. Munyah/Umayyah, governor of the Yemen 42, 164
al-Yamāmah 15, 18 n. 93, 43 n. 210, 163 n. 777
Ya'mar b. 'Awf. *See* al-Shuddākh
Ya'qūb b. Ibrāhīm al-Anṣārī, *rāwī* 139, 141
Ya'qūb b. Ibrāhīm al-Jūzajānī, *rāwī* 10
Ya'qūb b. Ibrāhīm b. Sa'd, *rāwī* 96, 103, 104, 106, 108
Ya'qūb b. Isḥāq al-Ḥaḍramī, *rāwī* 138
al-Ya'qūbī, Aḥmad b. Abī Ya'qūb xix, 13 n. 67, 14 n. 72, 17, 21 n. 111, 115 n. 565, 143 n. 714, 164 n. 779
Yāqūt b. 'Abdallāh al-Ḥamawī xx, 3 n. 15, 4 nn. 18 and 20, 7 n. 38, 8 n. 41, 13 n. 67, 14 n. 72, 15 nn. 78–81, 17 n. 89, 18 n. 91, 20 nn. 101–3, 21 nn. 112–13, 23 nn. 120–21, 123, and 127, 24 nn. 128–31 and 134, 25 n. 136, 27 nn. 140 and 148, 28 n. 156, 29 n. 159, 30 n. 166, 37 nn. 180 and 183–84, 38 nn. 188–89, 43 nn. 206–8, 44 n. 213, 45 n. 218, 48 nn. 238–39, 51 n. 246, 52 n. 248, 53 nn. 249–50, 252, 254, and 256, 54 nn. 258 and 261–62, 56 n. 272, 64 nn. 283–84, 65 nn. 288–90, 66 n. 296, 68 n. 302, 71 n. 314, 73 n. 322, 74 n. 325, 75 nn. 330, 333, and 335, 77 n. 340, 79 nn. 353–54, 119 n. 592, 164 n. 784, 165 n. 789
Yarfa', servant of 'Umar b. al-Khaṭṭāb 85, 87, 88, 134, 135
Yarmūk 3 n. 10
Yazdajird b. Shahriyār b. Kisrā (Yazdajird III) xv, 2, 51–54, 56, 58–63
Yazdgard. *See* Yazdajird
Yazīd b. 'Abd al-Malik, Umayyad caliph 154 n. 750
Yazīd b. 'Iyāḍ b. Ju 'dubah, *rāwī* 123, 131
Yazīd b. Mu'āwiyah 42, 76
Yazīd b. al-Muhallab 154 n. 750
Yazīd b. Qays al-Hamdānī 22–24
Yazīd b. Rūmān al-Asadī, *rāwī* 123
Yemen 15, 42, 118 n. 580, 122, 164 n. 782
Yūnus b. 'Abd al-A'lā, *rāwī* 105
Yūnus b. Abī Isḥāq, *rāwī* 143
Yūnus b. 'Ubayd, *rāwī* 103, 104
Yūsuf b. Yazīd, *rāwī* 143

Z

al-Zabīdī, Muḥammad Murtaḍā 58 n. 276, 148 n. 734
Zādhān, Abū 'Abdallāh/'Umar al-Kindī, *rāwī* 118
zakāh, alms 84 n. 376
Zakariyyā' b. Siyāh, *rāwī* 48
Zarah, lake 75 n. 333
Zaranj 75, 76
Zawīlah 14
Zayd, son of 'Umar b. al-Khaṭṭāb 101
Zayd, the younger, son of 'Umar b. al-Khaṭṭāb 100
Zayd b. Akhzam al-Ṭā'ī, *rāwī* 98
Zayd b. Aslam, *rāwī* 99, 110, 112, 121, 133
Zayd b. Thābit 15
Zaynab bt. (al-)Jaḥsh, wife of the Prophet 97
Zaynab bt. Maẓ'ūn, wife of 'Umar b. al-Khaṭṭāb 97 n. 442, 100
Zaynab bt. 'Umar b. al-Khaṭṭāb 97 n. 442, 101
al-Zīnabī b. Qūlah Abū al-Furrukhān 21, 24–26

Zirr b. Ḥubaysh, *rāwī* 96, 97
Ziyād, client of al-Ḥakam b. Abī al-ʿĀṣ 69
Ziyād b. Abī Sufyān, governor of al-Baṣrah 81, 82
Ziyād b. Ḥanẓalah 3, 5, 6, 34
Ziyād b. Labīd al-Bayāḍī, a Helper 162, 163
al-Zubayr b. al-ʿAwwām 86, 91, 101, 129 n. 640, 145, 146, 150, 151, 156, 159
al-Zubayrī, al-Muṣʿab b. ʿAbdallāh 3 n. 10, 91 n. 403, 116 nn. 569–70, 118 n. 585, 132 n. 659, 152 n. 744, 164 n. 781
Zuhayr b. Abī Sulmā, poet 136
al-Zuhrī. *See* Ibn Shihāb al-Zuhrī
Zunbīl 76